Crisis and Covenant

SUNY Series in Modern Jewish Literature and Culture

Sarah Blacher Cohen, EDITOR

CRISIS AND COVENANT

The Holocaust in American Jewish Fiction

ALAN L. BERGER

State University of New York Press

Published by
State University of New York Press, Albany

© 1985 State University of New York

All rights reserved

Printed in the United States of America

For information, address State University of New York
Press, State University Plaza, Albany, N.Y., 12246

Library of Congress Cataloging in Publication Data

Berger, Alan L., 1939–
    Crisis and covenant.

    (SUNY series in modern Jewish literature and
culture)
    Includes index.
    1. American fiction—Jewish authors—History and
criticism. 2. American fiction—20th century—History
and criticism. 3. Holocaust, Jewish (1939–1945),
in literature. 4. Covenants (Jewish theology)
I. Title. II. Series.
PS153.J4B47 1985   813'.54'09358   84–26813
ISBN 0–88706–085–4
ISBN 0–88706–086–2 (pbk.)

10 9 8 7 6 5 4 3 2

Contents

Acknowledgments

Crisis and Covenant emerged from, and was shaped by, my Judaism in American Fiction course. Together the classes and I discussed, argued, and probed many of the issues treated in this book. My students bore the brunt of my thought processes and helped to refine my thinking on the topic. While it is not possible to name all of my students individually, I wish to specifically mention Deidre Depke, Elisabeth Goldberg, Michael Maimon, and Sarah Matzkin.

Fruitful discussions were held with colleagues at Syracuse and elsewhere: Thomas Friedmann, Rabbi Irwin Hyman, A. Leland Jamison, Steven Katz, Robert W. Ross, and James G. Williams. I thank them for their interest, their support, and their wisdom. They have been teachers as well as friends. I have benefited also from the keen insights of Irving Greenberg. A debt of a different kind is owed to Lester Friedman and to Barry Glassner. As is frequently the case, others have indirectly contributed; scholars and participants in the conferences of the Anne Frank Institute of Philadelphia, the Bernard E. Olsen Annual Scholars' Conferences on the Church Struggle and the Holocaust, and the International Conference on the Holocaust and Genocide held in Tel Aviv. Further back in time, but no less important, Rabbi Solomon S. Bernards persuasively made the case for novels as texts in the teaching of Judaism, thus influencing my initial decision to begin such a course. Emil Fackenheim and Franklin Littell, in a Holocaust symposium held at Syracuse University nearly a decade ago, set forth issues whose impact time and continued research have served to increase.

I wish especially to thank Elie Wiesel whose witness and writings provided wisdom and inspiration in my attempt to seek a response to the Holocaust's devastation. He is truly the *zaddik hador*.

Syracuse University supported the writing of this book by making available a research grant. I also am grateful for the able assistance given by Denise Stevens of the Humanities Staff at the E. S. Bird Library, and to Stuart Sherman, M.A., who prepared the index. Portions of the manuscript were typed by Anne Brinton, Jane Frost, and Margaret Wood. The work in its entirety was transcribed patiently and with great skill by Jane Frost.

A note of thanks is due Sarah Blacher Cohen, the series editor, whose guidance and counsel were invaluable.

Support and encouragement at very crucial moments were provided by my wife Naomi Benau Berger.

This book is for our children: Ariel, Michael, and Daniel.

Chapter 1

Introduction: Jewish Existence

Jewish existence is fundamentally rooted in the notion of covenant. The covenant is the foundation of the Jewish proclamation of redemption, and it announced a special relationship between God and the Israelites based on two assumptions: the people's witness and divine protection. God's love for His chosen people was both inscrutable and freely given. Covenantal existence provided a means for interpreting the dialectical relationship between historical events and religious response. To put the matter directly, covenant meant a sanctification of history; historical vicissitudes have, therefore, resulted in corresponding covenantal reactions. Various crises in Jewish national existence were measured against the norms of divine promise and divine judgment. But always covenant meant that the Israelites were held to a higher standard of accountability. This expectation is expressed most clearly in the first three chapters of Amos, especially in Amos 3:2 "You only have I known of all the families of the earth; therefore I will punish you for all your iniquities." The actions of the nations, no less than the misdeeds of the Israelites, were also viewed as touchstones of the divine, justifying the assertion that in Judaism historical events have been understood as barometers of God's disposition toward His people. The covenant was seen as an eternal gauge by which both parties' fidelity could be measured. The Jewish claim of redemption was, moreover, based on the expectation of its decisive occurrence within, rather than beyond or in spite of, history. Anxious scrutiny of the historical on the part of the faithful led, how-

1

ever, to ambiguous conclusions. Manifestations of the divine could be either merciful, as in the Exodus, whose very facticity announced that redemption was historical, or there could be negative moments, expressions of divine wrath, such as the destruction of the Temple, Judaism's cultic center. Covenantal existence sought to express the dialectic between redemption and the discomforting counterevidence of history.

If covenant was a witness to God's sovereignty, and history the stage on which the divine drama was enacted, then it is equally imperative to note that covenant made binding claims on the chooser no less than on those chosen. For example, God's first covenant was with Noah and, through him, all mankind (Gen. 9:8–17). Here a divine promise was made never again to destroy the earth no matter the degree or extent of man's evil. This divine self-restriction becomes paradigmatic for subsequent generations of covenant interpreters in times of crises. Jews who live according to the covenant must, in each generation, affirm its contents while simultaneously asking if its terms are still binding. What, for example, happens when the covenantal promise of redemption is juxtaposed against the bleakness and rav- ages of history? While covenantal thinking is a normative element of Judaism, the tradition has witnessed major and profound revisions of covenantal understanding. These revisions have been occasioned by various historical convulsions; exile, ruinations of the Jerusalem Temple, and various pogroms all resulting in a recasting of the ever shifting, complex, and always ambiguous relationship between God and man. Decoding history became the central covenantal activity. But covenant affirmation has meant that in each generation an assent to the belief that no historical event, regardless of how devastating, could cast doubt on the eternality of Israel.

One profoundly important and far-reaching consequence of this ongoing covenant revision was the gradual shift in emphasis assigned each actor in the covenantal drama. For example, the severity of historical counterevidence to the redemptive claim led to the assertion that God was increasingly hidden. Consequently, in order that the covenant be maintained, a correspondingly greater emphasis was placed on the necessity of human endeavors. If the covenant was not broken, how could Judaism account for the unredeemed state of the world and the suffering of the chosen people? In order to keep to- gether the historical condition of the Jewish people, and the theolog- ical promise of redemption, successive expressions of Judaism sought to heal an apparent breach between God and the world which threatened to desanctify history and invalidate the covenantal redemptive promise.

Writing after World War II, Martin Buber eloquently stated the contrast between history and redemption for the Jews. He wrote "standing, bound and shackled in the pillory of mankind, we demonstrate with the bloody body of our people the unredeemedness of the world."[1] The inseparability of history and theology in Judaism is, however, nowhere more profoundly wrenching than in the Holocaust.[2] Elie Wiesel articulates this relationship.

> Well, it seems that for the first time in our history, this very covenant was broken. This is why the Holocaust has terrifying theological implications. Whether we want it or not, because of its sheer dimensions, the event transcends man and involves more than him alone. It can be explained neither with God nor without him.[3]

The Holocaust is the sheer mass of history's counterevidence to the viability of the covenant, to the image of God, and to the task of man.

To begin, we must pay attention to the various attempts to justify the ways of God with man which have emerged in response to successive pre-Holocaust crises in Jewish history. Asserting divine providence over the historical has led to distinctive notions of the covenant-history dialectic, even as it has profoundly altered the roles played by each of the covenantal parties. Let us look briefly at the covenantal assumptions of the following periods: biblical, rabbinic (rational), mystic (nonrational), modern, and contemporary.

Covenant Transformations[4]

The biblical model of covenantal dialectic with history is based on a recognition that the divine-human encounter in Judaism is paradoxical at heart, rooted in the twin moments of the Exodus; freedom from bondage and acceptance of moral responsibility. At the Red Sea, God is transcendent, overwhelming, and awe-inspiring. Before the mighty acts of the Creator of the Universe, man is helpless, a lowly creature who reacts to his omnipotent Creator. At Sinai, on the other hand, both God and man are transformed. Divine commandments require human response. Although the word partner is not used in the Bible, Sinai denotes the embryonic expression of a partnership between the divine and the human actors in the covenant relationship. God was seen as the senior partner in the biblical covenant.

Divine sovereignty over history was unquestioned, and divine-human encounter was a normative expectation. For example, Mircea Eliade writes of the messianic prophets' "steadfast will to look history in the face and to accept it as a terrifying dialogue with Yahweh."[5] Solomon's building of the Temple transferred the locus of religious power; priests, rather than prophets, became the new religious virtuosi and the Jerusalem Temple was viewed as the preeminent site of divine presence.

The first destruction of the Temple by the Babylonians, in 586 B.C.E., was followed by its reconsecration in 515 B.C.E., some years after the exiles returned to Jerusalem. The Temple as holy place and priests as holy men continued to be religiously authoritative. The second destruction of the Temple by the Romans in 70 C.E. resulted, however, in a major transformation of Judaism. The tradition became rabbinic rather than biblical/priestly; academies and synagogues replaced the Temple, and prayer and study stood instead of sacrifice. The resultant covenantal transformation had important implications for the relationship between history, as countercovenantal, and redemptive promise.

Thinking and writing in the aftermath of the Temple's second destruction, rabbinic authorities wished to protect the imperative of divine promise and the necessity of human expectation. Refusing to be swayed by the Temple's devastation, the rabbis contended not that God had been vanquished from history, but that His presence was increasingly elusive and concealed. Because the possibility of divine revelation (gilluy shekhinah) was no longer a normative expectation, the rabbis attributed religious authority to the everyday acts of believing and knowledgeable Jews. Man became a more nearly equal covenantal partner. For example, a majority vote on a legal matter in a rabbinic academy achieved priority over divine revelation (Baba Metzia 59b). Both biblical and rabbinic Judaism embraced the view that disaster in its national and personal dimension was attributable to sin. "We are punished for our sins" (Mi-penei-hata'einu) was the covenantal response to historical upheaval. The crushing of Bar-Kokhba's messianic rebellion in 135 C.E. also presented rabbinic Judaism with a massive covenantal challenge. The rabbis, however, continually penetrated beyond the apparent to the hidden meaning of historical events. Surely it is no accident that rabbinic wisdom asserted: "On the day the Temple was destroyed, the Messiah was born" (Berakhot 2:4). Rabbinic thought also sought to console Israel by asserting that God shared the nation's historical fate. The *Shekhinah* (divine presence) was with the Israelites in exile (Megillah 29a).

Rabbinic Judaism provided explicit witness to the covenant-history dialectic in the form of the midrashic framework. This framework enabled the rabbis to steadfastly refuse sovereignty to empirical events which ran counter to covenantal claims. Emil Fackenheim terms this attitude "midrashic stubbornness."[6] Rabbinic Judaism attested that the Messiah will appear to a generation which is totally guilty or completely innocent (Sanhedrin 98a). Would the rabbis have been so confident, one wonders, if they could have reflected on the fact that from 1939 to 1945, when six million of the covenant people were gassed, beaten, shot, brutalized, and exterminated, both guilt and innocence were overwhelmed by evil and indifference?

Messianic and mystical interpretations of catastrophe interpreted the meaning of historical disasters in a twofold manner; as requiring a greater human effort in the salvific process, and as demonstrating increasing divine hiddenness or withdrawal from history. The sixteenth-century kabbalah of Isaac luria, responding to the disaster of Jewish expulsion from the Iberian peninsula which had occurred fifty years earlier, testifies to the existence of a fundamental connection between theosophy and Jewish vocation. Exile, the historical situation of the Jewish people, when viewed through Luria's prism, became transformed into a holy mission whose successful completion would usher in the messianic age. Luria's system, which involves an elaborate and daring cosmological view, focuses on three vital events in the cosmic unfolding: *tsimtsum* (the divine self-exile which yields space for the creation); *shevirat hakelim* (breaking of the vessels which were to contain primordial light, the shattering of these vessels caused divine sparks to fall to earth); and *tikkun* (an ongoing act of repair or world restoration performed by man elevating the fallen divine sparks by means of proper *kavvanah*, intention or meditation). The Lurianic Kabbalah significantly elevates man's status in the covenantal relationship. Luria's cosmogonic myth of exile and redemption views God as a savior desperately in need of salvation, while testifying to the paradoxical view of God that was typical in medieval mysticism. He is both *en sof*, without limitations and transcendent, a radically hidden and unknowable deity; and He is imminent, a God revealed through His divine emanations.

Touching deep imaginal wellsprings, kabbalistic literature sought to account for the existence of evil and the demonic in cosmic terms. While kabbalistic theodicy is a complex phenomenon—at times suggesting that evil is an element within the godhead itself while, on other occasions, contending that evil is an independent reality—the *Zohar*, the basic text of Jewish mysticism, refers to evil as *sitra achra* (the other, or left, side). Unlike either rabbinic or philosophic interpretations of evil, kabbalah views the *sitra achra* with utmost seriousness, ascribing to it a status akin to the divine or viewing it as a byproduct in the creative process. For example, the *Zohar* interprets Job's afflictions as punishment for failing to sacrifice to the "other side" (Bo 34a). Kabbalah and hasidic thought suggest a daring transformation. Evil itself might, under appropriate circumstances, be a footstool for good. The *Zohar* admonishes that "man should be cognizant of both good and evil, and turn evil itself into good." However, this accomplishment is "a deep tenet of faith." The left side, in isolation from the side of good, is destructive. Combat between good and evil is coterminous with creation.

Shevirat hakelim, the breaking of the vessels, is an unavoidable element in the drama of creation. Specifically concerning its implications for post-Holocaust fiction, Wiesel testifies that:

> The story that I try to tell is, first of all, a story of night which the Kabbalah calls *shvirat hakelim*—the breaking of the vessels—that something happened at the origin of creation, a cosmic cataclysm. Our story is of the same nature. Something happened a generation ago, to the world, to man. Something happened to God. Certainly something happened to the relations between man and God, man and man, man and himself.[7]

Contemporary religious responses to the Holocaust in fiction adopt the Lurianic notion of man's restorative task: helping to free God by liberating divine sparks. These sparks are, testified the Ba'al Shem Tov, founder of Hasidism, everywhere. In all that man does, including the telling of tales, he is potentially capable of assisting God.

Covenant and Modernity

The advent of modernity and the widespread acceptance of Enlightenment premises constituted a massive challenge to the notion of covenantal assumptions concerning God's sovereignty over history, the meaning of theodicy, and the nature of the divine-human relationship. Although precise dates are difficult to ascertain, certainly a decisive turning point in the history of Jewish covenant cohesion came in the aftermath of the French Revolution. The portent of this sea change was articulated in 1789 by Clermont Tonnere's assertion: "To the Jews as a nation we must deny everything. To the Jews as individuals we must grant everything."[8] Entry into society at large required abandoning the Jewish corporate identity. Western European Jews emerged en masse from the ghettos where every aspect of their lives had been regulated by the *kehillah* (Jewish communal organization). Embracing their newly declared freedom, Jews viewed the secular state as providing an opportunity for political and civic equality heretofore unattainable. Jews in Western Europe drew the logical, but fatal, conclusion that the doctrine of human rights would be their salvation. One political result was the emergence of the hyphenated Jew (for example, the French-Jew, the German-Jew, and later, the American-Jew). Emphasis on assimilation led also to the phenomenon of Jewish self-hate (*jüdishe Selbsthass*) as a defining group characteristic. The anthropologist Raphael Patai contends that for the first time in its history of encounter with other cultures, Judaism took on the negative evaluation of Jews which was espoused by the majority culture.[9]

Jacob Katz, the social historian, notes that the ferment in modern Jewish experience is called by a variety of names: Enlightenment (or *haskalah*) stood for the intellectual climate of the time, Emancipation denoted political changes, and Early Reform designated religious transformation.[10] Whatever the title, however, Enlightenment and Emancipation proved unfortunate illusions for Jewry. Western Jewry soon fragmented into three types of orientation to the tradition. The *maskil*, man of reason, at first challenged and then ignored covenantal authority. Reform arose, in large measure, to prevent Jewish assimilation, and, in the process, reinterpreted the religious demands of covenant as ethical imperatives. Orthodoxy, for its part, remained firmly rooted in covenantal assumptions. Never fully accepted by Gentile society, *maskilim* and Reform Jews were only grudgingly permitted access to the non-Jewish world. In this assimilation process, covenantal thinking was viewed as a surmountable obstacle to full emancipation. Based on laws whose origins were in antiquity, and administered by rabbis who were increasingly viewed as obscurantists, covenantal claims diminished in persuasiveness in the wake of Enlightenment rhetoric about the role of reason and the political allure of Emancipation.

The issues of modernity for Judaism are complex and intertwined, encompassing the relationship between tradition and personal freedom, revelation and reason. The move to domesticate God, as it were, and to undercut revelation was not, of course, unique to the Jewish experience of modernity. Seventeenth-century science, eighteenth-century rationalism, and nineteenth-century evolutionary and political thought all combined to undermine religious explanations of the world and the very concept of revelation. The weight of history fell, however, hardest on the Jews. While embracing modernism as a social and political panacea, Jews never completely abandoned their identity, retaining what sociologists identify as certain distinctive traits or defense mechanisms, such as endogamy, a concern for the well-being of fellow Jews in remote corners of the world (*ahavat Yisrael*), observance of designated days of fast and feast, and a modicum of dietary reserve based on laws of *kashrut*. Jacob Katz notes that "in spite of the crumbling of tradition and the weakening of religious commitments, Jewish cohesion persisted."[11] Non-Jews, for their part, continued to perceive Jews as outsiders, non-Europeans, whose cultural and religious practices rendered them unassimilable and untrustworthy. Even assimilationist Jews were viewed with suspicion. The poet Heinrich Heine, himself a convert to Christianity, accurately predicted that at his death neither mass nor *kaddish* would be said.

Modernism and its secularizing impulse confronted Jews with a paradox. It soon became apparent that the word Jew had a social as well as a religious and biological definition for both Jews and non-Jews. For Jews, heredity, more than religious belief, became the determinative factor of their Jewish identity. No amount of legislation, therefore, could make Jews acceptable in the eyes of their Christian neighbors. At precisely the time that the formal elements of Christianity had been displaced as a legal norm by a secular code of civil law, the negative teachings of the Christian church concerning the Jews remained firmly in place. The eighteenth-century crack in the door of European social acceptance ended with a fatal slam of that door in the twentieth century. Modernity had confronted Judaism with a fateful choice, yielding spiritual identity to gain political rights. These rights were elusive, however, because there was no nation to guarantee them. This spiritual identity crisis was, in retrospect, a prelude to the physical eradication of Judaism which has come to be called the Holocaust.

The Contemporary Covenantal Crisis

The Holocaust has ended in a devastating manner the ambiguity of the hyphenated Jew. Neo-Maimonidean thought (attempts to reconcile reason and revelation, and an inability to decisively confront the radicalness and reality of evil), scientific assumptions concerning the role of language and meaning, and political promises have all proven to be deficient before the enormity of Auschwitz and life in the post-Holocaust world. The gaping wound in the body and soul of Israel remains unclosed. Covenantal thinking appears to have been rediscovered—in a manner of speaking—as the appropriate response to catastrophe.

Contemporary concerns about the status of the covenant and all that it implies—divine hiddenness, the evident victory of evil, and man's task of mending the world—combine in the works of scholars and novelists such as Arthur Cohen, Emil Fackenheim, Irving Greenberg, and Elie Wiesel. Wiesel gives voice to the concerns of this group. He observes:

> We all stood at Sinai; we all shared the same vision there; we all heard the *Anochi*. "I am the Lord. . . ." If this is true, then we are also linked to Auschwitz. Those who were not there then can discover it now. How? I don't know. But I do know that it is possible.[12]

It is not only possible but, for Wiesel, mandatory. "Any Jew born before, during or after the Holocaust," he writes, "must enter it again in order to take it upon himself."[13]

The Holocaust glaringly revealed the ambiguity of the relationship between past and present in Jewish existence. Fackenheim terms the catastrophe of what happened to European Jewry an epoch-making event; a time of testing, for all Jews, of the ancestral faith in the harsh crucible of present experiences. Unlike previous responses to catastrophe, neither self-blame nor mystical-mythological remedies appear sufficient to the task of covenant renewal. Our age is thus afflicted by the enormity of evil while at the same time being unable to console itself with traditional responses. One fact emerges, however, with great clarity: lack of sensitivity to the Holocaust means exclusion from the realm of Jewish concern. In fact, for Fackenheim and Greenberg the distinction between religious and secular Judaism has now been superseded. Jews are either authentic or inauthentic. A willingness to confront the Holocaust, to renew, in however modified a form, the covenantal framework of Judaism, is the touchstone of authenticity.

Literary Response to Covenant Crisis

Destructions of the Temple, expulsions, forced conversions, massacres, crusades, pogroms, and other disasters, all of which have
served as historical countertestimony to the covenant, found literary
expressions in communal elegies, *selihot* and *kinot*, and in midrashim.[14] *Kinot* and *selihot* are part of the genre of Lamentation literature and were recited in mourning over an individual, or at times
of national catastrophe. Midrashim are rabbinic commentaries which
serve as a national folklore and whose purpose is to instruct the people
on how they can live with the inscrutable ways of their God. In
general, Lamentation literature acted to preserve sacral communal
memory by providing "footnotes to update the biblical revelation of
divine purpose, to commemorate the martyrs and to praise and pe-
tition God."[15] The underlying assumption of this literature was that
suffering resulted from sin, and that martyrdom was an act of sanctification of God's name (*kiddush hashem*).

The *paytan* (liturgical poet) served a prophetic function, assumed
a community of readers who believed themselves firmly rooted in the
covenant, and bore witness to the continuity of faith in spite of the
vicissitudes of history. The metahistorical concept of *k'lal Yisrael* (community of Israel) collectively endured historical tribulations secure in
the knowledge that hovering above, and superior to, temporal events
was a Lord of History who would render final judgment on the enemies of Israel and the Jewish people.[16]

Lamentation literature, like so much else in Judaism, changed
dramatically in modernity. Traditional assumptions about God's
goodness and the victim's martyrdom no longer went unchallenged.
Compare, for example, the special *kinot* which were composed by
Ashkenazi and Sephardi poets after the Chmielnicki massacres of
1648, which extolled the victims' piety and called on God to help in
the hour of despair, and reaction to the 1903 Kishinev pogrom. H. N.
Bialik's poem "In the City of the Slaughter" ("B'Ir Haharegah") com-
memorates the terrible events in Kishinev.[17] Bialik's work, however,
questions not only traditional theodicy, but also criticizes the response
of the victims no less than the actions of the perpetrators. Sidra Ezrahi
is correct in claiming that "Bialik represents the lamentation tradition
in transition."[18] God, in Bialik's poem, is inscrutable and elusive. The
divine hand, which earlier generations of Jews had witnessed in historical events, is less certain. Bialik scrutinizes every aspect of the

pogrom and bitterly criticizes the Jewish men who, after watching their women being raped, ran to the rabbi asking if it was permissible to sleep with their violated wives. Analyzing the poem Ezrahi writes:

> the speaker displays neither pure piety nor unmitigated compassion; he is as repelled by the cowardice of the victims as by the brutality of the victimizers. In this poem it is human behavior, as well as divine providence that is being tested.[19]

This testing or questioning of human and divine action is one characteristic of authentic literary response to the Holocaust.

American Judaism and the Holocaust

The question of American Jewry's relationship to the Holocaust may be approached in terms of two contrary views. Arthur A. Cohen articulates the position that all Jews, whether or not physically present in the death camps, are survivors. Although the generation of the birth of Israel lacks direct experience of Hitler's kingdom of death, Cohen describes these Jews as

> the generation that bears the scar without the wound, sustaining memory without direct experience. It is this generation that has the obligation, self-imposed and self-accepted (however ineluctably), to describe a meaning and wrest instruction from the historical.[20]

A second position is held by Jacob Neusner who argues that the "Holocaust-Rebirth myth," the catastrophe followed by the emergence of the State of Israel, is not appropriate to American Jewry's historical experience.[21] The Holocaust for American Jews, argues Neusner, is an ethnic identifier, not psychologically decisive, and misleads Jews away from their religious role. Neusner is correct in warning that the Holocaust should not become a surrogate for American Jewry's attempts to express itself Jewishly in a creative way. Adopting a "Holocaust only" view of Judaism is to misread Jewish history and to dishonor the victims of mass murder. He is on less certain grounds, however, in thinking that too much attention is paid to the catastrophe.[22]

It is one thing to state that in 1945 two out of every three Jews in Europe who had been alive in 1939 were dead. Two-thirds of European Jewry and one-third of world Jewry had been murdered. These figures are awesome and important in and of themselves. They take on added poignancy, however, when translated into the idiom employed by Chaim Grade's Hersh Rasseyner. Hersh contends that a Jew is not cognizant of the true dimensions of the loss unless he knows that "it was not a third of the House of Israel that was destroyed, but a third of himself, of his body, his soul."[23] Would it not, under these circumstances, be odd for Jews to continue as if nothing had occurred? Moreover the quality of what was lost in the Holocaust can never be replaced. "Among the dead," writes Greenberg, "were over eighty per cent of the Jewish scholars, rabbis, and full-time students and teachers of Torah alive in 1939."[24] The Nazis were intent on inflicting just such an irreparable blow on the Jews. Adolph Eichmann, master bureaucrat of murder,

> was absolutely convinced that if he could succeed in destroying the biological basis of Jewry in the East by complete extermination, then Jewry as a whole would never recover from the blow. The assimilated Jews of the West, including America, would, in his opinion be in no position (and would have no desire) to make up this enormous loss of blood and there would therefore be no future generation worth mentioning.[25]

The long-range impact of this devastation puts into question the survivability of Judaism itself. There is no covenant without a covenant people.

The contemporary American Jewish community is the result of a terrible paradox. Precisely at the moment when America assumed leadership of Diaspora Judaism, there were pitifully few qualified Jews remaining to undertake the leadership task. Wiesel conjectures that many generations will pass before there is full realization of what was lost. American moral and spiritual leadership, he writes, "still derives from Eastern Europe and those few survivors who came over before or after World War II."[26] Unlike the Babylonian exiles of antiquity, American Jews do not in the main represent the cream of the religious crop. The spiritual deepening and theological maturing which occurred among the exiles in Babylon have not yet transpired among the Jews in America. Demographics here are revealing. Of the approximately five million seven-hundred thousand American Jews, roughly 60 percent affiliate at some point in their lives with a Jewish denomination or organization. Yet in a recent national sample, only

5 percent of this number identified themselves as "integral Jews"—
"those whose Jewishness is a full-time concern, the central factor of
their lives,"[27] whether expressed religiously, ethnically, or through
devotion to Jewish affairs. One must wonder whether the remaining
more than 90 percent represent the new *maskilim*. Wiesel, in fact,
foresees a serious crisis on the American Jewish horizon.

> The American Jewish community is going to go down because the moral
> reserve and the spiritual and intellectual baggage that are required sim-
> ply won't be there.[28]

The Holocaust continues to take its toll. Americans who were never
there are heirs of the terrible legacy.

The holocaustal assault on covenant Judaism was devastating,
but covenant remains the linchpin of Jewish expression while helping
to discern genuine from spurious literary response to the *Shoah*. We
are only at the beginning of the process of developing special criteria
for judging Holocaust novels. Alvin Rosenfeld has persuasively argued for a phenomenology of reading such literature. He writes:

> we lack a phenomenology of reading Holocaust literature, a series of
> maps that will guide us on our way as we pick up and variously try to
> comprehend the writings of the victims, the survivors, the survivors-
> who-became victims, and the kinds-of-survivors, those who were never
> there but know more than the outlines of the place. Until we devise
> such maps, our understanding of Holocaust literature will be only par-
> tial, well below that which belongs to full knowledge.[29]

Rosenfeld's suggestion is an important one for American Jewish novelists and their readers, "survivors who were never there but know
more than the outlines of the place." The spate of recent books analyzing literary response to the *Shoah* testify to the great diversity of
interpretive approaches. A question, however, remains. How does
one distinguish genuine from spurious Holocaust literature?

This book suggests that a covenant orientation serves as such a
criterion; by focusing attention on a normative element in Judaism,
and simultaneously analyzing the changes which catastrophe has
brought to covenant. Writers of dissimilar Jewish background and
training may, nonetheless, be evaluated in terms of covenantal awareness. Robert Alter's perceptive observation bears repetition here. He
writes, "one cannot . . . simply discount the possibility that some essentially Jewish qualities may adhere to the writing of the most thoroughly acculturated Jews."[30] One does hesitate to compare the writings

of Elie Wiesel with those of Philip Roth, and indeed there are enormous differences between them. Yet Roth's "Eli the Fanatic" is a Holocaust story, although one which utilizes covenant as a club with which to bludgeon assimilated American Jewry. Roth is concerned neither with the theological debacle nor the profound human suffering of the Holocaust. Nor is he apparently interested in appropriating Judaism as a personal resource. His concern lies in the psychosociological realm of evaluating the behavior of American Jews alienated from k'lal Yisrael and from the stern ethical demands of covenant Judaism.

The writers whose Holocaust fiction is analyzed in this book include both major and lesser-known figures in American Jewish fiction. Saul Bellow, Bernard Malamud, Philip Roth, Isaac Bashevis Singer, and Elie Wiesel are widely read novelists whose works have appeared over a long period of time. Arthur Cohen and Cynthia Ozick are Jewish writers whose works are now beginning to receive attention. Robert Kotlowitz, Hugh Nissenson, and Norma Rosen, for their part, enjoy a smaller reading audience, but are serious writers who deal with the problematic of Jewish existence. By focusing the study on covenant transformations in face of catastrophe, new light can be shed on the fiction written by the major figures, as well as illuminating important perspectives on the problem which are brought to bear by critically acclaimed authors whose work is of a high quality but which is not widely known. Franklin Littell, the theologian, compares the situation of Holocaust response to the ancient Israelite experience of wandering in the wilderness; for forty years the Israelites were in the desert before achieving redemption. Similarly, notes Littell, we also had to wait a certain period of time before responses began to come. It is necessary to be attentive to those voices which are now grappling with the issue of covenant and Holocaust, and which no longer appear to the listener as voices crying in the wilderness.

Contributions of American Jewish Holocaust Novelists

American Jewish novelists have been criticized for responding either insufficiently, or not at all, to the catastrophe of European Jewry. The question posed by Norma Rosen is, for example, typical. Have these writers, she asks, "developed a tone of voice for writing about the deepest concerns of Jews and the world?"[31] In essence, this is the wrong query or, more accurately, the wrong way to ask. Properly focused the question is, have these writers rediscovered Judaism's covenantal base? If so, how is the covenent reflected, shaped, modified, or abandoned in their literary works? This is no easy task to undertake because American Jewish fiction is for the most part innocent of theological maturity. But the Jewish tradition is increasingly experienced as fragmented and under radical assault for those living in the aftermath of Auschwitz.

The act of writing, once invested with sacral import, has also undergone great change in modernity. Narrative as transmitter of the collective faith and destiny of Judaism has given way, in many instances, to a solipsism which appears narcissistic and private; apocalyptic rather than prophetic in tone. The work of Norman Mailer, with its idealization of violence and murder, characterizes the post-traditional emphasis on apocalypse. Queried as to his view of the relationship of American Jewish writers to the traditional attitude of the sacredness of the word, Wiesel noted that:

> unfortunately American Jewish literature is sometimes lacking in this element of sacredness. Some of the writers distort what is Jewish, with too much vilification, too little understanding. Once upon a time a Jew had to know something in order to write. Now, people write who don't know anything about the Jews.[32]

Wiesel employs a neomystical and a messianic norm for determining authentic Jewish self-expression. This standard has a specific view of covenant which is simply not available to many native-born American Jewish authors. Nevertheless, certain of these novelists utilize—even as they reinterpret—the notion of covenant Judaism.

Viewing the post-Holocaust covenantal crisis through its religious, secular, and symbolic literary expressions the present work attests to a convergence of interests, if not methods, between theologians and novelists. The Holocaust works of Arthur A. Cohen, Cynthia Ozick, and Hugh Nissenson, for example, utilize biblical, messianic, and mystical themes in their attempt to maintain a covenantal perspective on the catastrophe. Their specifically religious focus has much in common with both Wiesel's trial of God (*din Torah*) and Isaac Bashevis Singer's recognition of evil's reality and its complex relationship to the realm of the sacred. Cohen, Ozick, Nissenson, Singer and Wiesel affirm that authentic religious response to covenant crisis is the norm of the present no less than of the past. Their works may be viewed as contemporary examples of *selihot* and *kinot*. Jewish literary secularism pursues the covenant theme by reinterpreting its demands in ethical and ethnic terms. For example, the importance of Jewish peoplehood is stressed in the Holocaust novels of Saul Bellow and Susan Schaeffer. The Holocaust short stories of Bernard Malamud and Cynthia Ozick also attest to the persistence of these values. In a bold literary move, Robert Kotlowitz and Hugh Nissenson have written novels which, while set in pre-Holocaust America, contain holocaustal warnings and convey the covenantal difficulties which stem from the breakdown of Jewish identity. The works of secular Jewish Holocaust fiction attest to the necessity of remaining open to the possibility of covenantal existence which, in turn, implies a denial of despair.

The Holocaust fiction of symbolic Judaism takes up the concern for covenant in a distinctively contemporary manner, reducing Jewish self-expression to psychological and sociological glosses on covenant religion. Frequently, the Jews in the Holocaust stories of Philip Roth, Edward Lewis Wallant, and Richard Elman, as well as in Bernard Malamud's novel of pre-Holocaust oppression, have either ambivalent or negative feelings about their own Jewish identity. Some flee into the religiously indeterminate Judeo-Christian tradition. Others, such as in Norma Rosen's Holocaust novel, are Christians who attempt to comprehend the Holocaust's shattering impact on all who live covenantally. Holocaust tales of symbolic Judaism retain, however, the notion that the covenant continues to make claims on Jewish existence. The fictional Jewish characters in these stories may not acknowledge these claims, or they may be admitted only grudgingly. Nonetheless, and in keeping with Alter's previously cited observation, symbolic Jewish Holocaust fiction points both to the presence of covenantal thinking and to its as yet unresolved post-Holocaust crisis.

The Holocaust is history's most murderous and emphatic denial of covenantal promise. The enormity of this Jewish and human disaster compels response even as the realization dawns that it defies meaning. The millennial struggle between covenantal claim and historical counterclaim in its twentieth century expression nearly resulted in the theological and physical destruction of Judaism. Viewing the contention of covenant and counterclaim through the eyes of a teller of tales, Wiesel asks, "What is Jewish history if not an endless quarrel with God?"[33] In the following pages we shall discover this quarrel's dimensions in the works of American Jewish novelists whose literary response to the Holocaust reveals both the despair and the hope which characterize post-*Shoah* Judaism.

Chapter 2

Holocaust As Watershed

$\mathbf{R}$eflecting on the enormity of the Holocaust and its contemporary meaning, Abraham Joshua Heschel draws a biblical parallel. The Israelites, he recalls, did not freely accept the Torah. Coming near Sinai, they had to be coerced into bearing the burden of the law. God raised the mountain over their heads, and said: "Either you accept the Torah or be crushed beneath the mountain" (Shabbat 88a). Heschel observes that "the mountain of history is over our heads again." As in antiquity, a choice must be made. "Shall we," he asks, "renew the covenant with God?"[1] Heschel's question is the one which we shall apply to our novelists. But Heschel's query, like Norma Rosen's concerning the Holocaust sensitivity of American Jewish writers, raises a host of issues. The death camps and crematoria signify the beginning of a new and terrible chapter in mankind's history. Auschwitz signifies, writes Wiesel, "the defeat of the intellect that wants to find a meaning—with a capital M—in history."[2] Consequently, traditional theological concepts such as covenant and election, an intervening deity and messianism, have undergone severe strain. On the literary plane the problems are no less intense: Is the Holocaust beyond artistic expression? What kind of language must be employed when, in the words of novelist and theologian Arthur A. Cohen, "the imagination can no longer invent larger than the enormity of the world?"[3] Who should write of the Holocaust? What, finally, is the role of the novelist in American Jewish culture?

Holocaust Problematics

Enquiring into the history, nature, and meaning of the Holocaust one is struck by the fact that the irrational scheme for eradicating the Jewish people was undertaken in a technologically efficient, bureaucratically competent, and rational manner, thereby demonstrating the enormous gap between skills and values in modernity. Students of the Holocaust are divided as to whether the catastrophe represents a violent break with the past (Wiesel) or a fulfillment of Western civilization (Richard Rubenstein). However one interprets the event, it is clear that post-Holocaust man is a tentative and marginal figure continually poised on the edge of abyss. It is in this context that Wiesel observes that "at Auschwitz not only man died, but the idea of man."[4] Rubenstein, too, is convinced that the Holocaust demonstrated that we live in an age that is "functionally Godless," thus forfeiting appeal to higher moral laws whose invocation will restrain government's murderous actions.[5] The many questions which face those who have come after the destruction can, I believe, be subsumed under three separate but interrelated headings; conceptual-terminological, historical, and theological. Conceptual-terminological queries revolve around the issue of uniqueness.

Was the Holocaust unique? If so, how? In one sense every event which occurs is unique because of the fact that it happened, when it happened, and where it happened. But when claims about uniqueness are made for the Holocaust, the claimants mean that there is something new and radically different about the nature and perception of reality. They mean that the Holocaust is a watershed event in Jewish and human history. It is the plumb line of which the prophet Amos spoke. Mirror and magnet, the *Shoah* reveals how little we know about ourselves, and how thin is the veneer called culture. Mankind's ethical, moral, and religious assumptions were all seared in the flames of Auschwitz. Alvin Rosenfeld approaches this issue via the medium of Holocaust literature which, he contends, "is an attempt to express a new order of consciousness, a recognizable shift in being."[6] Speaking from the philosophical view which links social ethics and the sociology of knowledge, Alice and Roy Eckardt contend that the *Shoah* is "uniquely unique."[7] The best known historical study demonstrating the singular character of the *Endlösung* is Lucy Dawidowicz's richly documented and meticulously researched *The War Against the Jews 1933–1945*. Dawidowicz observes that the "Final solution was a new phenomenon in human history," in which "one people made the killing of another the fulfillment of an ideology, in whose pursuit means were identical with the ends."[8] Steven Katz's penetrating comparative study of genocides concludes that the mass murder of the Jews was "unique in intent," that is, the extermination of every living member of a designated group.[9] All of these positions view the Holocaust as having shattered extant civilizational paradigms.

Negatively stated, the Holocaust was not *merely* mass murder or genocide. The victims of these tragic events are all equally dead, but the distinction is more than a semantic exercise. Accounts of the activities of Caesar, Ghengis Khan, and the Crusaders testify to the fact that mass murder is a constant phenomenon in human history. In the twentieth century, mass murder, coupled with mass indifference, reached an intensity of historic proportion. World War I witnessed the brutal death, by gassing and other means, of millions of soldiers. The genocide of the Armenian people by the Turkish Government also occurred at this time. The term *genocide* is, however, of more recent vintage. Coined by Raphael Lemkin, a Polish Jew and an attorney, genocide asserts two, contradictory, meanings. Yehuda Bauer correctly notes that initially Lemkin speaks of the extermination of a people; Lemkin then defines genocide as discriminatory mass murder of a nation's leadership, and the enslavement and corruption of those who remain. The second part of Lemkin's definition of genocide indicates that some people will live. Holocaust, by way of contrast, means all people are to be murdered. Bauer argues that Holocaust is the "farthest point of the continuum" which leads from mass brutalization through genocide.[10] Genocides and mass murders, horrible in their impact, are nevertheless undertaken for rational—if detestable—motives (for example, land appropriation, acquiring of wealth, mineral rights, and so on, and so on). The Holocaust was, however, perpetrated on pseudoreligious grounds in order to purify the cosmos by exterminating all Jews. There was no question here of surrendering, converting, or emigrating. Birth itself became a death sentence.

In addressing the historical dimension of the Holocaust and its place in Jewish history, let us begin at the beginning and ask an apparently simple question. How does the Holocaust undermine the covenant? The destruction of European Jewry has prompted Wiesel to write: "In the beginning there was the Holocaust." What compels a comparison of covenant and Holocaust? One pillar of covenant existence is of course the continuity of the Jewish people. At decisive moments and against all rational expectation, the Israelites are permitted to continue in history, thereby insuring that God's covenantal promises to the patriarchs and to the nation would be redeemed. This endurance is itself of great moral significance. It is no accident that Simon Stern, Arthur A. Cohen's literary messiah, observes:

> And to avoid that fatal decree, the ignominious insult of being forgotten after more than three millennia of our walking upon this earth, we must stay with what we have struggled to become—endurers who say over and again what must be.[11]

The biblical ethos is replete with examples of dramatic interventions whose purpose is to insure historical continuity. The *Akedah*, Abraham's willingness to sacrifice Isaac, is a cipher of the preciousness of this continuity. A second covenantal assumption, closely related to the first, is that Jewish endurance is bound to the promise of divine presence, chosen and chooser sharing a similar destiny. Biblical religion assumed that the Israelites dwelled under the protective wings of the *Shekhinah*. Rabbinic Judaism, as noted, interpreted covenantal obligation within a midrashic framework which required study of Talmud. In modernity, covenant fidelity was, as we have seen, frequently understood in ethical terms. Neither belief in divine intervention, adherence to the ritual of study, or human goodness could, however, withstand the Nazi murder machine.

Judaism has persisted in persisting. Each era of Jewish existence has endured its own Amalekites bent on the eradication of the Jewish people, but despite the ferocity of such assaults they all fell short of their goal. Romans, Crusaders, Cossacks, and modern secular rulers have tried—and failed—to subdue or obliterate Judaism. Seen in historical perspective, however, the intensity and totality of the assaults have increased with the passage of time. Raul Hilberg argues that the development of Europe's attitude toward the Jews underwent three stages: you have no right to live among us as Jews; you have no right to live among us; and, for the Nazis, you have no right to live. Conversion, expulsion, and extermination are the names given to these three stages.[12] But Judaism, although severely attacked, still remains an historical force even after the demise of National Socialism.

How is one to understand this Jewish endurance? Some view it in terms of God's grace, a mystery in the religious sense of the word. Martin Buber and Emil Fackenheim are eloquent spokesmen of this neo-Orthodox understanding. Others contend that the suprarational origin and meaning of Jewish survival is more intense than mere religion. Elie Wiesel writes that for him, "the essence of Jewish history is mystical and not rational."[13] Similarly, Heschel's position is colored throughout by his own mysticism. Certain scholars claim, more modestly, that the laws of Jewish historical development are unconventional, and behave differently than the so-called normal rules of history. The idiosyncratic position is articulated in a clear and concise manner by Henry L. Feingold. However one interprets the phenomenon of Jewish survival, it is plain that the *Endlösung* was a negative witness, so to speak, of Jewish singularity. Writing of the impact of the *Shoah* on covenant thinking, Cohen observes:

> The *tremendum* is more than historical. It is an elaboration of the most terrible of Jewish fears—that the eternal people is not eternal, that the chosen people is rejected, that the Jewish people is mortal. If there is one incontestable article of the Jewish unconscious, it has been the mythos of indestructibility and the moral obligation of tenacity. Six years, nonetheless, nearly concluded three millennia of endurance. Is it a wonder that Jews should regard the *tremendum* as a caesural fissure that acquires with each decade a more and more profound meta-historical station as the counter-event of Jewish history, the source of its revisionist reconsideration and self-appraisal.[14]

Cohen's eloquent and penetrating insight provides a framework within which one can understand the impact of the Holocaust on covenant thinking. In other words, for the first time in Jewish history, empirical events threatened complete obliteration of the mythic structure of Jewish existence—the counterevidence of history is overwhelming. But, one may object, such history is always awesome. Did not Jewish survivors, from the time of exile on, feel the sting of divine rebuke or the obligation to persist? This time, however, the question was, had the Jewish people been chosen for extermination? Wiesel opines that owing to the evil revealed by the Holocaust, the Jewish mission to the world is comparable to a "collective suicide mission."[15]

Theological Responses

At this point it is appropriate to examine the positions of selected covenant revisionists, bringing together their theological reflections on the nature and possibility of post-Holocaust covenant affirmation, and works of American Jewish Holocaust fiction. This section will focus on Arthur Cohen, Emil Fackenheim, Irving Greenberg, Richard Rubenstein, and Elie Wiesel. These thinkers are representative of a wide spectrum, although they by no means exhaust the kinds of

Holocaust thought now operative in the Jewish community. Cohen and Wiesel are themselves novelists as well as being moved by theological passions. Fackenheim and Wiesel were both in Nazi camps, although at different periods and under vastly different conditions. Fackenheim was released from Sachsenhausen concentration camp in 1939. Wiesel was liberated from Buchenwald in 1945. Greenberg and Rubenstein have suggested profound revision of traditional covenant thought. All of these thinkers view the Holocaust as decisive for covenant religion, and as an event which challenges traditional understandings of God, of the divine-human relationship, and the Jewish vocation in history. Concepts of language and imagery, ethics, and the notion of Jewish-Christian encounter are called radically into question by the extermination of six million Jews.

Arthur A. Cohen views the Holocaust as a unique event in Jewish and human history. "Anything," he writes, "we might have known before the *tremendum* of this event is rendered conditional by its utterness and extremity."[16] Traditional remedies such as the biblical assumption of punishment for guilt, or the mystical faith which transformed exile into a salvific opportunity, are inappropriate responses to the Holocaust. Offering what may be termed a three caesura paradigm of Jewish history, Cohen notes that the destruction of the Temple in ancient Palestine resulted in an abyss which the Jews closed by affirming their guilt. The second abyss, opened by expulsion from Spain, was breached by a mystical understanding of historical events (Lurianic kabbalah). The death camps were, notes Cohen, another caesura of the demonic. "This time," he writes, "the abyss opened and one-third of the Jewish people fell in."[17] Jewish thought progressed from guilt, to hope, to meaninglessness. Cohen calls for the creation of a new language. The Holocaust, or *tremendum*, must be sub-scended, penetrated writes Cohen, "to its perceivable depths."[18] For Cohen, divine speech is man's hearing.

Specifically concerning the task of the novelist, Cohen has observed that "the first work of a Jewish literature" is "the redivising of the narrative condition of the people of Israel and the Jewish people." Cohen views the conjunction between literature and theology as normative, engaging the moral and religious dimensions of life. He writes:

> The literary imagination—in my rendition—verges it would seem to the spinning webs of theology. But, has it not always been so? I think it no irony that the literary experience to which we go back again and again (not once only for the sake of hearing or mastering a special voice) are those that ambitiously engage the deepest question of human origins

and ends. Not that they succeed in demonstrating such meanings (for demonstration would fall to linguistic precisionism) not, for that matter, that they achieve coherence and conceptual clarity (for that is philosophy's task, or even that they project answers conterminous with those described by the great religions (for that one needs theological dialectic), but rather that they exhibit richly and deeply the complexities of being human in a dark age such as ours. That is the task of literature and, insofar as it succeeds in imagining the rivings of the human, it documents the ground of immanence, our suffusion by the world as it is.[19]

The idea of novelist as theologian, although not in the formal sense of the term, while not a new concept in Judaism, has assumed increased appeal and urgency in light of the Holocaust. Concerning this role, Primo Levi wondered if the stories of survivors are not in themselves a new Bible.

Emil Fackenheim sees the catastrophe as an epoch-making event which determines the valence of the past for contemporary Judaism. Fackenheim, with Cohen, views the *Shoah* as unique. It is unlike any other epoch-making event in Judaism. Its uniqueness, for Fackenheim, lies in two factors. No rational purpose was achieved by exterminating the Jews. "The Nazi murder of the Jews was an 'ideological' project; it was annihilation for the sake of annihilation—evil for the sake of evil." Secondly, the situation of the victims was without parallel. The Nuremberg laws defined a Jew as one who had three Jewish grandparents. Therefore, the one million five hundred thousand Jewish children murdered were killed "because of the Jewish faith of their great-grantparents." Fackenheim then reveals the dilemma confronting Jewish people in the post-Auschwitz universe. He writes:

> Had these great-grandparents abandoned their Jewish faith, and failed to bring up Jewish children, then their fourth-generation descendants might have been among the Nazi criminals; they would not have been among their Jewish victims.[20]

Fackenheim asserts that a "Commanding Voice" of Auschwitz bids Jews to remain Jewish even in the face of the catastrophe. Jewish steadfastness is commandment number 614 of Judaism. In fact, to abandon the faith would, Fackenheim argues, be handing Hitler a posthumous victory. Such abandonment occupies the role played by idolatry in classical Judaism.

Fackenheim's post-Holocaust theological reflections negate distinctions between religious and secularist Jews, both of whom were mandated by the Nazis for extermination. Instead he views Jews as being either inauthentic—those who flee from Jewishness—or authentic—those who affirm it. "This latter group includes religious and secularist Jews. These are united by a commanding voice which speaks from Auschwitz."[21] Fackenheim invests the very survival of Jews with theological significance. After Auschwitz, Jewish survival is no longer mere survival but a fundamental duty which has a suprarational resonance. Unlike Cohen, Fackenheim does not call for a new language, but utilizes, and transforms, the classical midrashic framework in approaching contemporary Jewish existence. Midrash embraces paradox, recognizing that oppositeness must be affirmed while continuing the task of seeking covenantal meaning in Jewish existence. What Fackenheim terms "the logic of Midrashic stubbornness," is exemplified by the rabbinic phrase k'b'yakhol "as it were." He writes:

In rabbinic theology . . . (k'b'yakhol) is a . . . technical term, signifying, on the one hand, that the affirmation in question is not literally true but only a human way of speaking; and, on the other hand, that it is a truth nonetheless which cannot be humanly transcended.[22]

The midrashic framework enables Jews to endure the vicissitudes of history while embracing the promise of covenant. The messianic age will be the time of solution for seemingly insolvable theological dilemmas. Therefore, midrashic thought insists on fragmentariness, being expressed in story, parable, and metaphor. Fackenheim examines, and rejects, several possible explanations of midrash's relationship to disaster (such as, midrashim of divine powerlessness, of protest, of martyrdom and of punishment for Israel's sins). The task of conflicting midrashim in confronting catastrophic events is "not how to explain God but how to live with Him."[23] Fackenheim boldly extends the notion of midrashic existence after Auschwitz by positing the necessity of "Mad Midrash." Midrashic madness is,

the Word spoken in the anti-world which ought not to be but is. The existence it points to acts to restore a world which ought to be but is not, committed to the faith that what ought to be must and will be, and this is its madness. After Planet Auschwitz there can be no health without this madness, no joy, no life. Without this madness a Jew cannot do—with God or without him—what a Voice From Sinai bids him do: choose life.[24]

Mad midrash is Fackenheim's attempt to respond to the Holocaust by utilizing a modified form of rabbinic interpretation.

Irving Greenberg argues that the Holocaust is an orienting event for Jews, Christians, and humanists. The extermination of European Jewry is radical countertestimony to the sanctity of life and the integrity of man. Greenberg poses the ultimate touchstone for any attempt at responding to the Holocaust: "No statement should be made that would not be credible in the presence of the burning children."[25]

Greenberg contends that traditional faith responses are not adequate in confronting Auschwitz. Instead, he posits the notion of a post-Holocaust moment or dialectical faith. Neither classical theism nor the Jewish death of God positions are viable theologically because both views treat the Holocaust under extant categories. The *Shoah*, in Greenberg's view, signals the end to final solutions, "even theological ones."[26] Moment faith, for its part, moves between hope for redemption (Jerusalem) and the sheer countermass of historical events (Auschwitz). The dialectic operates between "moments when redeemer and vision of redemption are present, interspersed with times when the flames and smoke of the burning children blot out faith though it flickers again." For Greenberg, while Auschwitz must not be permitted to "overwhelm Jerusalem," neither may Jerusalem negate Auschwitz.

Greenberg suggests three theological models for those living in the Auschwitz universe: Job, the suffering servant, and controversy with God. The Book of Job rejects easy pieties or facile denials. Whatever the measure of Israel's sufferings, she may, like Job of antiquity, restore contact with the divine out of the whirlwind. Universalizing the lessons of the Holocaust, Greenberg then discusses the suffering servant interpretation based on Isaiah 53. Struck for the sins of all humanity, the suffering servant testifies that the state of the world is, despite claims to the contrary, unredeemed. The servant's existence stands against absolutizing "the relative status quo." Treatment of the suffering servant serves as "a kind of early warning system" of the inherent sins of culture. The third model is characterized by anger and controversy with God. Prominent in the writings of Wiesel, this mode is biblical in origin and Greenberg views its contemporary application as renewing the intensity of the divine-human relationship. It is a radical form of "protest from within."[27]

Greenberg also negates the distinction between religious and secular, while advocating what he terms the covenant's voluntary nature.

It makes no essential difference if the Jews involved consciously articulate the covenantal hope or express a belief in the God who is the ground of the covenant. The witness is given by their actions. Actions speak louder than words. People who profess God but gas men, women and children or burn them alive are atheists whatever their words may be. People who profess to be atheists and to be without hope yet who actively uphold the covenant, even at the cost of their lives, betray their true position by their actions. If anything, their denials only add to the hiddenness of the Divine. Therefore, their theological language is the appropriate one for this time, more appropriate than those who go on speaking as if God were visible and fully performing under the previous terms of the covenant.[28]

Greenberg's notion of voluntary covenant is based on the original covenant and emerges logically from his view of God's increasing hiddenness in history. The voluntary covenant depends on recognition that the apparently secular can in fact be deeply religious, and that being humanly responsible is a revelatory act.

Voluntarily embracing the covenant is, for Greenberg, a positive counterevent to the massively negative testimony of Holocaust. Voluntarily living a Jewish life is, therefore, an "affirmation of God's presence" and is analogous to the situation of the voluntary convert to Judaism whose action attests that, although the Jews are hounded by history, he—the convert—testifies to hope.[29] Incorporating the Holocaust into the national life of Israel and the Jewish people is accomplished by ritual, pilgrimage (both to sites of death camps and to Israel), the telling of the tale in film, books, and other media, and by "a range of acts of justice and restored dignity." Greenberg, with Fackenheim, argues that reverence for life—*kiddush hahayyim*—constitutes the central post-Holocaust religious testimony.

Richard Rubenstein views the Holocaust as having ended once and for all the Jewish notion of a superintending God of history. In fact, traditional theological categories are inadequate to cope with either of the two monumental upheavals in twentieth-century Jewish life, the Holocaust and the religious meaning of the state of Israel. The Holocaust is, for Rubenstein, as for Cohen, Fackenheim, and Greenberg, the touchstone of authentic Jewish theology. He has written that "the problem of God and the death camps is the central problem for Jewish theology in the twentieth century."[30] Unlike the aforementioned, however, Rubenstein contends that God, the covenant, and chosenness were murdered with the Jews of Europe. Rubenstein argues that the classical triad upon which Judaism rested, God, Torah, and community, now is reduced to two pillars; Torah and community.

Rubenstein reached a "theological point of no return"[31] in his postwar discussion with Heinrich Grüber, a Protestant clergyman who had risked his life to save many non-Aryans, including Jews. Grüber viewed Hitler as an instrument of God's will, much as had been the case of Nebuchadnezzar. Relying on the Biblical notion of punishment for sin, Grüber advanced the position that Europe's Jews had—somehow—deserved the Holocaust. Rubenstein's response is to assert that, if such thinking and such murderous actions are the result of the doctrine of chosenness, then the doctrine must be discarded. A God who either permitted, or was powerless to stop, the extermination of His people, is worthy neither of their belief nor their lives. Jews must abandon their attempts to sanctify history and return to nature, a form of neo-Paganism, which means that Jewish religious experience will be "predominantly cyclical and ahistorical in nontechnological matters."[32]

Community and ritual are all that remain to post-Auschwitz Jews. But the Rubensteinian idea of community lacks the classical Jewish mythic structure of covenant and a superintending deity. The metahistorical coming of the messiah is, for Rubenstein, obliterated by the sheer mass of history. Steeped in existentialism, psychoanalytic interpretive categories, and a kind of mystical neo-Paganism, Rubenstein reveals the depth of his covenant abandonment in contending that we treasure our religious community precisely because human existence is hopeless and without meaning.[33] Ritual practices are, however, "so authentically rooted in human need that they are unlikely ever to be dispensed with." Rubenstein is also convinced that the doctrines of covenant and election resulted in two thousand years of training in powerlessness which, in a manner of speaking, prepared the Jews mentally and physically to acquiesce in their own destruction. In place of God and covenant, hallmarks of survivalist or powerless Judaism, Rubenstein calls for a language of force and potency.

Elie Wiesel is a survivor of Birkenau, Auschwitz, Monowitz, and Buchenwald through whose firey gates he entered as a young student of Jewish mysticism and the Talmud. He testifies for the millions who were slaughtered; his books serving as a bridge between the wreckage of civilization and the possibilities of rebirth. Wiesel contends that "everything that has to do with writing is sacred." He testifies that for him:

> writing is a *matzeva*, an invisible tombstone erected to the memory of the dead unburied. Each word corresponds to a face, a prayer, the one needing the other so as not to sink into oblivion.[34]

Yet, Wiesel shoulders a double burden. He has written that "the concept of a theology of Auschwitz is blasphemous" for both believer and nonbeliever. On the literary plane, Wiesel notes the inadequacy of language when writing about the death camps: "A novel about Auschwitz is not a novel, or it is not about Auschwitz." The contradictory and simultaneous demands which the Holocaust makes are silence and speech.

For Wiesel, the novelist has an awesome and sacred task. "We have to write a new Talmud," he opines, "just as we did after the destruction of the Second temple . . . in order to accentuate the new beginning."[35] Wiesel's new covenant has been termed, by Michael Berenbaum, "an additional covenant."[36] It "can no longer be between humanity and God or Israel and God, but rather between Israel and its memories of pain and death, God and meaning."[37] Wiesel's additional covenant has three characteristics: solidarity of the Jewish people, witnessing to the sheer endurance of Jewish existence, and the sanctification of life. The God of Wiesel's new covenant is a diminished deity who—in the kabbalistic mode—depends for His existence on the actions of man. Wiesel's neomystical response to the catastrophe is a powerful witness to the significance of moral, or prophetic, madness—the willingness to stand for the sacredness of life as a guide for living in an Auschwitz universe which is marked by brutality, depersonalization, and widespread indifference. Wiesel's emphasis on witnessing is, however, a difficult and tenuous task, one which attests to the increasing ambiguity of the divine-human relationship in the post-Holocaust world.

Collectively, these thinkers hold that the Holocaust was unique and, consequently, the history of the world must now be clearly demarcated into pre- and post-Holocaust periods. Theologically, God has been either seriously diminished (earlier, the kabbalists contended that the *Shekhinah* was along with the Jews weeping and in exile) or, for Rubenstein, vanquished entirely by the events of 1939 to 1945. Failure to engage the catastrophe means that one has not come to full human consciousness. All of the positions attach great significance to the necessity of community, *k'lal Yisrael*, thereby embracing a prophetic rather than an apocalyptic stance. Even Rubenstein's insistence on the divinity of holy nothingness is made against the background of the importance of ritual and communal existence, thereby advocating the emergence of Jews who have transcended the limitations of mythic Jewish history while nonetheless remaining Jewish. Each of the positions takes seriously the reality of evil and the moral importance of Jewish endurance. The issues they raise collectively serve as benchmarks of what is authentically Jewish writing.

Theology and Literature

Literary encounters with the *Shoah* have yielded a variety of characters whose views personify these main currents in Jewish Holocaust theology. For example, Isaac Bashevis Singer's Tamara (*Enemies, A Love Story*), a survivor of both Hitlerian and Soviet enslavement, typifies a Rubensteinian Jew who has abandoned the mythic structure of Jewish history but has retained strong communal bonds. Singer's troubled Herman Broder (*Enemies, A Love Story*), a refugee who had been hidden from Hitler's terror in a Polish hayloft, exemplifies Rubenstein's own theological dilemma: How can one accept a God who permitted Auschwitz? Saul Bellow's Artur Sammler (*Mr. Sammler's Planet*) is a literary embodiment of Irving Greenberg's refutation of enlightenment assumptions. Emil Fackenheim's impassioned and powerful comments on the "614th commandment," are expressed literarily in the works of Wiesel. Susan Schaeffer's Anya (*Anya*), a survivor, is a secularist who finds comfort in a tradition which she might just as logically have abandoned. Anya's faith is eloquent testimony to the elusive quality of post-Holocaust distinctions between religious and secular Jews. Hugh Nissenson and Robert Kotlowitz have written novels which underscore Judaism's perilous encounter with modernity and its Holocaust portents; loss of belief in God, fragmented communal life, assimilationist impulses, and Jewish self-denial. These authors explore the possibility of a covenantal Jewish existence similar to Rubenstein's moral but godless, Judaism.

Jewish writers whose encounter with the Holocaust has not changed their orientation, display great ambivalence about the tradition. On the one hand, even the most thoroughly acculturated among them, such as Philip Roth and Richard Elman, have written Holocaust stories. But these tales lack an understanding of either Judaism or the Holocaust. Roth's "Eli the Fanatic," for example, utilizes, in a highly superficial manner, hasidic survivors of the Holocaust to symbolize an authenticity which, in the author's view, is lost to assimilating American Jewry. Similarly, Roth's *The Ghost Writer* does great violence to Holocaust history. Yet Roth's Holocaust fiction may also be viewed as a goad for American Jewry to rediscover covenantal norms from which they have departed in so radical a fashion. In this case, Roth's work, which might indeed be only satire, can also stand as a modified version of Greenberg's position that the Holocaust is an orienting event.

Is the Holocaust Beyond Artistic Expression?

The entire enterprise of making art from the Holocaust is controversial and problematic. Michael Wyschogrod contends that it is forbidden to make art out of Auschwitz because art takes the sting out of suffering.[38] And indeed, initially, the Holocaust was viewed as a barrier for writers no less than for theologians. Art assumes meaning, but Hitler's kingdom of death systematically destroyed the concept of rationality. T. W. Adorno, for example, observed that "language itself had been damaged, possibly beyond creative repair, by the politics of terror and mass murder."[39] Bureaucratic manipulation of language soon became perversion. Jews were "liquidated," "resettled," or singled-out for "special handling," not murdered. Those who choose to respond to the Holocaust need to recognize the gap which exists between ordinary language and the death camp experience. Primo Levi compares "free words, created and used by free men who lived in comfort and suffering in their own homes" to the linguistic world of the camps (*Lagers*).

> If the Lagers had lasted longer a new, harsh language would have been born; and only this language could express what it means to toil the whole day in the wind, with the temperature below freezing, wearing only a shirt, underpants, cloth jacket and trousers, and in one's body nothing but weakness, hunger and knowledge of the end drawing nearer.[40]

Can this world be spoken of or written about?

Addressing the dilemma of whether speech or silence is the appropriate reaction to the Holocaust, Fackenheim writes, "silence would, perhaps, be best even now, were it not for the fact that among the people the floodgates are broken, and that for this reason alone the time of theological silence is irretrievably past."[41] Consequently, the earlier advocacy of silence (Adorno, George Steiner, Wiesel), has been overturned even by the advocates themselves. George Steiner's essay on silence[42] and his reflection *The Death of Tragedy*[43] were followed by a provocative novel *The Portage to San Cristóbal of A.H.*,[44] a tale of the purported arrest and interrogation of Hitler—discovered hiding in South America. Neither total silence nor continued speech, it seems, is appropriate. Man is *homo narrans*. But one needs to work dialectically between speech and silence, recognizing that—however many of the facts are known, and whatever new details concerning the methodology of murder are uncovered—the Holocaust ends where it began, with the death of reason and the defeat of man.

Who Should Write of the Holocaust?

We are confronted by an ever-increasing body of literature and criticism by both survivors and those who have come after. At the very least, we are required to distinguish what constitutes authenticity in these works. Although literary criteria cannot be ignored, the quest for the authentic requires the writer and the reader to distinguish between substance and shadow. Perennial questions about the relationship between form and content pale before the enormity of how to write about the Holocaust. The *Shoah* has been discovered, so to speak, by Americans. Novels, movies, and television programs have conveyed various distortions of the event, thereby influencing the lives and perceptions of millions. There is a bad joke that says it all: "Have you heard about the Holocaust? Oh, you mean the movie?" What culture does with the facts of mass systematic murder reveals a great deal about society's values and its future.

An extreme view holds that only those who endured the death camps should be permitted to speak. Testimonial literature—chronicles, diaries, journals, memoirs, novels, and poems written by those who survived and by those who did not—bears witness to the sheer otherness of the death camps—"laboratories," Hannah Arendt called them—"in which the fundamental belief of totalitarianism that everything is possible is being verified."[45] Although there is merit in the claim of Arendt and Fackenheim that because the death camps were literally beyond belief, first hand literary reports may be of less use than ex post facto interpretations, this author takes it as axiomatic that works by victims constitute Holocaust literature *stricto sensu*. The stance in favor of recognizing as authentic only the works of survivors involves, however, more than a genre issue; it raises two problems. Judaism is a tradition of midrash making. All formative events in Jewish history have elicited response both from those who were there and those who were not present or, in Cohen's words, those who were really and those who were literally present. Exodus has entered the liturgy. All Jews are required to experience the flight to freedom from Egyptian bondage. Secondly, the saved remnant is dying. Soon there will be no more first-hand accounts written. Thus, an unintended consequence of restricting access to the Holocaust event will be the gradual cessation of attempts to confront the reality of the demonic. Generations will grow up who do not know the Holocaust and its implications.[46]

More is at stake than reminiscence of a mythic past. The covenantal framework is, as we have seen, a creative and flexible, but permanent, point of orientation for Judaism on its historical sojourn. Events of the present are weighed against ancestral paradigms. Consequently, epoch-making events must be incorporated into the liturgical and ritual life of Israel. Covenant is the key to Jewish self-understanding. If history triumphs over covenant, Judaism ceases to have a *raison d'être*. It is for this reason that Greenberg has proposed that the Holocaust be ritually incorporated into the life of *k'lal Yisrael* thereby taking its place in—rather than terminating—the ongoing saga of Jewish existence. He writes:

> In the decades and centuries to come, Jews and others who seek to orient by the Holocaust will unfold another sacral round. Men and women will gather to eat the putrid bread of Auschwitz, the potato-peelings of Bergen-Belsen. They will tell of the children who went, the starvation and hunger of the ghettoes, the darkening of the light in the Mussulmen's[47] eyes. To enable people to reenact and relive there are records, pictures, even films—some taken by the murderers, some by the victims. That this pain will be incorporated in the round of life we regret—but we may hope that it will not destroy hope but rather strengthen responsibility, will, and faith.[48]

Greenberg's position is cogent testimony to the centrality of post-Holocaust witnessing on the part of all Jews, and others, who ponder the question of man's destiny in the age of Auschwitz. For Jews it is a mark of continuity with the tradition, respect for their slaughtered brethren, and an affirmation of their Jewish commitment and destiny. Non-Jews will be reminded of what happens when human obligation and compassion are no longer esteemed civic virtues.

Trivializing the Holocaust

Wiesel told an interviewer that "twenty years ago they [American publishers] ignored the truth by refusing to listen. Now they ignore it by trivializing it."[49] Let us look at two examples, one Jewish and the other non-Jewish, of trivialization. The *Shoah* has been ritually incorporated into the fiction of certain Jewish writers as a series of stories parents tell to keep their children Jewish and well-behaved. Nessa Rapoport's *Preparing for Sabbath* exemplifies Jewish misuse of the Holocaust.[50] Here the catastrophe appears no more than a heuristic device for maintaining ethnic identity, much in the manner described by Neusner.

Recent American fiction of the Holocaust treating its non-Jewish victims tends, for its part, toward triumphalism and false universalization.[51] *Sophie's Choice*, for example, fails to comprehend the Jewish specificity of the Holocaust. Ahistorical in method, Styron's novel deals not so much with an epoch-making event, but with human existence in extremity, sexuality, slavery, and sterotype. This kind of Holocaust novel encourages trivialization by ignoring the interconnection between the destiny of Judaism and the fate of Western civilization. Styron draws the incredible conclusion that Jews are insensitive to the Holocaust. Cynthia Ozick has pinpointed the underlying error in ersatz universalization of the disaster. "Jews are no metaphors," she writes, "not for poets, not for novelists, not for theologians, not for murderers, and never for anti-Semites."[52] *Sophie's Choice*, while capitalizing on the Holocaust fad, if one may use that term, raises a serious problem. It may well be the case that Styron accomplishes in the literary world what the so-called revisionists—the falsifiers and deniers of history—are trying to achieve among academics and the gullible public, de-Judaizing the Holocaust.

American Jewish Writers and the Holocaust: A Critique

The suggestion has been made that response to the Holocaust requires an alliance of the chronicler and Job—witness and man of faith—present during the time of destruction.[53] Whatever the intrinsic merit of this suggestion, which I think is considerable, it excludes American Jewish novelists who, spared by historical circumstance, could only be "witnesses through the imagination." Lacking knowledge of Judaism in many cases, its non-English languages, its history, its culture, and its ritual life, Jewish-American novelists testify to the truth of Joseph Blau's observation: "it is one characteristic of modern Judaism in all its varieties that constancy to the ancestral faith has been more of a problem than has adaptation to the surrounding world."[54] Many American Jewish writers in fact seem to prefer viewing themselves as American writers who are also Jewish, the surrounding world being a more familiar and accessible subject than the ancestral faith. Jewish writing, a genre dear to the hearts of literary critics, is not restricted to Jews, and bears no necessary relationship to writing as a Jew. The difference is comparable to, say, enjoying a chopped liver sandwich as opposed to reading a page of Talmud. Nevertheless, as the gruesome truth became known, American Jewish novelists had before them not only the enormity of the extermination project, but the realization—slowly dawning—of their own vulnerability.

The initial silence of American Jewish novelists in responding to the Holocaust requires analysis. Some have suggested that these writers did not wish to stir up latent American antisemitism.[55] The obverse of this position is the stance adopted by Arthur Miller who observed that writing about the bad traits of the Jewish people would merely provide ammunition for antisemites. The assumption behind both of these contentions is that if one remains silent about one's identity, the oppressors and potential oppressors will then cease their oppression; it is as if all those good German-Jewish citizens had never been marched to the gas chambers protesting their allegiance to Germany. In this context, Norma Rosen's cogent observation takes on added poignancy: "The Holocaust is the central occurrence of the twentieth century. It is the central human occurrence. It cannot therefore be more so for Jews and Jewish writers. But it ought, at least, to be that."[56]

Many events have, collectively, served as a catalyst in bringing the Holocaust trauma closer to the center of the American Jewish literary consciousness: the Eichmann trial, which incidentally served a similar purpose in Israel; the Six Day and Yom Kippur Wars; the writings of Elie Wiesel; unrelenting hostility from the extreme left and right; international antisemitic campaigns spearheaded by the Soviet Union; a rising sense of ethnic and religious awareness on the part of American Jews; and the earlier mentioned television and movie productions. These factors have led an increasing number of Jewish writers to a dual realization: Jews are still singled out, even in a secular context, as "a people dwelling alone" and, second, Jewish destiny is inextricably linked to the fate of Israel. On the mythic plane, some time must pass before the enormity of a great historical tragedy is assimilated into human consciousness and expressed in works of art, myth, or mysticism. Spanish exile, as we have noted, was incorporated into the Lurianic kabbalah only some fifty years after the event.

But the question remains: Did the silence of Jewish-American novelists indicate a period of reflection? Or did it reveal the depth of the American acculturation process?

Twentieth-century American Jewish literature has experienced three major periods, each of which reflects a certain relationship between Jewish and American identity. Initially, the immigrant novel focused on the difficulty of being both a good American and a good Jew. Abraham Cahan's *The Rise of David Levinsky* chronicles the pitfalls inherent in the perceived either/or dilemma confronting the immigrant Jew. Anzia Yezierska, a little-known contemporary of Cahan, also writes of this struggle and is among the earliest to offer a female perspective of the times. For these writers Judaic values seemed on a collision course with secular American values. The second era of Jewish fiction is characterizable by the assimilated nature of its Jewish figures. Here the values of American culture; individualism, civic religion, and suburban living, became the norm against which to evaluate fictional Jews. Literature of this period satirized middle-class values which, somehow, were identified with Judaism. The works of Philip Roth come immediately to mind. The third manifestation of Judaism in American Jewish fiction has witnessed the appearance of Jewish characters to whom covenant Judaism is the norm. These fictional Jews evaluate American culture in terms of its relationship to Jewish (Hebrew or Yiddish) standards. Arthur Cohen and Cynthia Ozick are significant names here, but so are Mark Helprin, Robert Kotlowitz, Jay Neugeboren, and Hugh Nissenson.

The movement of Jewish-American fiction toward Jewish specificity or high seriousness was, as noted, prompted by many events. But the fact remains that many Jewish novelists have not dealt with the catastrophe of European Jewry, having told us neither plainly, nor in symbolic terms, anything about Auschwitz or post-Auschwitz man. For those novelists who have written Holocaust stories, I suggest that one criterion for authentic Holocaust fiction *lato sensu*, is recognition of what the catastrophe involves: its Jewish specificity, its continuing trauma, and its moral, societal, and theological implications.

The Role of the American Jewish Novelist

The theological worth of literature is a fundamental tenet of Jewish existence where the telling of stories and the learning of faith are inextricably woven together. Biblical *mashal* (parable), rabbinic midrash, and medieval elegy were communal utterances of faith and hope. Those who composed their words were viewed as inspired individuals able to commune with God or to discern some facet of His inscrutable will in contemporary events. The theological distinctiveness of tales in Judaism rests on the assumption that, in Greenberg's words,

> the story touches levels conscious and unconscious, cultural and personal, that neither formal literature nor philosophy can ever reach. In fact, to be a Jew is to hear stories and claim them as one's own; to live accordingly and to keep telling them to someone else.[57]

Literary art implies theological vocation. Scribal craft and prophetic narrative virtuosity retained their hold on the Jewish imagination even with the advent of modernity. Two examples—both provided by Jewish historians—are instructive. The last reported words of the secular nationalist Simon Dubnow, shot in the back by the Nazis, were "*Yidn— Fahrschreibt! Fahrschreibt!*" ("Jews, record! record!")[58] Do not omit one word of what is happening to our people. Lucy Dawidowicz contends that the Jewish historian writing even a fragment of the history of the Holocaust may actually be involved in a "secular act of bearing witness to Auschwitz and to the mystery of Jewish survival."[59] Narrative, even in a secular context, serves a transcendant purpose: preservation of *k'lal Yisrael*. Can we apply Dawidowicz's bold assertion to novelists who, unlike historians, are committed not only to report and interpret events, but to prophesy?

There are various interpretations of the novelist's post-Holocaust task, ranging from the political to the theological. Steiner has, for example, written that Jews need to tell about the Holocaust, to be on their guard, to warn their children, to know the signals, so that "we can tell the noise when it comes and be on our toes and know how to react."[60] The literary critic Edward Alexander shares Steiner's perception contending that American Jewish novelists must begin to equip their readers for tragedy.[61] Cohen, as we have noted, has argued that novelists must redivise the narrative condition of the Jewish people. Wiesel's seriousness of purpose stems from his realization that he speaks for and about the victims of the cataclysm. Consequently, his observations establish a norm for those who write Holocaust fiction, especially *lato sensu*. Wiesel observes:

> I believe that every writer today, no matter who, Jewish or not Jewish— but particularly Jewish—must write with the Holocaust as background,

as criteria. Once he takes this as a background, as a yardstick, he will be careful in writing.[62]

America's Jews are of course addressed by a variety of individuals; rabbis, academics, so-called Jewish professionals, theologians, and novelists. It is, therefore, artificially restrictive to contend—as Philip Roth has—that American Jews are forced to choose between rabbis and novelists. Yet historically, rabbis were scholars, writers and story tellers. Maimonides and Naḥam of Bratzlav are but two examples, although the latter did not teach by writing but utilized tales and parables. Indeed certain American rabbis have also been writers—Chaim Potok and Milton Steinberg. The plain fact is that although American Judaism comprises 45 percent of world Jewry, it is by no means a monolithic, religiously informed group. It is, rather, composed of many strands—religious and ethnic—all of whom (wittingly or otherwise) are attempting to cope with modernity, with America, with Judaism, and with the idea of covenant. It is, however, true that novelists are increasingly viewed as more representative and interesting than other articulators of the Jewish experience.[63] Novelists can raise the ultimate Holocaust problems about God and man and meaning without having to provide ultimate solutions. They are, moreover, able to address these fundamental issues without being limited by denominational politics. Provocative and serious, the best of the Jewish novelists are grappling with the problematic of post-Holocaust Jewish existence in a manner which finds extraordinary resonance among their audience.

American Judaism lacks the cohesion and resources of traditional Jewish society which, as Jacob Katz tells us, based its existence "upon a common body of knowledge and values handed down from the past."[64] This type of society, as noted in chapter one, began disintegrating in the eighteenth century. The modern experience of communal dissolution and theological stagnation has meant the loss of reliance on classical texts and rabbinic authority for clarification and resolution of Jewish and human problems. Consequently, many American Jews depend on novels, rightly or not, for their knowledge about fundamental Jewish issues. Increasingly it is the case that American Jewish novelists, whether grudgingly or willingly, have assumed the role of theologians of Jewish culture. We should not assign them a role which the novelists themselves hesitate to accept. But many writers view themselves as performing a task of utmost seriousness. Wiesel has observed that survivors wrote for the "extraordinary purpose of saving mankind." This lofty ambition may not be uniformly shared by the novelists in this study. However, it does establish a criterion by which to measure their literary response to the *Shoah*. Chapter three analyzes novelists whose writings remain within the midrashic framework while addressing the Holocaust's impact on covenantal Judaism. The work of novelists discussed in chapter four is secular in outlook and views the midrashic framework as having been severely strained by the catastrophe of European Jews. The fiction of the novelists in chapter five assumes that the Holocaust has shattered this framework.

Chapter 3

Holocaust Responses I: Judaism As A Religious Value System

What one critic terms "Act II" of American Jewish writing[1] is in fact a religious revival. Stunned by the Holocaust and its theological implications, novelists such as Arthur A. Cohen, Hugh Nissenson, and Cynthia Ozick are exploring the possibilities of authentic Jewish life after the catastrophe. As such, their Holocaust fiction forms a contemporary midrash to an ancient Jewish question: How is it possible to live after a destruction? (Ezek. 33:10). Traditionally, answers to this query have upheld the covenant while fortifying a sense of Jewish vocation. Like the Babylonian exiles, the rabbis in Palestine, the mystics of Safed, and the pious Jews in pre-Holocaust Europe, these writers are turning inward: seeking guidelines from within traditional sources by which to approach the issues of theodicy, divine concealment, and human responsibility in the post-Auschwitz universe. The vicissitudes and sheer awfulness of contemporary history prompt these novelists to seek a hidden, more profound, meaning in events. Symbolically, the work of this group is influenced by the assumptions of rabbinic midrash, by the Jewish mystical tradition, especially the sixteenth-century kabbalah of Isaac Luria, by messianism, and by the genre of hasidic tales.

Cynthia Ozick's "lesson of the shofar" serves as a collective symbol for this new type of Jewish-American fiction which eschews American culture as normative. Only by sounding into the shofar's narrow end, this group believes, will their work be spread across the land. This fiction exemplifies what Ozick terms "liturgical literature": it has "a choral (communal) voice, the echo of the Lord of History."[2] Akin to a theological meditation, this literature views the novelist's task as prophetic; announcing that no matter what the devastation, a remnant shall be saved (*shear yashub*), and the tradition renewed.

The Holocaust and American Diaspora Jewry

The works of this new group testify to the realization that the ambiguities of Diaspora existence have been clarified with devastating certainty by the destruction of European Jewry. But there is an inherent and inescapable tension in the notion of Diaspora. While nurturing creatively Jewish expression in literature and religion, it has been the historical fate of Diaspora communities to experience devastation and upheaval. Nonetheless, and in spite of their familiarity with the historical record, Ozick and Cohen foresee a religiously creative and morally significant role for Judaism in America. With Yavneh for Ozick and Bene Brak for Cohen, America is seen as crucial to the resuscitation of post-Holocaust Judaism. Ozick has written that American Jewish culture comprises the "Aggadists, the makers-of-literature" and must assume a role equal to that of Jerusalem—place of "the healers, the health-bringers, the safe-keepers, in reconstructing contemporary Jewish life."[3]

The relationship between Israel and the Diaspora is, however, complex. Ozick employs Yavneh as "an impressionistic term, a metaphor suggesting renewal"; although she has now considerably modified her earlier optimism. America will nurture Judaism, but only for a brief historical moment, until Israel "consolidates itself against savagery."[4] Israel is the enduring home of Judaism and the place to which all Jews must eventually go. Cohen, on the other hand, views Israel differently. His use of Bene Brak, like Yavneh an academy established after the second destruction of the Jerusalem Temple, challenges the assumption that "For out of Zion Shall Go Forth the Law" (teaching). His survivors emphatically choose life in America rather than embark on a postwar journey to Palestine. Jewish separateness and religious creativity can only flourish, for Cohen, in New York City. Nissenson, less occupied with geography, is concerned with locating "a sense of the numenous. A sense of the holiness of life."[5]

All of these novelists take seriously Emil Fackenheim's notion of the centrality of Auschwitz for Jewish consciousness. Fackenheim writes:

> The Jew after Auschwitz is a witness to endurance. He is singled out by contradictions which, in our post-Holocaust world, are world wide contradictions. He bears witness that without endurance we shall all perish. He bears witness that we can endure because we must endure; and that we must endure because we are commanded to endure.[6]

Fackenheim, as we have seen, invests the very survival of Jews with a theological significance which surmounts the distinction between religious and secular. "The North American Jewish hero," writes Fackenheim, "is he who has confronted the demons of Auschwitz and defied them."[7]

Act II Holocaust fiction employs distancing devices in treating the catastrophe. Geographically, the locales are America or Israel or pre-Holocaust Europe. In terms of time, the world portrayed is either shortly before the destruction, or—with the exception of Cohen's *In the Days of Simon Stern*—post-Holocaust. Only two of the writers in this group address daily life in the camps, Ozick's "The Shawl,"[8] and portions of Nissenson's "The Law"[9] which reconstructs a survivor's wartime experience. The ongoing trauma of Holocaust survival itself is stressed. Cohen, Ozick, and Nissenson, unlike their predecessors in Act I, assume a Jewishly literate audience and utilize esoteric symbols and concepts of the Jewish religious tradition.

Hasidic Tales

Hasidic tales are the best known modern genre in which a conscious attempt is made to have literature express messianic, mystical, and mythic themes. While not all of a single style, the hasidic tale is a *hieros logos*, a sacred story, one in which the narrative itself bears salvific import. Telling hasidic tales is, moreover, akin to performing an action. Like the rabbis of old who believed their prayers had cosmic ramifications, those who told and heard hasidic tales were engaged in religious activity. For example, the Ba'al Shem Tov, (Besht) specifically compared the telling of tales praising *zaddikim* (wonder-working mystics and holy men) to being engaged in mystical activity. The sacral power of hasidic tales is well known, and perhaps nowhere better revealed than in the following story. The Besht, when faced with a difficult spiritual problem, would go to a certain place in the woods, meditate, and light a fire. The problem would then be resolved. As the legend goes, the Maggid of Mezhirech, successor to the Ba'al Shem Tov, could only go to the same place in the woods. The Maggid was unable to light the fire. However, meditation in prayer was still possible. And this was sufficient. The next generation, personified by Rabbi Moshe Leib of Sassov, knew where the holy place was, but could not light the fire. Nor did Rabbi Moshe know the secret meditations accompanying the prayer. However, knowing the secret place in the woods was sufficient to accomplish the task at hand. Rabbi Israel of Rishin, representing the fourth generation, had also to perform a task. His generation could not light the fire, forgot the prayers, and did not recall the place. But they could tell the tale. And this was sufficient.

Concerning the Holocaust, hasidic tales serve as both examples for, and warnings to, contemporary men and women. All of Wiesel's literary works are touched by the hasidic imprint. Two of his books, however, attempt to directly utilize the lives, teachings, and struggles of *zaddikim* as models for human aspiration and divine revelations: *Souls on Fire: Portraits and Legends of Hasidic Masters* (1972), and *Four Hasidic Masters and Their Struggle Against Melancholy* (1978). The portraits which Wiesel so masterfully paints concern holy men who live intensely on the cutting edge between covenant and history; individuals for whom the divine promise of redemption—while flawed—is nonetheless present. More recently Yaffa Eliach's *Hasidic Tales of the Holocaust* (1982) presents an electrifying and humbling collection of tales which testify to human faith in divine stewardship during the catastrophe. Based on interviews with survivors, witnesses, friends, and family members, these tales bear contemporary witness to hasidism's continuing emphasis on the theological worth of literature.[10]

Considering the Evidence

Arthur A. Cohen

Cohen's *In the Days of Simon Stern* (1973) is a rambling novel which freely weaves together various messianic, kabbalistic, and talmudic interpretations of the Jewish vocation, and explanations for theodicy. A pastiche of philosophical and theological ruminations, Cohen's work emphasizes the reciprocal nature of the divine-human relationship. Millennial Jewish endurance and apartness continue in our time. The book extols the virtues of Hebrew as the sacred tongue (*leshon hakodesh*), the "language of anticipation, of new beginnings and salvation." English, for its part, is the second language of the world. It is in English that the world "heaves and groans." Cohen's novel liberally utilizes Hebrew and Yiddish words. In the political sphere, Cohen reacts to American Jewry's naïve trust in Roosevelt and the democratic process. Simon Stern notes that: "If Jews wish to endure, they, alone . . . must be responsible." The Holocaust has put an end to the phenomenon of hyphenated Jewry. It is no longer possible to live life as an American-Jew, a German-Jew, a French-Jew, or other. The choice is either/or. One can be a Jew or refrain from making such a claim. But the choice must be consciously made. "In the past being Jewish was eternal being. No longer. It's an option of knowledge or stupidity."[11]

The novel is composed of four books, each with a prologue, two epilogues, and an appendix. The form of the book, as well as the title *In the Days (Be Yemei)*, indicate that it can be viewed as an addition to the Bible. In actuality, however, the book encompasses a series of tales within the larger story. These component tales may be read as examples of the hasidic genre. They contain apparent miracles, extol the divine meaning of storytelling itself, reflect the paradox of necessary evil in the universe, and are ruminations on the meaning(s) of the messiah. The various episodes are presented in hagiographic form, devotedly recreated by Nathan of Gaza, Simon Stern's blind scribe.

Simon's tale begins in Eastern Europe where a strange, mad, female seer foretells the birth of a son to Abram, Simon's father. His son, she predicts, will be responsible for the deaths of his parents. And he will be the messiah. Born in New York, Simon is physically undersized but a mental wizard. A student of *halaka* (normative Judaism) and kabbalah, Simon's "passion became money." By the outset of World War II he has amassed sixty million dollars primarily through the real estate business which he has operated according to *halakic* precepts. However, he continued to live modestly with his parents on the lower East Side, preferring never to travel uptown. A fire caused by faulty wiring, which Simon had been told to correct, claims the lives of his parents and further scars Lubina Krawicz, the Stern's crippled non-Jewish tenant.

Following his parent's deaths, a second crisis occurs. Simon trav-

els uptown to hear Chaim Weizmann speak at a Madison Square
Garden rally. The news is horrendous. Two million Jews have already
been murdered by the Nazis. Simon vows to rescue a remnant of the
death camp survivors, and recruits assistants for the task. Dr. Fisher
Klay, Viennese born Ph.D., is chairman of an organization called "The
Committee of Rescue." Although a secularist, Klay shares Simon's
concern that Jews must remain apart from society at large. The two
men establish "The Society for the Rescue and Resurrection of the
Jews." This group will contain "a remnant whose strength shall be
in mutual love and helpfulness and disdainful removal and estrange-
ment from all others" (p. 207).

Simon and Klay sail to Europe. There Simon adds to his staff.
Rabbi Lazare Steinmann, Russian-born, has "been on the losing side
of every major conflict of the century." But Steinmann himself makes
a crucial distinction between empirical events, transient in nature,
and moral laws, which exercise an abiding claim on men. Wrong in
all things pragmatic, he claims "I don't think I have ever been morally
wrong." At Buchenwald Simon chooses two additional people; Nathan Gaza and Janos Baltar. Nathan is descended from a family of
rabbis and scribes. Baltar, a half-Jew, is a "homicidal maniac, nothing
more or less; . . . a kind of inverted Christ," who opened the wounds
of the world and forced them to bleed again. The embodiment of evil,
Baltar engages Simon in lengthy philosophical discourses about
theodicy.

The death camp remnant is installed in the Shearith Housing
Center, a lower East Side Citadel which Simon has constructed behind
a tenement facade, a small Bene Brak, where the remnant can "rebuild each other's flesh and spirit," witnessing that "despite all, everything, Jews will endure." The compound is built according to the
specifications of Solomon's Temple. This third Temple is fated, like
its two predecessors of antiquity, to be destroyed. Inside the compound there are secret rooms, concealed passages, and hidden en-
trances. The outside world must not know what the Jews are doing.
Within the compound ritual Jewish existence and prayer life are en-
couraged. The Jews are forced to choose between the messianic Simon
Stern and the maniacal Janos Baltar, who had smuggled two million
dollars' worth of arms and ammunition into the compound. It is the
explosion of this material which destroys the rebuilt Temple, and
Baltar.

Simon's tale concludes with Blind Nathan's report that the messiah travels, after the Temple's destruction, uptown and into Central
Park. The implication is that Simon Stern is to embark on his messianic

task in the world, on behalf of all its inhabitants. As Nathan tells us, Simon Stern "joined himself to the large world."

In the Days of Simon Stern responds to catastrophe by reminding Jews of the complexity of evil, the mystery of the divine-human relationship, and the vocation of endurance. Interpreting a passage from Isaiah (God makes alive and kills), Simon articulates a kabbalistic view: "God contains within Himself the possibility of good and evil." But Simon argues that evil, far from being a flaw in the cosmos, is complexity. This complexity consists of the fact that even evildoers can act with nobility and heroism. Simon illustrates his point with reference to Janos Baltar.

> The very heart of the struggle between good and evil, between Baltar and ourselves, is that we are not all good and he could not be wholly evil (p. 308).

This mixing of the realms, so to speak, demands a remedy.

> Repentance.[12] Turning. Turning away. Turning back. Returning. These motions of regeneration are what the Jewish people must stand for (p. 308).

Simon's life and deeds, his homilies and his discourses, may all be viewed as reactions to the question posed in his father's posthumously delivered letter: "Why is it always so, that good should come out of evil?" (p. 167). The answer, for Cohen, depends on whether one views the world through a philosophical or a mystical prism. Against an unnamed "German philosopher" (Husserl), whose demand is that understanding requires bracketing one's experience, isolating the world into autonomous units, Cohen has Simon advocate viewing existence in the kabbalistic mode. The universe is a great chain of being. Everything is interconnected. Simon notes that:

> We should not want to reduce down to the essence, but to build up toward everything, to embrace and hug as much as we can, to make our eyes wide-angled apertures extending the horizontal breadth of our sight, however much it foreshortens our vertical vision (and that's right too, for the vertical vision is inside a man and what really counts is that he have a broad sight to support his vision) (pp. 316–17).

Simon's messianic mission is proclaimed by three different sources: the female seer, Nathan of Gaza, and an unidentified figure whose characteristics suggest that he is the prophet Elijah. Elijah, link between the generations, identifies himself to Simon merely as a "visitor by profession and a storyteller." His visit occurs while Simon is in mourning for his parents. Simon is neither awake nor fully asleep. He dreams.[13] Elijah, who validates his metaphysical prowess by entering and leaving Simon's room through a locked door, relates "The Legend of the Last Jew on Earth." (pp. 118–153). Don Rafael is a medieval Spanish Jew who, despite hardships, trials, and eventual execution, remains firm in his Jewish conviction. He attests: "I endure and my endurance is an offense." Though it be an offense, endurance also is an example. Don Rafael's martyrdom served as catalyst for the appearance of a new generation of those who were called Jews. Elijah's visit, wisely conceived, is important as it serves to identify Simon with the Jewish messianic tradition (Elijah never dies but is carried to heaven in a fiery chariot), to announce that as Jewish persecution has been overcome in the past so must it be now after the Holocaust, and to establish the very possibility that such divine-human encounters can still occur.

Nathan of Gaza is an obvious reference to the prophet of Sabbatai Zvi, the seventeenth-century pseudomessiah. Nathan differs from his predecessor both physically, he is blind and not ascetic; and theologically, he does not confuse Simon with God. Much is made of Nathan's blindness. Like Saul Bellow's one-eyed Artur Sammler, Nathan's insight is more penetrating than visual perception. Alvin Rosenfeld suggests, in fact, that from a literary point of view,

> the Holocaust has worked on its authors in a double way . . . simultaneously disabling them and enlarging their vision, so that they see with an almost prophetic exactness. Holocaust writers . . . are one-eyed seers, men possessed of a double knowledge: cursed into knowing how perverse the human being can be to create such barbarism and blessed by knowing how strong he can be to survive it.[14]

Simon observes that "we must learn to see as blind Nathan sees or we are all to remain murderers" (p. 354). Baltar, however, does not regard Nathan's insight as paradigmatic. Threatened by the scribe's knowledge of his illicit arms smuggling, Baltar threatens to kill Nathan.

Nathan's primary theological insight is that Simon has wrongly attributed divinity to himself. Simon's "enormous acts of salvation," observes Nathan, have resulted in "palpable ineffectualness." Consequently, Simon grew impatient with the historical process of salvation. It was this impatience rather than theological arrogance, however, which prompted Simon's actions. In Nathan's words:

Simon's resolve to transform us, to wither our ancient limbs of submission and paralyze our habitual kneebending to historical fortune, struck me then as uncharacteristically ungenerous (p. 366).

Simon was guilty of attempting to "force the end";[15] hastening the messianic era by imposing human will on the historical drama of exile and redemption, Simon had overstepped the bounds of his salvific mission.

The figure of Simon is employed to illustrate the complexity of evil. He is a *lamed-vov zaddik*, one of the thirty-six hidden righteous men whose presence supports the world's existence.[16] He has confronted the Holocaust's evil and rescued the pitiful remnant at Buchenwald. Yet Simon has borne terrible witness to the truth that evil is part of every man, himself being at least partially responsible for his parents' death. Fisher Klay articulates this complex relationship between good and evil, calling Simon "our *sitra achra*. Our demon and our redeemer in one" (pp. 386–87).

Cohen's novel moves toward an historical end time. On the microcosmic level this movement is seen in Simon's efforts to unify the downtown and uptown Jewish communities. Downtown Jews are those of Eastern European origin who are less assimilated, more traditional, and less affluent than their uptown counterparts. The latter are Central and Western European acculturated Jews, economically stable, and theologically Reform. It is helpful to recall here that rabbinic speculation on the messiah's tasks included the assertion that at the end of time the messiah will reconcile all the differences between Jews.[17] On the macrocosmic scale, while Simon realizes that "everything is embedded in particularity," he also begins to travel, joining himself to "the large world." While Nathan asserts that "the Messiah is a Jew," his task is universal in scope.

Simon Stern realizes, after the compound's Temple is destroyed, that it must be rebuilt again. The sense of destruction and reconstruction which form the essence of traditional Judaism is here elevated to the position of a pivot around which all else rotates. Simon articulates what might be termed Judaism's prophetic mission: "The world is unmerciful and the Jews announce the principle of justice. Always the same. The world does—in its gentile fecklessness—and the Jews stand to the pulpit and pound the principle" (p. 431). Failure to take part in the redemptive drama puts one on the side of the criminals. The murderers, announces Simon, are everywhere, "they are the ones who do not pay attention." This announcement applies to Simon himself, unaware of Baltar's scheme, and failing to repair the faulty wiring; as well as to American Judaism which had, in the view of many, paid insufficient attention to European Jews during the Holocaust.

In the Days of Simon Stern portrays the terrible uncertainty of the divine-human relationship after Auschwitz. Simon is chastised for confusing himself with God while simultaneously being profoundly aware of the differences between himself and the Creator. But the novel is no less an indictment of the divine. A "merciless narcissus," God is forced to choose between the ways of the world and the Jews. Simon contends that:

> I wish merely to unfold a logical demonstration to God, that this and this is the way of the world, thus and so is the way of your creatures, choose then who you wish to be. Choose, dear God, if you wish to remain our God (p. 265).

Simon's recasting of the covenant theme, viz, God's choosing the Jews, implies that post-Holocaust Jews must, as suggested by Wiesel and Greenberg, assume a much more active role in their relationship to the divine. Fisher Klay articulates this position in his question to Nathan. "Do you imagine," he asks, "that the work of redemption is done without the cooperation of the redeemed?" Redemption is cooperative. We are conspirators, observes Klay, "to save the saver." Although specifically referring to their attempt to assist Simon by providing him details of Baltar's arms scheme, Cohen is here suggesting that the kabbalistic notion of man as the redeemer of God may be the only way to save both man and God in the aftermath of Auschwitz.

In the Days of Simon Stern is ambivalent in its assessment of the American Diaspora. Jews are free but not safe. Their particularity must be hidden behind a facade. But the issue goes deeper than concealment from society at large. After all, the Marrano phenomenon demanded the same guise from Jews of the Iberian Peninsula. On one level, the debate may be viewed as a choice between America and Israel. Inasmuch as this is the case, Cohen's view is clear. Rabbi Steinmann observes that Simon Stern is a visionary who builds castles in the sky. However, David Ben-Gurion was an "unskilled engineer who built castles in the sand." But it is premature to conclude that America is the new Promised Land.[18] For Cohen, to live in history is to be unredeemed. Luria's kabbalah taught that the messiah would come only as visible proof that the world had been restored. In this sense history, as such, remains a snare. *Tikkun*, world-restoration, is a continual process. It is not accidental that Nathan observes "the war of the survivors . . . will continue," perhaps for centuries (p. 238).

Cynthia Ozick

Cynthia Ozick has written that "stories ought to judge and interpret the world." But universal meaning can only be derived from particularistic experience. "Literature," she has written, "is the recognition of the particular."[19] Responding to the Holocaust requires not only an encounter with, but a struggle to redeem from, evil. Ozick's "redemptive literature" is embedded in biblical, rabbinic, and mystical symbolism. Her Holocaust fiction expresses two types of response to the disaster. On the one hand, she emphasizes the survivors' singularity as covenant witnesses. A second type (analyzed in chapter 4) treats post-holocaust Jewish identity by merging holocaustal and feminist concerns which stress character portraits of secularist survivors.

"Bloodshed" (1976), her earliest novella of the Holocaust, reports the visit of Bleilip, an acculturated Jew, to his cousin Toby who lived in a new hasidic community near New York. A lawyer (secular rabbi), he is no longer a practicing attorney but has become a full-time fundraiser, the quintessential expression of suburban American Judaism. Bleilip was a contented secularist who "liked his life excessively" (p. 58). Apparently repulsed by the religious ambience of the nascent community, he nonetheless was awed by its inhabitants; all or most of them were either survivors or children of survivors.[20] He knew their Holocaust experiences made them wholly unlike American Jews.

Invited to *mincha* (evening prayers), Bleilip is an auditor at the rebbe's explanation of the contemporary meaning of the ancient rite of *Azazel*; the sacrificial killing of a scapegoat symbolically laden with the community's sin.[21] He hears the rebbe contend that post-Auschwitz Jews stand *"instead of"* the goat whose horns were adorned with a crimson sash. Contemporary Jewish existence is cursed for having to live without the messianic presence. The rebbe laments:

> In the absence of Messiah . . . we are not free, we are only *instead of* . . . instead of choice we have the yoke, instead of looseness we are pointed the way to go, instead of freedom we have the red cord around our throats, we were in villages they drove us into camps, we were in trains, they drove us into showers of poison.[22]

Interrupting his discourse, the rebbe points an accusing finger at Bleilip as the embodiment of faithlessness. To the surprise and dismay of his faithful disciples, the rebbe orders Bleilip to empty his pockets. Doing as commanded, he reveals that he has two guns, one toy and one real. The rebbe, reflecting his experience with euphemism and deception at the hands of the Nazis in Auschwitz ("soap" stones and "shower" heads) states, "it is the toy we have to fear" (p. 71).

There follows a discussion between Bleilip and the holy man which can only be described as theological in character. The rebbe observes that "it is characteristic of believers sometimes not to believe. And it is characteristic of unbelievers sometimes to believe." He then elicits from Bleilip a startling confession. The secularist believes in God, "now and then." The rebbe concludes their discussion with the remarkable observation that Bleilip is "as bloody as anyone" (p. 72).

"Bloodshed" is a novella which incorporates mystical paradox. The rebbe (hasidic mystic) and the atheistic Bleilip are the same age, and both are plagued by theological uncertainty. Bleilip was initially unable to recognize the rebbe. In fact, the holy man is described as disfigured, with a pitted nose, wearing a worker's cap, and looking like a common laborer. It is impossible to recognize the hidden saint (*nistar*). When Bleilip states that he is visiting "with the deepest respect," the rebbe responds: "We are not South Sea Islanders sir, our practices are well known since Sinai." The rebbe is a believer, like Cohen's Simon Stern, in influences or turnings. Turnings from folly, error, and a mistaken life. He tells Bleilip that despair must be earned. Like Naḥman of Bratzlav, great grandson of the Ba'al Shem Tov, this modern hasidic leader embraces Naḥman's most enigmatic paradox: "There is nothing so whole as a broken heart."

Bleilip's trip (dare we think of it as a pilgrimage?) to the community is made voluntarily to visit a distant relative. Ozick implies by this device that even the most apparently acculturated of Jews is unable to resist the magnetic bond of peoplehood. The Besht frequently testified that all Jews were limbs of the *Shekhinah* (divine presence), and only Sabbatai Zvi, the apostate messiah was cut off from the possibility of salvation. But first Bleilip must be made to see the sterility of his own life. He vaguely remembers fragments of his boyhood reading about Judaism and about the hasidim, but Bleilip considered them "actually christologized: everything had to go through a mediator." Listening to the rebbe's talk, Bleilip is seated like a child at a school desk, able to discern only words and phrases of what was being said in Hebrew, and in Yiddish. Ozick symbolizes the beginning of Bleilip's initiatory process—dissolution of the old self, a return to childhood—which marks the commencement of his transformation to a questioning member of the faith.

The rebbe becomes Bleilip's guru, however, only after first empirically demonstrating his occult powers. Like Cohen's Elijah figure, Ozick's rebbe must prove himself. This he accomplishes by reporting Bleilip's inner thoughts—all laden with despair—which he discerned by means of his mystical insight. It was Bleilip's despair which the rebbe had articulated in his remarks on *Azazel*. The rebbe publicly rebukes Bleilip: "Man he equates with the goats. The Temple, in memory and anticipation, he considers an abattoir. The world he considers a graveyard" (p. 68). His relative's "white stare" indicated to Bleilip that this was not the rebbe's usual way.

Dismissing his followers, whom he addresses as "little fathers," the rebbe attempts to reach Bleilip at the latter's level of Jewish comprehension. Rather than deliver a learned talmudic exposition or an esoteric mystical sermon, which would be far beyond Bleilip's capabilities, or interests, the rebbe engages him in a rational mode of discourse concerning the dangers of modernity's illusions. The *zaddik* descends, so to speak, in order to redeem sinners. In classical hasidic terminology, Ozick's rebbe is engaged in *yeridah le-zorekh aliyyah*— "the descent in behalf of the ascent." The gas chambers which the Nazis called shower rooms, the toy gun, secularism, all exemplify the deceptiveness of modernity. The rebbe's fingers, which he calls "toys," are deformed as a result of a Nazi experiment in Buchenwald.

Bleilip embodies the religious uncertainty of modern man who, although skeptical of organized religion and feeling himself blocked from access to the transcendent, nevertheless longs for meaning and certitude. Bleilip, for example, had hoped to at least glimpse the effect of the rebbe but "never supposed he would get to the rebbe himself." On the other hand, Bleilip "hated accuracy in a survivor." Far better, he thought, was "some kind of haze, a nostalgia for suffering." Ozick combines the figures of rebbe and survivor as links with authentic Judaism. Survivors are bridges between American Jews and the vanished world of Eastern European piety, testifying to the Holocaust's centrality even for American nonwitnesses. Bleilip's vocabulary, "habitually sociological," provides a measure of the difference between American and East European Judaism. Against sociological Judaism, Ozick places the specifically mystical figure of the rebbe. Bleilip, in fact, misterms the holy man, calling him a rabbi (a Torah scholar) rather than a rebbe (a mystic who has achieved *devekut* or communion with God).

Men of faith must deal with despair. To be a believer in a Lord of History and the covenant requires one continually to search for a hidden or deeper meaning amidst the chaos of existence. Bleilip's toy gun has been interpreted by one critic as "the rascally, crafty, cheating and evasive hand of the demonic."[23] But existence itself is a confrontation with the demonic. The rebbe espoused the hasidic dictum that "every man should carry two slips of paper in his pockets. On one paper should be written: 'I am but dust and ashes.' On the other: 'For my sake was the world created.' " The Holocaust has laid bare the danger implicit in the kind of humanism which defines itself solely according to the latter assertion. Bleilip, by confessing to the rebbe his belief, although inconsistent, in God, has taken the first step toward opening himself to the true nature of evil in the post-Holocaust world, and to the possibility of covenant renewal. After the Holocaust it is impermissible and inauthentic to refrain from taking evil and suffering seriously. More than mere categories of classifying human experience, the reality of evil and the overwhelming nature of suffering unleashed by the death camps compel one to rethink all of one's basic assumptions, both humanistic and theological. Bleilip's metamorphosis means that he is a likely candidate for Greenberg's notion of voluntary covenant.

"The Shawl" (1980), another in the Ozick corpus of Holocaust fiction, is a unique story because it directly confronts the horrors of a death camp experience.[24] The tale, told from the perspective of an omniscient narrator, concerns three Jewesses; Rosa, her infant daughter Magda, and her adolescent niece Stella. The story centers around Rosa's unsuccessful attempt to keep Magda—who is wrapped in a mysterious shawl—alive. In the brief space of two pages Ozick paints the familiar but no less terrifying landscape of death and torment which was the fate of Europe's Jews; forced marches, starvation, dehumanization, the filth of death camps, murder, and the indifference of the world. She spares no detail of Jewish misery. For example, Rosa contemplates giving Magda to a stranger during the course of their march toward certain death. Rosa thinks, however, that if she left the line of prisoners she would be shot. But supposing she managed to hand the shawl-wrapped infant to an unknown woman, would the stranger take the precious package? Or would she drop it, splitting Magda's head open? Countless thousands of Jewish women had to confront this dilemma, one which makes King Solomon's decision seem a pale thing in comparison.

Both on the march and in the camp itself, the shawl provides life-giving sustenance. When Rosa's own sore breasts were dry, Magda sucked on the corner of the shawl and "milked it instead" (p. 33), with the smell of "cinnamon and almonds" emanating from Magda's mouth. Ozick twice describes the nurturer as a "magic shawl"; one which could "nourish an infant for three days and three nights." Although pitifully undernourished, Magda lived long enough to walk. Rosa gave the child almost all of her own food. Stella, on the other hand, was envious of Magda whom she gazed at "like a young cannibal," and to whom she gave no food. Rosa's premonitions about Magda's impending death grew increasingly strong. The Jews were, writes Ozick, "in a place without pity." (p. 33). Toddling across the roll call area without her shawl Magda is murdered by a guard who throws her onto the camp's electrified fence. Rosa, watching from a distance, is helpless; able only to stuff the shawl into her own mouth in order to swallow "the wolf's screech ascending now through the ladder of her skeleton." Rosa tasted "the cinnamon and almond depth of Magda's saliva," drinking the shawl dry.

Ozick has masterfully combined covenant Judaism and a mystical parapsychology as responses to the pervasive hopelessness of the death camps. The magic shawl is a literary symbol of the tallit. Although women were freed from the so-called time-bound *mitzvot* (commandments), such as wearing a prayer shawl, Jewesses have donned this ritual object. The Talmud tells, for example, that Rabbi Judah the Prince, editor of the Mishnah (second century C.E.), affixed *tzitzit* (tallit fringes) to his wife's apron (Menahot 43a). Wrapping oneself in a prayer shawl is tantamount to being surrounded by the holiness and protection of the commandments; as well as conforming to the will of God. The wearer of the tallit is a member of the covenant community. Ozick's shawl/tallit is a talisman which protects both Rosa and Magda when they either wear or hold it. Separated from the shawl, Magda dies. The shawl saves Rosa as well. If she had screamed at her daughter's murder she would herself have been murdered since the Nazis, amplifying the edict of Pharaoh, had decreed that having a Jewish child was an offense punishable by death.

Rosa is also portrayed as being literally above the earth, or able to overcome history. Ozick employs a variety of words to suggest that Rosa, like her subsequent literary heir Feingold in "Levitation," can fly. For example, Rosa, while on the march, was "already a floating angel." Magda's mother "flew, she could fly, she was only air" (p. 33). Magda, for her part, is also described in flight imagery. Riding on the shoulders of her Nazi murderer, she is "high up, elevated." She appeared—hurtling toward the death fence—as a "butterfly

touching a silver vine" (p. 34). Rosa is also clairaudient; she hears
"grainy sad voices" coming from the fence. What do these phenomena signify?

Ozick strongly implies that the camps, designed to turn Jews into
matter and then to destroy that matter, although successful to an
awesome and staggering degree, were not able to achieve complete
domination of the Jewish soul. The peculiar aroma of cinnamon and
almonds, itself so out of place in the midst of death, corpses, and
wind bearing the black ash from crematoria, evokes a quasimystical
image of the *besamim* (spice) box. Jews sniff the *besamim* at the *havdalah*
ceremony which marks the outgoing of the Sabbath, thereby sustain-
ing themselves for the rigors and tribulations of the profane or ordinary days of the week. By utilizing the prayer shawl and spice box
imagery, and paranormal phenomena usually associated with the
mystical element of Judaism, Ozick's tale conveys the message that
the bleakness of the historical moment is not the final chapter in
Jewish existence. Jewish religious creativity and covenantal symbolism can occur even under the most extreme conditions. The eternality
of Israel is symbolized when Rosa and Stella survive the death camps,
and come to America (see chapter four).

"Levitation," another piece of Ozick's Holocaust fiction is, in the
Ozick tradition, a tale of remembrance and warning.[25] Like "Bloodshed," "Levitation" employs a strategy of revealing the difference
between authentic and inauthentic Jews, employing Holocaust memories and awareness as touchstones of authenticity. Bleilip, the acculturated Jew of "Bloodshed," is measured against the yardstick of
hasidic mystical piety and survivorship. He is portrayed as being
sensitized to strive for redemption. If anything, the Jewish situation
in "Levitation" has deteriorated. Feingold has married a Christian.
He and Lucy are novelists, "anonymous mediocraties." What saves
Feingold, while differentiating him radically from Lucy as well as the
acculturated Jews of America, is the voice of an anonymous refugee—
friend of a friend—who is mysteriously present at the Feingold's
party. The voice reminds Feingold of the pain and suffering which
occurred during the Holocaust. A time when "the eyes of God were
shut. Shut . . . like iron doors" (p.13).

The novella is comprised of three main sections. As the reader
moves through them the seeming closeness of Feingold and Lucy is
revealed as an unbridgeable chasm. Their inadequate marriage is hinted
at in Ozick's initial character portraits. Feingold "had always known
he did not want a Jewish wife" (p. 3). Consequently, he married a
minister's daughter. But he immersed himself in the history of Jewish

martyrdom, writing about Menachem ben Zerach, survivor of a fourteenth-century Spanish massacre who had hidden under a pile of corpses until rescued by a "compassionate knight." Lucy had always "hoped to marry out of her tradition." As an adolescent she "became an ancient Hebrew" while listening to her father read a psalm to his congregation. She spent much of her time reading European romances. The notion that each spouse is out of place occupies the entire novella.

The Feingolds are fascinated by power, although powerless themselves. They have a party for literary celebrities, none of whom attend. Those guests who do appear—mediocrities like their hosts—congregate in the dining room where all the food is. Lucy observes that the "living room's got nothing." Feingold is distressed because the evening is sure to be a social disaster.

Ozick's literary device for indicating a transition to the major issue is the lighting of a fire in the fireplace. Lucy has previously announced—in response to a guest's request that the fireplace be lit—that neither the fireplace nor Feingold's grandmother's candlesticks are ever used. The flames reveal the presence of Feingold's seminary associate. Lucy is uneasy with her husband's "theological" friends. Here, Ozick merges both literature and mysticism. Mysticism has to do with light, clarity, vision. The very titles of classic Jewish mystical texts such as the *Bahir* and the *Zohar* translate as Brightness and Splendor. Moreover, Ozick is retelling the hasidic parable concerning the power of a tale (see p. 42). In Ozick's version, Feingold lights the fire while the anonymous refugee tells the tale.

Section two accentuates the differences between Feingold (Jews) and Lucy (Christians), heightening the irony of their earlier fascination with each others' tradition. Now Feingold is absorbed by talk of God or historical atrocities. For example, he is interested in the historical coincidence of Magna Carta and the Jewish badge of shame. Lucy, for her part, is apprehensive about too much Jewishness. Feingold's seminary friend had administered her conversion, and she felt every encounter to be an examination. Lucy did, after all, sometimes speak about Jesus to the children. At this point in the tale Ozick has accomplished Lucy's religious isolation. She is the only non-Jew in the living room. The Jews in the dining room are the inauthentic, acculturated kind:

the humorists, the painters, film reviewers who went off to studio showings of *Screw on Screen* on the eve of the Day of Atonement (p. 12).

Lucy is, moreover, annoyed with Feingold. He is having one of his spasms of fanaticism; recalling the historical episodes of Jewish martyrdom. In her view, "Feingold was crazed by these tales, he drank them like a vampire." She wishes he would be normal. All those with sense, thought Lucy, "the humanists and humorists . . . would want to keep away." Lucy's elevation of the behavior of humanists as normative stands in sharp contrast to the collective failure of this group during the catastrophe. Writing of resistance in the death camps, Wiesel states that the first to give in and to collaborate, in order to save their lives, were the intellectuals and the humanists. They had, notes Wiesel, nothing to lean on.[26]

The tale's third and major section is introduced by Ozick's description of the refugee survivor. Unlike the rebbe in "Bloodshed" around whom a congregation formed, this survivor is an outsider. Face shielded, unknown to all but one of those assembled, the refugee possesses great moral stature. He is the voice for whom Feingold has been waiting. The tone of the survivor's utterance compels Lucy to think of the passage in Genesis when God calls to Adam: "Where are you?" All the Jews are riveted by the refugee's words. Lucy, however is irritated. Jews were intense all the time. She wonders if Jewish intensity is a condition of being chosen.

The testimony begins. Witness to and victim of the concentrationary universe, (the French term *universe concentrationnaire* symbolizes the metaphysical otherness of the death camps), the survivor speaks of its horrors. Lucy could feel nothing. She has seen all the movies. The only way she could enter the Holocaust kingdom was by reference to crucifixion. She visualizes hundreds of simultaneous crucifixions, "a hillside with multitudes of crosses, and bodies dropping down from big bloody nails. Every Jew," thought Lucy, "was Jesus" (p. 14). Nevertheless, she listened to the tale.

The survivor's voice is an instrument upon which is played the Jewish dance macabre. In telling his tale, the anonymous guest ranges from whisper to full voice. His oral power is stunning. Employing his voice as an artist utilizes a brush, the man's whisper "carved" the Jewish victims "like sculptures":

there they stood, a shadowy stone asterisk of Jews, you could see their nostrils, open as skulls, the stony round ears of the children, the grandmother's awful twig of a neck, the father and mother grasping the children but strangers to each other, not a touch between them, the grandmother cast out, claiming no one and not claimed, all prayerless stone gums (p. 15)

The refugee's voice "pinched them [the victims] and held them, so that you had to look." Lucy is compelled to "look and look." Transformed by the tale, the fingers of the listeners are stretched out. The room begins to levitate.

Like some metaphysical pied piper, the survivor—link with the past and reminder of Jewish particularism—is leading the Jews away. The room "rose like an ark on waters." Lucy describes it as a "chamber of Jews" which levitated "on the little grains of the refugee's whisper" (p. 15). Abandoned, she realizes that only Jesus could lead her. The anonymous messenger from the land of the dead had a power, but only for Jews. Even as the room ascended, Lucy knew that the man was already "in the shadow of another tale," one which she promises herself not to hear.

At this point in the story Lucy experiences a glorification. Her own illumination consists of witnessing a sexually suggestive pagan dance, performed by Calabrian and Messinain shepherds and goatherds in a New York City park. The accompanying songs are erotic. At the performance's conclusion Lucy "sees how she has abandoned nature, how she has lost true religion on account of the God of the Jews." Lucy's enlightenment enables her to see what is eternal:

> before the Madonna there was Venus; before Venus, Aphrodite; before Aphrodite, Astarte. The womb of the goddess is garden, lamb, and babe. She is the river and the waterfall (p. 18).

Jewish attention to theologizing history is, for Lucy, a stumbling block. Ozick's concern with the struggle of Judaism against Paganism, both as a movement and as an impulse within individuals, runs throughout her writings. For example, "The Pagan Rabbi," one of her early short stories, treats the seduction of Rabbi Isaac Kornfeld, "a man of piety and brains" who hanged himself in a public park attempting to achieve pantheistic unity.[27] Judaism, for Ozick, must always reject pagan deifications of nature in favor of seeking the divine or covenantal elements within and pointing beyond history.

Even as the living room ascends higher and the voices of the Jews become barely audible, Lucy knows the one primary word which is uttered—Holocaust.

> How long can they go on about it? How long? A morbid cud-chewing. Death and death and death. The word is less a human word than an animal's cry; a crow's. Caw caw. It belongs to storms, floods, avalanches. Acts of God (p. 19).

She is concerned about this Jewish obsession with the Holocaust. Lucy thinks that "history is bad" for Feingold. It makes him seem little. For her part, Lucy is not ashamed to admit that the shootings, the gas, and the camps bore her. Atrocity can leave one jaded; repetition breeds indifference.

Returning to the dining room, surrounded by cocktail-party chatter, Lucy is thankful for the "relief of hearing atheists." The humanists—compassionate knights all—bantered about art and romanticism. Above, and beyond, the party "Feingold and the refugee are riding the living room." "All the Jews," writes Ozick, "are in the air" (p. 20). Unlike the *luftmenschen* Jews of Eastern Europe, favorite satirical targets of their "enlightened" Western European literary brethren, Ozick's Jews are literally airborne in their attempt to escape the surrounding culture. However, Ozick's tale here argues that in order to avoid the cynicism of skeptics and the indifference of secularists, authentic Jews must actually leave the world. Far from criticizing those who refrain from adopting the cultural fashions of the moment, Ozick employs a contemporary variant of the *Luftmensch* as religious ideal.

Unlike Bleilip in "Bloodshed," Feingold and his fellow seekers cannot hope to authentically confront the Holocaust and affirm the covenant while remaining in the confines of New York City, or even by traveling to its suburbs. Bleilip is further distinguished from Feingold in his orientation to the secular. Bleilip's reconversion to Judaism, one is led to believe, will not remove him from this milieu. Rather, he will attempt to embrace the covenant while remaining in the world. Feingold, on the other hand, is unable to elevate his environment and must overcome it physically as well as theologically. The sheer superficiality of culture—parties, second-rate novels, the religious dominance of Christian symbols as seen in his earlier fascination with the compassionate knight—is matched only by its power either to deaden or to diffuse Jewish religious sensibility. The irony in Ozick's resort to levitation resides in the attempt to avoid, at least symbolically, the historical—that element which Jews have always viewed as the arena for the actions of their covenant deity.

Ozick offers a tough-minded and uncompromising portrayal of Judaism. One in which confronting the Holocaust is the litmus test of Jewish authenticity. Like Cohen, she disdains interaction between Jews and Christians. Christians simply are unable to feel Holocaust pain as do authentic Jews. Ozick also shares with Cohen the technique of distancing the Holocaust by writing in an American setting. She steadfastly contends that the Holocaust touches the lives of all Jews, those who were there and those who were not. Curiously absent from

Ozick's literary interpretation, however, is the dialectical movement between silence and speech as authentic responses to the catastrophe. Her survivors do not reflect or agonize over these impulses. Nor does the author, despite her insistence on its centrality, struggle with the singularity of the Holocaust. Ozick's Holocaust tales teach lessons rather than ask questions.

Hugh Nissenson

Nissenson's Holocaust fiction is concerned with examining the relationship between the covenantal God and the historical situation of His people. Nissenson, who spent several years in Israel and chronicles his experiences there in *Notes From the Frontier* (1965), explores the nuances of this relationship as it is expressed by European, Israeli, and American Jews. His Holocaust writing, like that of Ozick's, reflects two types of response: the religious affirmation of covenant and a secular view in which the covenant is seriously impaired because of the ravages of history. Concerning the religious response, Robert Alter noted that "Nissenson is . . . the only genuinely religious writer in the whole American Jewish group." "His fiction," writes Alter, asks whether "the God of the Kaftaned grandfather (can) still be the God of the buttoned-down grandson, especially with the terrible shadow of the Holocaust intervening between then and now?"[28] Nissenson's Holocaust fiction employs both the midrashic framework and Jewish mystical interpretation in seeking an increasingly hidden deity.

A Pile of Stones (1965), Nissenson's first published collection of short stories, focuses on the religious ambiguity of post-Holocaust covenant faith[29] asking if redemption is possible in a world of diminished deity. For Nissenson, the question about God also implies a question about man. For example, the book's epigraph, "Let me go for the day breaketh" (Gen. 32), symbolizes the divine-human relationship in Jewish covenantal thinking. Chapter 32 of Genesis is paradigmatic for the meaning of Israel, recalling the nocturnal struggle between Jacob and a mysterious divine figure or angel who, at daybreak, after smiting Jacob's thigh, renames him Israel. This dialectical movement of divine presence and hiddenness, Israel's holding on and letting go,[30] which recalls Greenberg's moment faith, forms the core of Nissenson's characters' post-Holocaust covenant struggle.

Nissenson first explores the essence of covenant faith in its pre-Holocaust dimensions. Poland forms the setting for two tales which focus on the binding nature of choosing and of being chosen. "The Groom on Zlota Street" recounts the experience of Yechiel, a pious Jew who resists the inroads of modernity on traditional life. Yechiel sells carriage whips in Warsaw while living with his impoverished relatives. With his young cousin David in tow, Yechiel goes to the Gentile groom on Zlota Street where, as he well knows, he will be offered many rubles for allowing the groom to pull his scraggly beard. Yechiel deliberately chooses a thrashing at the hands of the groom rather than permit the man his "pleasure." This covenant test, so to speak, involves a choice. Yechiel, bruised and sitting in the snow, tells David: "There's always a choice to be made. Remember that and rejoice. . . . Praise Him. . . . God provides" (p. 39). Nissenson's seller of whips is himself whipped, but refuses the temptation of renouncing his Jewish dignity. The youth remains true to his name; Yechiel (God will live—forever).

"The Prisoner" shifts covenantal models; from the Sinai example of "The Groom on Zlota Street," which depends on human choice, Nissenson now uses the Red Sea paradigm of compelling man's acquiescence. A Jew who had been a Torah student of the Kotsk sage is in jail for anti-Czarist activities. Prior to his political efforts, the hapless Jew, enraged after watching a pogrom, had ripped off his clothes and, mouth foaming, beaten his rabbinic mentor. Now the prisoner experiences a number of pantheistic mystical suffusions. His *ruach*—breath and spirit together—had to be held back with all his strength, "because it too seemed on the verge of being—becoming part of the rest (straw on the floor, fingernail dirt, the chains which bound him, his own body)—dissolved—with joy. If I let go, it would rush out, and merge—roar out. Roar with joy" (p. 62).

The prisoner is theologically shaken by the horror of the pogrom. Nevertheless, he is obsessed with God's holiness. Even the violent rape of a young girl which he had witnessed seemed—at the time of his mystical experience—"in order, significant, meaningful. . . . More. Good. . . . No, holy" (p. 63). The evident conflict between historical experience and hope overwhelms the prisoner. He "cried in a stifled voice," "Make Him stop, why don't you? Tell me how to make Him stop. . . . Hasn't He done enough? Why can't He let me alone? (p. 63).

Nissenson denies his prisoner the secular alternatives of atheism or revolutionary socialism. The burden of covenant existence is not so easily shaken off, demanding as it does a life lived in creative tension between historical events and redemptive moments. Covenant has a "once and for all" mark, but its terms must continuously be affirmed and "renegotiated" by each generation. Nissenson's centrally Jewish characters struggle with the perennial Jewish dilemma of divine-human coexistence.

Nissenson's post-Holocaust Jews also search for a means of living with a deity whose ways are frequently inscrutable. This quest intensifies when attempts are made to account for the suffering of the innocent. "The Blessing" is a short story which frames these issues around responses to the death from cancer of an eight-year old Israeli boy. The child's aunt Esther and Rabbi Levinsky are survivors of Bergen-Belsen and Auschwitz. Their covenant faith has been deepened by their Holocaust experience, and they struggle "not so much to accept the suffering inflicted upon the innocents in the camp, but—to sanctify it." Learning of her nephew's death, Esther recites the traditional benediction upon hearing evil news: "Blessed art Thou O God our Lord who art the True Judge in Israel."

Yitshaak, the boy's father, is, on the other hand, unable to reconcile the theological assertion of "a true judge," and the death of his son. The Israeli, unlike the European Jews, cannot grasp the elusive and painful message of covenant dialectic, he refuses to attend his son's funeral. Yitshaak realizes that the difference between himself and the survivors is that their faith had "taken—the condemnation of innocence—into account." Aunt Esther, although not a theologian, powerfully describes the dynamics of covenant faith when she tells the grieving Yitshaak "one must struggle every day." Esther, who still recites daily prayers, "blessed God, her tormentor," because—Yitshaak thought—of the promise of peace. Esther's struggle is waged between the poles of history and redemption. But Yitshaak, although having had a religious upbringing, cannot accept the tradition's teachings on tragedy as a balm for his own personal grief. The faith of Holocaust survivors symbolizes authentic covenant espousal.

The centerpiece of *A Pile of Stones* is "The Law," a remarkable short story which illustrates the perplexities of post-Holocaust covenant Judaism while underscoring the difference between those who were in the camps and those who were not. Uncle Willi, an eloquent survivor of Bergen-Belsen, has written an unpublished book recounting his experiences (*Mein Erlebnis*). He and his wife Helene have a son Daniel who, though a brilliant student of history, is a stutterer. Danny is preparing for his bar mitzvah at which he is to recite his Haftarah portion from the Book of Numbers—"It's some of the Law." The tale's other central character is Willi's nephew Joe, who is writing his doctoral dissertation on the Alien and Sedition Act.

Nissenson adroitly weaves together the Holocaust past and the Jewish present showing their inextricable connection. During preparation for, and some unease about the performance of, Danny's bar mitzvah, Willi Levy tells of his own initiatory experiences in Bergen-Belsen. Heinz, *Herr Hauptsturmfuehrer*, Berger was Willi's reality instructor. Nissenson portrays the ambiguity of good and evil in the dialogue between the Jew and the Nazi. Both Willi and Heinz were the same age and had received a middle-class German education. Willi, the scion of an assimilationist German-Jewish family, had never become a bar mitzvah and could recite no more than five of the Ten Commandments, and not even those in proper sequence. The SS man's family, for its part, boasted three generations of pastors. Heinz tells Willi that in order to please his own pastor father "I would learn whole passages of the Bible by heart; your Bible, Levy." Heinz could recite the Decalogue as it was written in the Bible.[31]

Nissenson depicts the doubleness of good and evil in a manner similar to that of Cohen and Ozick. For Cohen, Simon Stern the purported messiah, and Janos Baltar, embodiment of evil are the same age. Moreover, it is helpful to recall Simon's contention that "we are not all good and [Baltar] could not be wholly evil." Ozick's rebbe in "Bloodshed" is the same age as Bleilip, the secularist. For Ozick, however, the ambiguity concerns the thin line separating believing and agnostic Jews, rather than good and evil per se.

Willi Levy, standing in the rain at Bergen-Belsen, is taught the Ten Commandments by Heinz Berger who beat him "like some dog." He remembers the Nazi's actions.

> As if he were training some animal. . . . That whip across the back, the bridge of the nose, the eyes . . . all afternoon . . . until I could repeat it all word for word. "I am the Lord thy God who brought thee forth out of the land of Egypt." He hit me in the Adam's apple. I could hardly speak. The rain came down my face (p. 150).

Nissenson has skillfully illustrated that being a Jew depends on both external and internal factors. The Nazi Party's Nuremberg Laws imposed a definition of Jewishness from the outside. But an individual Jew must also affirm his own Jewish identity. Nissenson's story takes seriously the talmudic definition of a Jew: One who is born of a Jewish mother (Kiddushin 68b). There have been, however, many attempts to avoid, evade, or deny Jewishness. The continuing mystery of Jewish survival does not depend on the actions of assimilationists, but rather on those Jews who strive to discern the hidden ways of covenant in history.

Willi views his encounters with Heinz as symbolizing the long and baneful history of Jewish-Christian relations. The Jews were chosen, in part, to witness for the law. The yoke of the law is, in turn, what Judaism demanded of Christianity. The law, observes Willi, "makes a man different from a beast." Willi told of Heinz's murdering a seven-year-old girl in front of her mother. Several days later the Nazi had forgotten the incident. Christianity hated the law's yoke.

> They were murdering, humiliating us because . . . we had come to embody that very Law that bound them too—through Christianity (p. 155).

Willi himself is unsure of the Holocaust's meaning. But he knows that the law must be passed on, "the way we always have," from father to son.

"The Law" emphasizes that covenant affirmation in face of historical disaster is a normative component of Jewish history. For example, returning from the Babylonian Exile, Ezra read the law to the assembled community (Neh. 8:1–11). Danny's trauma combines communal and personal elements of the Jewish historical experience in modernity; he is the child of a survivor and has an uncontrollable stammer. The congregation grew increasingly restive as Danny stood to chant. It was raining outside as it had rained when Willi recited the law at Bergen-Belsen. Unable to stare down the crowd, Danny began to recite: stammering "the blessing he had made up his mind to assume the burden of what the reiteration of the Law of his Fathers had demanded from the first" (p. 162).

Willi is unlike American Jews. A survivor, he asks: "What good are words to describe such things?" Nonetheless, he continually speaks of his experiences, illustrating the conflicting and simultaneous claims of speech and silence concerning the Holocaust. Willi knew, for example, that words could never convey the overwhelming hunger felt by the victims. Yet he had a way with words. His tale may be told but not understood. *Mein Erlebnis* is unpublished and unpublishable, it is experientially and linguistically unavailable to those born in America. Can anyone not physically present in the camps know their message?

"The Law" is an open-ended story stressing the continuing, if camouflaged, nature of covenant tradition in modernity. Danny, without really comprehending, has chosen to receive God's covenant and Willi's testament. Willi's son is brilliant but inarticulate. Searching for meaning, he arises early each morning to pray to a God whom he has never experienced. Helene, a refugee who left Germany in 1936, thinks it a mistake for Danny to endure the bar mitzvah ritual. Public exposure of his stammer will only embarrass both the boy and the family. She thinks it far better, and less damaging, to have a party without religious or ritual significance at home. Helene also feels it wrong for Willi to tell Danny his Holocaust tales.

Joe is the American counterpart to the pre-Holocaust Willi Levy. Like Willi, he has had no bar mitzvah, is not especially concerned about Judaism, and is innocent of any knowledge about the Holocaust. Joe is surprised when Willi asks if the eighteenth-century Alien and Sedition Act, which permitted deportation of newspaper editors who criticized the American government, was directed against Jews. Nissenson may wish to suggest here that no country is immune from governmental repression. More likely is the interpretation that Joe's position represents the ethnic and religious amnesia—Ozick quotes her father's diagnosis of the ailment *Amerikaner geboren* (which she translates as being autolobotomized out of history)—suffered by many American Jews in avoiding their Jewish identity. For Nissenson, re-membering and telling the story of the *Shoah* is a ritual (in Greenberg's sense of the term); a barometer of authentic Jewish existence and a way of affirming covenant.

"The Law" stresses the point that God's absence or hiddenness during the *Shoah* does not free man of the obligation of partnership. Willi's case illustrates that even the assimilationist Jew feels the mag-netic pull of the Jewish catastrophe. Consequently, passing on the tradition from father to son becomes, in the sense of Fackenheim's argument, a divine imperative which binds both religious and secular Jews. On the other hand, Nissenson's pre-Holocaust Jews, Yechiel and the prisoner, contend with their own experiences of history's counterevidence to redemption: Jew-hating Gentiles and pogroms. Throughout their stories these characters are in a dialectical relation-ship with God. Those who, like the prisoner, accuse God of indif-ference or cruelty are, in the end, unable to resist His majesty or His grace. The tension is unbearable but inescapable.

"The Law" focuses on a different facet of divinity, presenting a literary form of Luria's notion of *tsimtsum*. God is, in the kabbalistic idiom, self-limiting. Hence, man is required to search harder in order to find Him. Danny's bar mitzvah is, for example, an act of faith in a radically hidden God. Only Jews who accept these obligations are permitted by Nissenson to achieve a form of transcendence over his-torical oppression. Nissenson, like Cohen and Ozick, utilizes the sto-ries of survivors to link his readers to the Holocaust. However, Nissenson also writes around the events, telling of the *Shoah* by in-direction (see this volume, chapter 4). Unlike either Cohen or Ozick, he focuses on individual rather than communal responses, and varies the geographic locales of the covenantal struggle.

The Holocaust fiction of Cohen, Ozick, and Nissenson views the catastrophe of European Jewry as an overwhelming presence in the consciousness of their principal characters. This presence, in turn, causes the main actors to adopt a covenant model which increases their awareness of God's guilt no less than His mercy. As such, this fiction is distinguished from other American Jewish works on the Holocaust and invites comparison instead with two European-born Jewish novelists who have written Holocaust stories set in America. Elie Wiesel's *The Accident* (originally published by *Editions du Seuil* in French as *Le Jour* [1961]) and *The Fifth Son* (*Le Cinquième Fils*, Editions Bernard Grasset [1984]), and Isaac Bashevis Singer's *Enemies, A Love Story* treat the theological and psychic anguish of Eastern European Jewish survivors living in New York City. The *Accident* and *Enemies* represent their author's first book-length account of post-Holocaust Jews in an American context.

Elie Wiesel

The Accident (1962),[32] written shortly after the inception of Wiesel's remarkable literary career, represents a genre which Robert Alter terms the "parabolic novel." The primary action, as it were, resides in the theological ruminations and discussions of the main characters. For Wiesel survivors are "Messengers of the dead," who do not belong among the living. The paradox of these messengers is that while they are links to the destroyed universe of European Jewry, their testimony is too overwhelming to be understood. Frequently, the survivors lie because their truth is too awful to be believed. Asceticism is another distinguishing characteristic of those who came back from the kingdom of death. But beyond the physical aspects of asceticism there resides a far more troubling dimension. Survivors "have been amputated; they haven't lost their legs or eyes but their will and their taste for life" (p. 75). *The Accident* explores this amputation by pursuing the theme of suicide. Against the background of the deuteronomic injunction to "choose life," suicide is, next to idolatry, the most dramatic rejection of covenant Judaism.

Contrasting starkly to the psalmists' rhapsodic utterance that "no place is empty of Him," Wiesel compares the planet earth to a railroad station where children see their parents carried off by a train. "And," observes Wiesel, "there is only black smoke where they stood." Everything, "love, happiness, truth, purity, children with happy smiles, women with mysterious eyes, old people who walk slowly, and little orphans whose prayers are filled with anguish," has taken the train which went straight to heaven. Wiesel terms this journey the "new exodus," from one world to another. In antiquity, Exodus meant a profound transformation from bondage to freedom. In modernity, Wiesel's new exodus is no less profound. It is the transformation of flesh and hope into smoke and ashes. The Nazis have reversed the creation process: God made order out of chaos, Nazis made chaos out of order; their death camps brought forth cosmic upheaval. This change is symbolized by Wiesel's reflection that we live in a stupid time. "Everything is upside down. The cemeteries are up above, hanging from the sky, instead of being dug in the moist earth" (p. 106).

Eliezer, the main character in *The Accident*, is a survivor, a veteran of Israel's War of Independence, and the New York correspondent for an Israeli newspaper. Struck by a cab while crossing Times Square, he is severely injured, and spends ten weeks hospitalized in a body cast. The accident was in fact an attempted suicide. In the artificiality and indifference of New York City Eliezer is convinced that to continue living is a betrayal of the slaughtered.

Resolution of this spiritual despair is initiated on two levels: the physical and the theological. Dr. Paul Russel saves Eliezer's life. Gyula, the hasid, begins the redemption of his soul. Russel and Eliezer are bound together. Roughly the same age, both speak the mature language of men who are in direct contact with death. Yet the two are very different. Each is an ambassador of a power. The doctor's fingers touch life. Eliezer's have confronted death. Dr. Russel cannot understand Eliezer's refusal to help during the long and dangerous operation. Worse, Dr. Russel accuses Eliezer of being on the other side, the side of death. In kabbalistic thought the "other or left side" (*sitra achra*), when existing apart from the right side, is viewed as unrestrainable evil. Applied to Eliezer's life, his immersion in the other side—the death camps—made him different from others. Dr. Russel, for example:

> looked at me steadily, stubbornly, to catch in me that which eluded him. In the same way primitive man must have watched the day disappear behind the mountain (p. 73).

Tales of the Holocaust transform their listeners. Eliezer describes himself as a storyteller whose "legends can only be told at dusk," like Hegel's night bird of Minerva who sings only when it is too late.

To listen to his tales is, moreover, dangerous. "Whoever listens questions his life." The heroes of such tales "are cruel and without pity. They are capable of strangling you."

Dr. Russel is aided not only by Gyula but by Kathleen who tries unsuccessfully to counterpose love against death. In her efforts she, too, is overwhelmed by the dead. She grows to fear Eliezer who thinks her reaction is a fitting one. Survivors, he muses, must serve to mirror the fear of others. Even Eliezer and Kathleen's lovemaking lacks passion. Coupling on earth, according to kabbalistic teachings, stimulated and imitated the primal union above between God and the *Shekhinah*. Professor Werblowsky writes that in fact Luria's kabbalistic interpretation of union represents nothing less than "the first system in the West to develop a mystical metaphysics of the sexual act."[33] But this act had to be accompanied by the correct *kavvanah*, for the reunification of God and the *Shekhinah*, in order to achieve the desired reverberations in the world above.

Theologically, *The Accident*, while indicting God, "I hadn't been able to understand for a long time what God had done to deserve man," refuses to abandon Him. Irving Greenberg suggests that *Night* (1960), the first of Wiesel's books and the most directly related to his Holocaust experiences, represents a "Rubenstein phase" through which Wiesel passed.[34] If so, *The Accident* marks the first attempt to enter a new phase which permits the reconstruction of covenant tradition. While the image of God in *The Accident* is pessimistic, "death is only the guard who protects God, the door keeper of the immense brothel that we call the universe" (p. 93), Wiesel calls on man to help resuscitate this deity. This book was the first one of Wiesel's in which life triumphs, albeit tentatively, over death. Suicide is rejected owing largely to the efforts of Gyula, who is both friend and guru to Eliezer. Like Dr. Russel, Gyula has an obsession: "to pit himself against fate, to force it to give human meaning to its cruelty." Suffering, attests Gyula, belongs to the living, not to the dead. Far from any naïve plea to abandon the past, Gyula calls instead for an emphasis upon living.

> If your suffering splashes others, those around you, those for whom you represent a reason to live, then you must kill it, choke it. If the dead are its source, kill them again, as often as you must to cut out their tongues (p. 118).

Eliezer himself has no illusions about the supposed moral value of suffering. "Suffering," he observes, "brings out the lowest, the most cowardly in man. Saints are those who die before the end of the story" (p. 49). The story's denouement is triggered by Gyula's portrait of Eliezer. Somber in tone, except for his eyes, which have been painted a bright red, the portrait confronts Eliezer with a choice. Either he learns to live with his past, or he will be consumed by it. Without saying a word, Gyula sets fire to the portrait, asserting that "it is man's duty to make (suffering) cease, not to increase it. One hour of suffering less is already a victory over fate."

Wiesel, the Job of Auschwitz, testifies to the decisiveness of the Holocaust.

> The Holocaust is beyond all frameworks. What happened . . . was so unique; even within the framework of our own history, it is unique. It was a mutation on a cosmic scale and it always implies more than man— it implies God, it implies history, it implies metaphysics.[35]

Yet, for Wiesel, the essence of Jewish history is, as we have noted, mystical and not rational. Thus, while he has written that the "Torah has become an orphan," Judaism must begin anew. Contending with God, Wiesel remains firmly rooted in the Jewish tradition of theological protest. Wiesel has in fact been described as "the *Tanna Kamma* (master teacher) of the new Talmud, trying to explain why God's prayers, as well as man's, remain unanswered.[36] Strongly autobiographical, like all of Wiesel's novels, *The Accident* emphasizes the singularity of survivors and the constant presence of their past. Man is called on to redefine and recast his relationship to God whatever the environment, whether it be New York City or the more familiar European landscape of Wiesel's later novels. The seeds of Wiesel's neohasidic, post-Holocaust Judaism, which require man to assume the awesome burden of covenant by contending with God and by being responsible for one's fellow human beings, are sown in *The Accident*.

The Fifth Son,[37] Wiesel's newest and most symbolic literary encounter with the *Shoah*, marks a significant departure from his earlier works. Combining literature and pedagogy, history and theology, Wiesel has written a new *Haggadah* for children of Holocaust survivors and, by implication, all others who wish to wrest covenantal meaning in the post-Auschwitz world. In a move characterized by both its boldness and subtleness, *The Fifth Son* reverses the theme of Wiesel's long held view that it is impossible for a nonwitness to imagine Auschwitz. Here, Wiesel the witness attempts to imagine how it is to be a nonwitness. Theologically, Wiesel advocates guidelines by which the second generation can remain within the midrashic framework while simultaneously advancing criteria for post-Holocaust Jewish authenticity. Wiesel in fact dedicates the book to his son Elisha, and all the other children of survivors. Steeped in talmudic, messianic, and mystical teaching, the novel explores ways of communicating divine silence by telling tales whose purpose is to inform, but more importantly to transform their listeners.

Wiesel's new *Sh'ma Yisrael* prayer is a meditation focusing on a survivor family and their American born son, a college student who comes of age during the radicalism of 1960's America. The appearance of this novel gives credence to the contention that a new genre of Holocaust fiction is slowly emerging: books written by or about children of survivors.[38] Reuven and Rachel Tamiroff are survivors whose six year old son, Ariel, had been brutally murdered by a Nazi whom the Jews, with gallows humor, had dubbed the Angel. Both Ariel and Angel are symbolic names which will be discussed below. After the war Reuven conspired to assassinate the Angel. Reuven's American son discovers both his parents' past, his own identity, and the fact that the Angel is still alive. The son's mission of vengeance to Germany provides the vehicle whereby he travels between dreams and reality, individual and collective destiny.

The Passover commandment to tell thy son, and the traditional *Haggadah*'s injunction that each person shall feel as if he himself were freed from bondage provide the novel's context. In Wiesel's haggadic reshaping, Exodus and Holocaust, freedom and extermination, the sovereignty of God and the partnership of man form the background for a meditation on the contemporary meaning of the Jewish vocation which, after Auschwitz, means an intensified struggle against Death (the word is always capitalized), a synonym for Evil or the kabbalistic *sitra achra*. Theologically, Wiesel continues his portrayal of Jews who balance precariously between the pain and despair of Jewish memory and the hope of Jewish destiny; a destiny which is forever clouded by that memory.

In seeking to portray theological guidelines for the fifth son— who symbolizes American Judaism—Wiesel's novel maintains his view on the paradigmatic nature of silence. "Silence," he observed elsewhere, "is enriching. God's voice is heard in silence—true silence— and sometimes is silence."[39] Linking divine and human silence, Wiesel wrote that "silence more than language, remains the substance and the seal of what was once their (the victims) universe, and . . . like language it demands to be recognized and transmitted."[40] *The Fifth Son* also speaks of ethics in focusing on the relationship between the offspring of victims and victimizers. Rejecting the notion of collective guilt, the Tamiroff's American son feels sorry for young Germans who are "unjustly marked". They are in fact faced with a paradox.

> If they are content it is because they are insensitive; if they are not, it is because they are honest. In other words, in order to be honest they must feel guilty (p. 196).

There are no easy post-Holocaust choices for people of conscience.

Consisting of 25 sections, not termed chapters, not, in fact, designated at all, Wiesel successfully erases time distinctions, just as he shifts scenes between Europe and America, and narrators between past and present. The novel opens with a query emphasizing this attitude toward alledgedly normal boundaries, "Was it Dawn or dusk?" (p. 13). At the novel's conclusion the American son assumes the name and identity of his murdered brother, symbolizing thereby the fact that the Jewish people, as a whole, form the book's implicit cast of characters. One's name is obtained, much in the manner of Jacob (Gen. 32), from finding out who one is. The power of a name is its granting of a destiny. Wiesel has, in fact, insisted on the transrational nature of the Jewish mission, writing: "Whatever he chooses to do, the Jew becomes a spokesman for all Jews, dead and yet to be born, for all the beings who live through him and inside him."[41]

Epigrammatically, Wiesel unfolds the search for identity undertaken by the Tamiroff's nameless American son. Emphasizing the difference between survivors and nonwitnesses in all his works, Wiesel here contends that survivors' children are, to use Gyula's term, splashed with their parents' suffering. The Tamiroff's son observes "I suffer from an Event I have not even experienced" (p. 192). Consequently, children of survivors are as different from their nonwitnessing peers as survivors are from others. But the meaning and experience of the Holocaust elude the grasp of survivors' children. "From a past that made History tremble," observes the son, "I have retained only words" (p. 192). In one of his letters to Ariel, Reuven speaks of the survivors' difficulty in witnessing to others about the Holocaust.

> I am searching for a special course: one that lies between words and silence. As I am searching for a special time: one that lies between life and death. No, let me correct myself: between the living and the dead. I am searching for you, my son (p. 26).

The Fifth Son differs, however, from Anya and Mr. Sammler's Planet, novels which convey psychological problems associated with post-

Holocaust parenting (see this volume, chapter 4). Wiesel is consumed by the moral and theological questions of life after Auschwitz: what is the relationship between good and evil, and, as in his autobiographical memoir *Night*, what of God's justice? Writing to Ariel, Reuven asks the covenantal question:

> Is it true that God always intervenes? Did he save our generation? He saved me. Is that reason enough for me to tell Him of my gratitude? (p. 42).

Reuven's protest is, like that of Wiesel's, a protest from within the tradition. Reuven, whose name may be read "see, a son" (Reu-ben), is, like Eliezer in *The Accident*, a messenger of the dead.

Wiesel's covenant seekers include his favorite characters: madmen, messianists, and mystics. Bontchek, a teller of tales, and Simha-the-Dark, a kabbalist and merchant of shadows, who attempts—unlike Cohen's Simon Stern—to "force the end" through manipulation and permutation of numbers (Gematria), are Reuven's European companions in America. Bontchek and Simha are the boy's teachers, combining to tell tales of the plight of the ghettoized Jews of Davarowsk and mystical midrashim. Each of the book's main characters expresses a dimension of Wiesel himself. The juxtaposition of Simha (joy) and Dark reveals the tension which characterizes much of post-Holocaust Jewish existence.

If Wiesel wishes the second generation to maintain his quarrel with God, he is no less adamant in insisting that they recognize the crime of man. The ultimate crime of the Nazi killers lies in the fact that "They have killed eternity in man" (p. 176). But man and God are, according to kabbalistic thought, interdependent. God requires man, as we have seen, to elevate imprisoned divine sparks, thereby restoring cosmic wholeness and ending the *Shekhinah*'s exile. Killing man is, therefore, simultaneously homicide and deicide.

Echoing the theme of cosmic chaos expressed in *The Accident*, "the cemeteries are all in the sky," Simha describes events which occurred in the ghetto on Yom Kippur. Commanding the hapless Jews of Davarowsk to pray, the Angel tells them to "imagine that I am the Lord your God" (p. 152). In response, Simha's wife, Hanna, speaks for the assembled Jews. "Faith in God, yes; faith in our ancestors, yes again. Faith in Death, never" (p. 154). As reprisal, two hundred Jews, including Hanna, were murdered. Wiesel presents the cruel inversion or parody of the *Unetane Tokef* prayer, which occurred with fatal frequency in the Nazi kingdom of death. This prayer, a communal affirmation made before the opened Ark on Rosh Has-hannah and Yom Kippur, that God is the Supreme Judge of the world, asks how many—in the coming year—shall pass away, and how many will be born; who shall live and who will die; who will achieve the full number of their days, and who will not. No matter the degree of sin, however, there remains a chance for redemption. The prayer's final line states: But Teshuvah (repentance), Prayer, and Good Deeds can avert the severity of the decree. Wiesel's profound theological disappointment is in a God who, while promising to avert His own decrees, was apparently helpless to avert those made by the mur-derers of His chosen people.

Wiesel's testimony, as history told by an insider, is meant to accomplish two goals. Like the *Haggadah*, it recalls for the present generation the extraordinary circumstances confronting the Jews: new kinds of killers who kill "without passion," and the unprecedented life and death situations confronting the *Judenräte* (Jewish councils). Wiesel presents this information to counteract both the trivialization and outright denial of the Holocaust. The Tamiroff's son observes, at novel's end, that his contemporaries "create small circumstances out of great events" (p. 219).

The whole issue of covenant destiny is encompassed by the names Ariel and Angel. Ariel may be translated several ways: Altar of God, Lion of God, Mountain of God, or Hero. The name may also, however, stand for shade—in the sense of shadow—or underworld and refers to the destruction and degradation of Jerusalem (Isaiah 29:1–4). Je-rusalem is thus apostrophized as an altar but also sacrificed on the altar. Underscoring the notion of covenant renewal, however, God promises to rebuild His holy city. By utilizing the term Angel, Wiesel emphasizes the more than human power which the Nazis exercised over the Jewish people, as well as combining ghettos and death camps. Joseph Mengele, the infamous Angel of Death, made his absolute and merciless selections at Auschwitz.

The Passover *Haggadah* serves as both text and context for Wiesel's novel. The text is a compilation of prayers, midrashic observations, biblical and mishnaic excerpts. Various additions have been made throughout the course of time. In fact, the notion of four sons: the wise, the wicked, the simple, and the child, is a rabbinic innovation based on the biblical injunction, mentioned four times, commanding parents to tell their children about the exodus from Egypt. These four attitudes may also, incidentally, be seen as reflecting society's un-derstanding of the Holocaust, as well as representing stages through which an individual or a society may pass. Reuven tells his son that prior to the war, he, the father, had begun as the wise son, but then—

lured by the attraction of secular culture—he had rejected Judaism, thereby becoming the wicked son. The *Haggadah* defines the wise son as one who seeks knowledge and has the wisdom to ask the right question. The wicked son, on the other hand, separates himself from the community and ridicules the tradition. *The Fifth Son* attests that, after the Holocaust, the four traditional models are no longer adequate. Wiesel is also urging second generation American Jews to reject the role of wicked son. They, like Reuven before them, are surrounded by alien temptations. New York is, for example, identified as a place of misanthropes where Jewish ritual ceremony—especially the bar mitzvah—has lost religious significance.

The *Shoah* has overturned traditional models of understanding even as it challenges Jews to remain within the midrashic framework. Wiesel's reinterpreted Passover marks the extension of his earlier work as a covenant revisionist. Unlike Nissenson who, in "The Law," employed a traditional ritual—the bar mitzvah—to indicate covenant fidelity, Wiesel has adjusted the traditional Passover in response to the monumental nature of the Holocaust's covenantal challenge. While the Seder continues to serve as link between generations, its primary focus in Wiesel's retelling has become the Holocaust.

The contents of Wiesel's mystical *Haggadah* are revealed during the first Seder after Rachel has been institutionalized, unable to cope with the loss of Ariel. The young Tamiroff hears his father read the *Haggadah*'s explanation of why this night differed from all others: Because we were slaves in Egypt long ago. The boy, however, contends that this night differs because his mother is in exile. Simha agrees, extending the implications threefold.

> Your mother is in exile. Just like the *Shekhina* who is also in exile. That is why your joy is not complete and neither is ours. And neither is the Lord's (p. 32).

The *Shekhinah*, the Jewish People, and God are dramatically altered in the aftermath of extermination. The exile of the *Shekhinah*, so vital in kabbalistic theology, is, like "The Breaking of the Vessels," no mere figure of speech. Gershom Scholem observes that:

> The exile of the Shekhinah is not a metaphor, it is a genuine symbol of the 'broken' state of things in the realm of divine potentialities.[42]

It is the possibility of achieving *tikkun*, (repair, restoration, or mending), that occupies Wiesel's literary mystics and messianists, forming the core of his theological instruction to the second generation while sharply distinguishing his response from Rubenstein's assertion of the essential theological despair of the post-Auschwitz human situation.

The Passover Seder serves, on another occasion, as the background for affirming life and the necessity of messianic waiting. Simha admonishes Reuven that "the duty of a Jewish father is to the living." The dead, states Simha, are not part of the *Haggadah* (p. 35). Simha tells two tales in place of the traditional Passover response concerning the exodus from bondage. The first concerns the elusive and somber beauty of the *Shekhinah* whose shadow, hovering over the ruins of Jerusalem, transfixed a Roman officer. The second tells of the Ushpitzin Rabbi who successfully intervened with God on behalf of a notorious sinner, only to be told by a heavenly voice that he was wrong to look for additional sinners because, "If God chooses to look away, you should do the same" (pp. 32–33). The Rabbi, concludes Simha, "understood that some things must remain in the shadows, for the shadows too are given by God" (p. 33).

Shadows play an important role in the novel and can be understood on a variety of levels. Children are shadows of their parents both in the sense of being replicas, and being only insubstantial. Children of survivors both are and are emphatically not their parents. Shadows may also be understood as Wiesel's warning that not everything is ultimately knowable to mere rational enquiry. Simha's use of shadows also refers to messianic yearning and to the kabbalistic notion that evil itself is part of the divine. The name Ariel, as noted earlier, also conveys this duality. Stressing the mystical understanding of shadows, the *Zohar* interprets a passage about dwelling in booths (the festival of Sukkot), as meaning that "when a man sits in this abode of the shadow of faith, the Shekinah spreads her wings over him from above" (Emor 104a). Those who seek covenantal guidance in the post-Holocaust world must simultaneously embrace the shadow of faith and struggle to dispel the shadows of despair.

Messianic yearning occupies a significant place in *The Fifth Son*. Concerning the relationship between messianism and Passover, rabbinic testimony asserted that Messiah was to be viewed as a "second Moses" who would come to free Jews—from their political bondage in the wake of the Temple's second destruction—on the evening of Passover (Midrash Rabbah, Mekhiltah and Yalkut on Exodus 12:42). This messianic impulse is intimately bound with the Jewish vocation. From the anticipation of redemption to the Warsaw Ghetto uprising, Passover encompasses the totality of the Jewish historical experience.

Indeed, contemporary Seders include readings about both the Holocaust—somewhat mitigating Simha's earlier contention that the dead do not form part of the *Haggadah*—and the plight of Soviet Jewry. Wiesel's broadening of the Seder is thus seen as a response to the complexity of the post-Auschwitz divine-human encounter, while attesting to the wisdom of Greenberg's contention that the Holocaust's implications "need to be incorporated into a host of areas: culture, scholarship, liturgy, and observance."[43]

The Fifth Son raises, and rejects, apocalyptic responses to the post-Holocaust Jewish situation. The American son, seeking a name and an identity, begins composing letters to Ariel, asking why Good should not be rejected, and injustice embraced as a means of bringing Messiah (p. 177). It is significant that Wiesel frames these salvific queries in a manner which suggests that only the dead can respond. "To survive," he observes, "one needed not to exist" (p. 16). When, later in the tale, the son goes to Reshastadt (evil city), he thinks of himself as traveling to the "other side" and he hears the "rustling of the wings," both of these images are associated with evil. The son realizes the transformative effect of such encounters: "I am and I am not myself" (p. 201). These words spoken by an American Jew, are meant both as a rejection of America's nihilism and a repudiation of its innocence.

Sanctification of life, one of the ingredients of the additional covenant, plays a crucial role in *The Fifth Son*. Wiesel contrasts justice with vengeance in telling of the Davarowsk ghetto. The Nazis appointed Reuven head of the ghetto, in which capacity he acted as a *zaddik*, treating all the Jews equally and eschewing special privileges for his own family. Rabbi Aharon-Asher teaches Reuven the Jewish way of approaching issues, contending that it is important not that Reuven believe the tradition but that he know it. The rabbi is a saint, and eventually a martyr, who goes to the mikveh (ritual bath) even in the midst of winter. His counsel is against the taking of life: both revenge and suicide are forbidden by Jewish law. Utilizing examples from the teachings of Rabbi Akiba who lived in the aftermath of an earlier historical cataclysm (the second destruction of the Jerusalem Temple), Aharon Asher offers both solace and guidance to Reuven.[44] Reuven and his companions on the ghetto council swear an oath of revenge against the Angel. Aharon-Asher declines the oath, explaining "It's not the executioner I'm defending, but the Law" (p. 155). Wiesel's use of the pious rabbi as a spokesman for justice even in face of unparalleled cruelty is meant as a model for remaining Jewish and thereby influencing one's culture. Elsewhere, Wiesel commented on the relationship between Judaism and culture observing that the Jew's mission was "never to make the world Jewish but, rather, to make it more human."[45]

Haunted by their alleged murder of the Angel, Reuven and Simha scrutinize Jewish texts for clues to their possible redemption. The two men speak of Moses's slaying of the Egyptian overseer. Murder, they conclude, is justified, perhaps, but never just. Moses was, for example, denied entrance to the Promised Land because of this action. The novel's other rabbi, the mystical Zvi-Hersch, in a dream segment reminiscent of Cohen's rendition of the prophet Elijah, appears to know—without being told—that the Tamiroff son wishes to murder the Angel. Zvi-Hersch not only witholds his blessing from the youth, but disapproves of Simha's mystical efforts at hastening Messiah, contending that "Simha . . . is treading on dangerous ground. Kabbalah is the privilege of the initiated" (p. 189).

In a bold literary move, Wiesel portrays an encounter between the younger Tamiroff and the now respectable Nazi. Affirming his belief in the transformative power of tales on their listeners, Wiesel has the American Jew symbolically assume the identity of Ariel, and all the other dead Jewish victims. Musing on what is and is not within his power as storyteller, the narrator (Wiesel himself) observes:

> I shall speak. I shall tell the tale. The *Angel* must be, will be, unmasked.
> I shall describe the solitude of the survivors, the anguish of their children.
> I shall relate the death of my little brother. I shall set forth, I shall recall
> the wounds, the moanings, the tears. I shall speak of the voices of dusk,
> the mute violence of night. I shall recite the *Kaddish* of dawn (p. 214).

Recognizing both the tale's efficacy and the teller's limits, the narrator concludes by observing, "The rest is no longer within my scope" (p. 214).

Transmuting vengeance, the narrator curses the killer; putting upon him the mark of Cain. Come to kill the Angel, the son ends by pronouncing a malediction upon him. In a scene reminiscent of God's condemnation of the Serpent (Gen. 3:14–15), the young Jew tells the murderer:

> You will never know peace. Wherever you are you shall feel like an
> intruder pursued by the dead. Men will think of you with revulsion;
> they will curse you like the plague and war; they will curse you when
> they curse Death (pp. 214–15).

Wiesel's character leaves the Angel walking backward, "I stare at him saying to myself over and over: he must look at me as long as possible" (p. 215).

Wiesel's image suggests a backing into the future and brings to mind the figure of Walter Benjamin's angel. Benjamin's concern for meaning in history led him to utilize the figure of an angel whose face was turned toward the past while his back is turned toward the future into which he is being blown by a storm from paradise. The question arises whether the angel will merely gather the accumulated debris of history as he travels inevitably toward the end. Or will he engage in the work of *tikkun*, the world-restorative task kabbalists assigned man? There is a crucial difference between Wiesel and Benjamin. Wiesel wishes the executioner to look at his victim. Benjamin's angel, on the other hand, is apparently given the opportunity of repairing the world.[46]

Wiesel's own anguish over the Jewish vocation is seen in the young Tamiroff's observation concerning his father's failed assassination attempt. "What foolishness," he tells his father and Simha, "to believe that in this society, justice could be done by the victims of injustice; what an idea to want to write history in terms of ethics and generosity. How naive can one be?" (p. 170). This passage reflects Wiesel's concern, reported earlier, that the Jewish mission is a suicide mission. Are Jews able to fight evil?

Wiesel underscores the problematic of struggling against evil without oneself becoming evil. He tells a parable about an Israeli police officer interrogating an Arab prisoner. To what lengths should the officer go? At what point does the effort to uncover a plot to murder innocent civilians begin to dehumanize the interrogator? Force measured against moral constraints has become the crucial post-Holocaust question. In a significant message to his own generation, the Tamiroff's son contends that all hatred is self-hatred.

The Fifth Son weaves skillfully between the dialectical poles of hope and despair. Survivors have children testifying thereby to a future, perhaps messianic, hope. Reuven proclaims a version of Fackenheim's 614th Commandment in confiding to his son, why should the enemy be the only one to multiply? Wiesel's challenge here, as elsewhere, is the difficulty of confronting not the future, but the past. The task of the witness is essentially unable to be realized. Wiesel, speaking through the Tamiroff's son articulates this theological "mission impossible."

> There were so many events, so many mutilated, buried destinies, that I could spend my life and that of my people evoking them. Even if all

the Jews in the world were to do nothing but testify, we would not succeed in filling more than one page. However, the Book contains six million pages (p. 210).

Summing up his life at the novel's end, the narrator (Wiesel) speaks of having moved heaven and earth, risking damnation and madness by interrogating the memory of the living and the dreams of the dead. But all to no apparent avail. Forever haunted, he wonders when he shall be able to live his own life. But survivors play the ultimate pedagogic role. Bontchek is, for example, young Tamiroff's "inexhaustible guide and teacher" endlessly telling of the Davarowsk ghetto. "I am his prisoner," muses the son, "without him, my imagination won't be fueled" (p. 101). The second generation is linked forever to the experiences of the survivors.

Wiesel views Jewish fate during the Holocaust as being inextricably bound to human destiny. The American son contends that:

from afar I glimpse the immense shadow, not unlike a monstrous, poisonous mushroom, linking heaven and earth to condemn and destroy them (p. 219).

Universal nuclear destruction may be Rubenstein's holy nothingness. However, Wiesel knows that Holocaust witnessing is a dialectical process. The survivor is described as a bridge. But to whom? The novel refers to only one American, Lisa, the son's political activist girlfriend, who helped discover the Angel. By novel's end, however, she is not part of the tale. Who will bear the burden of memory? On the other hand, the son is a professor who has many students: all of whom are potential witnesses. But this observation must be viewed against the son's earlier contention about societal distortion of the Holocaust.

novels in which everything rings false, essays that are all pretentiousness, films in which facts are embellished and painted and commercialized. None has anything in common with the experience the survivors carry within (p. 193).

Was there, in fact, an encounter with the Angel? Or was this symbolic testimony; the imagined act of confrontation designed to rescue human dignity and affirm divine judgement?

Wiesel has written a profound and profoundly challenging meditation. His post-Holocaust deity is both diminished and implicated. *The Fifth Son* presents, nonetheless, a theology of history which refuses to yield to despair. This position is articulated by Rabbi Aharon-Asher in the midst of the Davarowsk ghetto. Speaking to a despondent Reuven, the rabbi reflects on the endless persecution of the Jews.

> It means that we live in spite of Death, that we survive Death! It means that our history, our prodigious history, is a permanent challenge to reason and fanaticism, to the executioners and their power! Would you really want to desert such a history? (pp. 39–40).

In the post-Holocaust world it is crucial that the second generation continue to witness to the mystery of Jewish historical continuity. Wiesel's emphasis on silence stems from his immersion in mysticism which is here combined with an expectation that Messiah, even though he may tarry, will arrive. *The Fifth Son* attests that the hour is late, but not too late; the situation is desperate, but not irreversible, the obstacles are many and increasing, but not insurmountable. "To be a Jew," wrote Wiesel elsewhere, "is to have all the reasons in the world not to have faith in language, in singing, in prayers, and in God, but *to go on* telling the tale, *to go on carrying on the dialogue*, and to have my own silent prayers and quarrels with God."[47] The American Ariel, wiser than Simha, attests that he will follow the hasidic practice of waiting for the Messiah, even though he may come too late. In an earlier novel, for example, Wiesel wrote that Messiah is not one man, but all men. "As long as there are men, opines Wiesel, "there will be a Messiah."[48] This espousal of messianism represents Wiesel's criterion of covenant authenticity for second generation Jewish encounters with the Holocaust.

Isaac Bashevis Singer

Isaac Bashevis Singer's *Enemies, A Love Story* represents the mature phase of the author's work and reflects the theological turmoil of post-Holocaust Jewish existence.[49] Ostensibly, Singer's story centers on Herman Broder, a man with three wives, a murdered culture, and an ambivalent relationship to the God of Jewish tradition. Married in Europe to Tamara, a Jewess whom he despises, Herman fathers two children. Separated from his family by the Nazis, Broder is hidden in a hayloft by Yadwiga, a Polish peasant who had been the Broders' servant. After an eyewitness reports that the Nazis murdered Tamara and the children, Herman marries Yadwiga and comes to America. He lives in Brooklyn amidst, but apart from, the Jewish community.

Masha, a Jewish survivor, is Herman's mistress and later becomes his third wife.

The book is structured such that each of the central characters has his/her own tale and represents an aspect of Jewish existence after the catastrophe. Tamara, a secularist, had been a prisoner in both Nazi and Soviet slave labor camps. No longer able to believe in the God of Abraham, Isaac, and Jacob, Tamara retains her identification with the Jewish community. As bad as the Soviet camps were, she laments, at least there the Jews were a community. This is not the case in New York. Masha and her mother Shifra Puah, both Jewishly literate survivors, share an apartment. Shifra Puah desperately wishes for a grandchild to whom she can pass on the names of the murdered. Bearing the agony of survival, she envies the dead. Masha, for her part, alternately prays and blasphemes. Sexually licentious, she undergoes an hysterical pregnancy. Herman, opposed to all institutional religious and philosophical systems is, nonetheless, well versed in kabbalah and occultism. He recalls that while in hiding he compulsively held a pencil and wrote, even his dreams "a combination of a story book, cabbalistic revelations, and scientific discoveries" (p. 42).

Enemies distances the horrors of the camps by means of flashbacks depicting the traumatic events in Poland and Russia. Yet the details which are given leave nothing to the imagination. For example, Tamara's father's beard is ripped off his face, along with pieces of his cheek. The Nazis force an eighteen-year-old daughter of a famous rabbi to drown in a pool of human excrement. But Singer is manifestly concerned with the ongoing trauma of Holocaust survivors. Theologically, his characters contend with God and underscore the fragility of covenantal religion; Masha observes that God has made a profound mistake in judgment.

> If it had been God's purpose to improve his chosen people by Hitler's persecution, He had failed. The religious Jews had been practically wiped out. The worldly Jews who managed to escape had, with few exceptions, learned nothing from all the terror (p. 46).

Singer's survivors share a bond which unites them, while simultaneously emphasizing the ineffable distance separating them from Diaspora Jewry in America. Like Wiesel, Singer underscores the chasm between those who survived and those who were safe in the United States.

Singer's theological position admits of no easy classification. But the norm against which he evaluates all subsequent expressions of Judaism is Eastern European folklore and mystical piety with its sense of reverence for creation, its belief in demons, and a steadfast commitment to the God of the covenant. The only authentic Jews in Singer's work are either dead, or survivors. The best among the latter are authorally removed to Israel. Singer's investment of Israel with great religious potential stands in sharp contrast to the assessment of Arthur Cohen. Reb Abraham Nissen Yaroslaver, Tamara's uncle, is a case in point. A learned man, an Alexandrover Hasid, Reb Abraham Nissen:

> wanted to settle in the Holy Land to save himself the arduous journey through the underground caverns which the dead must traverse before reaching the Holy Land, there to be resurrected when the Messiah came (p. 224).

He wished to be buried on the Mount of Olives, not among the shaved Jews in a New York cemetery.[50]

Although a believing and pious Jew, Reb Abraham rejected the strain of orthodoxy which saw nothing theologically unusual in the slaughter of six million Jews. He refused to seek comfort in the classical theological assumption, "For Our Sins We Are Punished." On the contrary, Reb Abraham was "plagued by doubts." He wonders: "How could those who had lived through the destruction believe in the Almighty and in his mercy." He "had no sympathy for those orthodox Jews who tried to pretend that the Holocaust in Europe had never taken place" (p. 224). The ambiguity of the divine-human relationship displayed here is reminiscent of the discussions in Cohen, Ozick, Nissenson, and Wiesel. For example, Reb Abraham and Ozicks' rebbe both articulate the notion—especially prominent in post-Holocaust theological speculation—that covenantal faith is a dialectical process, or a moment-faith as Greenberg terms it.

Herman Broder is a study in religious paradox. On the one hand, he is convinced that authentic Jewish religious existence has come to an end.

> Everything has already happened.... The creation, the flood, Sodom, the giving of the Torah, the Hitler holocaust. Like the lean cows of Pharaoh's dream, the present had swallowed eternity, leaving no trace (p. 143).

Broder appears as the literary proponent of Richard Rubenstein's theological position. God, for Rubenstein,·is either ineffectual (powerless) or a "cosmic sadist." In any case, divine hegemony over history has ended. Broder muses over this last point, refining it somewhat. "If," he opines, "a God of mercy did exist in the heavenly hierarchy, then he was only a helpless godlet, a kind of heavenly Jew among the heavenly Nazis." The forces of evil and the demonic have presumably triumphed once and for all. On the personal level, Broder was convinced that he "had not sealed a covenant with God and had no use for Him." Herman did not "want to have his seed multiply like the sands by the sea" (p. 226).

Broder encompasses three distinct tendencies in Jewish modernity. He begins with the assumption of covenantal adherence as normative: "If we don't want to become like the Nazis, we must be Jews." There is, however, an unrelenting combat for the soul of post-Holocaust Jews. Herman opposes talmudic Judaism with both kabbalistic ideas and the stance of atheism. On the one hand, he speaks lovingly of the Gemara (Babylonian Talmud). A link with the Jewish past, the Gemara provided a fence against the temptations and illusions of modernity.

> These writings were home. On these pages dwelt his parents, his grandparents, all his ancestors. These words could never be adequately translated, they could only be interpreted. In context, even a phrase such as 'a woman is for her beauty's sake' had a deep religious significance. It brought to mind the study house, the women's section of the synagogue, penitential prayers, lamentations for martyrs, sacrifice of one's life in the Holy Name. Not cosmetics and frivolity (p. 158).

This could never be explained to an outsider. Nevertheless, Herman, despite his knowledge of *halaka*, is unable to live a life of faith.

Post-Holocaust Jewry is described by Reb Abraham as a "time of moral chaos." Herman's search for clarity amidst this confusion focuses on a singular interpretation of kabbalistic teaching. He had been convinced for some time that "occultism was a valid subject for those who still sought the truth." Long ago William James termed occultism *"diabolical* mysticism, a sort of religious mysticism turned upside down."[51] Filtered through Broder's perspective, this type of orientation focuses on the relationship between sexual acts and mysticism.

> At moments when Herman fantasized about a new metaphysic, or even a new religion, he based everything on the attraction of the sexes. In the beginning was lust. The godly, as well as the human, principle is desire (pp. 48–49).

Broder's preoccupation with sex stems from mystical interpretations of the relationship between the human and the cosmic condition. He describes his lovemaking with Masha as a ritual frequently lasting till daybreak. "It reminded Herman of the ancients, who would relate the miracle of the exodus from Egypt until the morning star rose" (p. 122). Singer's intentional use of the word ritual casts the sexual act in a special light. Writing in his autobiographical *A Little Boy in Search of God*, Singer observes that "in heaven Torah and love were two sides of the same coin. In cabala books coupling was performed for the glory of God.";[52] The primal union between God and the *Shekhinah* prominent in Lurianic mythology had, as noted, been sundered by "the breaking of the vessels" and the subsequent exile of the Jews. This rupture could be repaired only with human assistance. Acts performed with the correct *kavvanah* could mend the shattered cosmos. Moreover, the *Zohar* taught that "it is the yearning from below (acts of man on earth) which brings about the completion above" (in the celestial spheres). Herman translated for Yadwiga "a mystical hymn about holy apple orchards." This hymn originated in the sixteenth-century kabbalah of Isaac Luria and was a metaphor of the restorative aspect of sexual union.

In a similar manner, Broder's theodicy is based on mystical beliefs. He affirmed the existence of hidden powers and a whole range of parapsychological phenomena. Herman's acceptance of metempsychosis, a specific type of reincarnation, is based on the teachings of the twelfth-century text *Bahir*, which speaks of *gilgul* or the rebirth of souls under specific conditions. Concerning *gilgul*, he

saw in Tamara's return a symbol of his mystical beliefs. Whenever he was with her, he re-experienced the miracle of resurrection. Sometimes, as she spoke to him, he had the feeling he was at a seance at which her spirit had materialized. He even played with the thought that Tamara wasn't really among the living, but that her phantom had returned to him (p. 122).

Kabbalistic themes notwithstanding, Broder seems intent on embracing a type of atheism or, in Rubenstein's terminology, neo-Paganism. History is, for example, not the arena of God's mighty acts. Rather, Broder adopts a cyclical view of historical events. The past is as present as today.

Cain continues to murder Abel. Nebuchadnezzar is still slaughtering the sons of Zedekiah and putting out Zedekiah's eyes. The pogrom in Kesheniev never ceases. Jews are forever being burned in Auschwitz (p. 33).

Promises of progress were, according to Herman "no more than a spit in the face of the martyrs of all generations." The entire world was a slaughterhouse. Singer is, in fact, willing to risk trivializing the Holocaust by claiming that killing of animals is, on one level, comparable to the fate of Europe's Jews.

> At every opportunity, he [Herman] pointed out that what the Nazis had done to the Jews, man was doing to animals. How could a fowl be used to redeem the sins of a human being? Why should a compassionate God accept such a sacrifice? (p. 134)[53]

The complexity of Broder's theological position is revealed by his ambivalent attitude toward the divine. Herman, for example, "sometimes prayed to God when he was not fighting with him." Elsewhere, Singer writes that as a boy he found some comfort in the "cabala books." While describing the earth as the meanest of all worlds, populated by evil spirits such as Lilith, Naamah, and so on, and stressing that the earth was the farthest removed from God and His mercy, these books nonetheless insisted that God had granted man the greatest of all gifts, free will. Consequently, man could choose between good and evil, and the struggle was never ending. Unfortunately, the choice was almost always on the side of evil. Singer writes of the deep impression made upon him when, as a boy in Poland, he discovered that several kabbalistic works were concerned with the powers of evil, demons, devils, and the like, as well as with magic. The Gemara's discussions of Jewish and Gentile demons also exercised great appeal for him.

The theological cost of survival has been steep. Broder and Masha contend, with Rubenstein, that chosenness was mocked and destroyed by the Holocaust; only a type of sham Judaism remains. Theology has deteriorated into profane ritualism in America. Describing Herman and Masha's experience in a "strictly kosher" hotel near the Canadian border, Singer writes that the guests—some of whom were refugees from Nazism—gathered to hear a pro-Stalinist speech from a Yiddish poet as well as impersonations and jokes from an actor and actress. For Herman the situation was blasphemous. He mused: "The vulgarity in this casino denied the sense of creation. It shamed the agony of the holocaust" (p. 113). Differing radically from the early Ozick, Singer is pessimistic concerning the resuscitative capacity of American Jewish expression. Individual Jews may succeed in their personal struggles with their demon adversaries. Collectively, however, American Judaism in Singer's view is theologically adrift, lacking even an awareness of what was lost in the death camps.

Singer's pessimism is strongest in his description of the American rabbinate. Rabbi Milton Lampert, for whom Herman ghost wrote articles and speeches, is a study in contrast to the classical rabbi. The rabbinic model, as it evolved from the pharisaic tradition, was a holy man and scholar, one whose concern and expertise was in interpreting Torah, shaping and transmitting the tradition, and reflecting on *halakic* matters. Rabbi Lampert, on the other hand, made a fortune in real estate, having neither the time nor the patience to study and write. Lampert also shares in what Singer perceives as the general failure of American rabbis to believe in God. God has become an ironic or merely nostalgic concept; an idea the loss of which, at the very least, would not hinder anyone in becoming a rabbi. Nonetheless, Rabbi Lampert continued to support Herman, was concerned about the welfare of Masha and Yadwiga, and involved himself in the fate of the Jewish community.

Herman Broder is consumed by Holocaust obsessions. He sees Nazis everywhere and thinks it only a matter of time before they invade America. This perception is shared by Masha who expresses a fear common to survivors. Vacationing with Herman at Lake George, Masha asks, "Where are the Nazis? What kind of world is this without Nazis? A backward country, this America" (p. 104). Herman's viewpoint is that evil is persistent: "If one Hitler is dead, there are a million ready to take his place." His fear of deportation is exceeded only by his quest for hiding places against the inevitable invasion.

Amidst the welter of talmudic, kabbalistic, and atheistic expressions found in *Enemies* there is a constant theme that the Nazi death and Soviet slave labor camps did serve, in their own way, a higher intention. Tamara, for example, recalls the saintly people whom she encountered in the camps. Some were holy figures who shared their meager rations with others and maintained their faith till the end. Tamara like Shifra Puah, and Eliezer in *The Accident*, believes that only true saints were murdered in the camps. She in fact opines that there may have been a divine purpose behind her suffering. "At least I had the privilege of knowing these saints. Perhaps that was God's purpose in my miserable adventure" (p. 98). Tamara's great moral authority, in contrast to Herman's ethical confusion, stems from the fact that she has returned from the dead (an eyewitness had reported her murdered). Like Bellow's resurrected Artur Sammler, Tamara serves as a critic of the nature and culture of man. Unlike Sammler, she is steeped in knowledge of Jewish ritual life and committed not only to the supramundane implications of *k'lal Yisrael* but to Jewish specificity.

Singer views the options for post-Holocaust Jewry as being extremely limited. There is, on the one hand, the response of classical Judaism. In order to avoid the temptations and seductions of the secular world, one had to turn to God. Herman mused: "There was only one escape for him: to go back to the Torah, the Gemara, the Jewish books" (p. 156). Addressing the issue of doubt, he reasons in typical pilpulistic fashion, "Even if one were to doubt the existence of oxygen, one would still have to breathe." Repentance, *teshuva*, was predicated on the shunning of Gentile culture. Demons and the world of hidden powers, for their part, threatened man's feeble efforts at constructing a meaningful world. Herman compares Jewry to a hothouse growth, "kept thriving in an alien environment nourished by belief in a messiah, the hope of justice to come, the promises of the Bible—the Book that has hypnotized them forever." History, however, had finally overtaken the Jews. In a scene reminiscent of Wiesel's *Night*, which asks whether in all of history a people had ever said *kaddish* for themselves as did the Jews in the death camps, Singer shares a dream with his readers. Broder fell asleep and:

> dreamed of an eclipse of the sun and funeral processions. They followed one after another, long catafalques, pulled by black horses, ridden by giants. They were both the dead and the mourners. "How can this be?" he asked himself in his dream. "Can a condemned tribe lead itself to its own burial?" They carried torches and sang a dirge of unearthly melancholy. Their robes dragged along the ground, the spikes of their helmets reached into the clouds (p. 116).

Herman's theological quest for metaphysical certainty, however, leads always to the same conclusion; there is no certainty in a Holocaust universe.

A second option that Singer sees for post-Holocaust Jewry is to disappear completely. Suicide, in the form of physically ending one's existence or in the guise of assimilation, plays a prominent role in *Enemies*. By the time the story has ended, Masha is dead and Herman has disappeared. Broder had earlier observed that his Jewish neighbors wanted to teach Yadwiga a Judaism which "the years in America had diluted and distorted." Tamara notes that her physical appearance has changed since arriving in New York.

> They put nylon stockings on me, dyed my hair, and polished my fingernails. God help me, but Gentiles have always prettied up their corpses, and Jews nowadays are Gentiles (p. 75).

Tamara is, in fact, echoing the sentiments of Reb Sender in Cahan's *The Rise of David Levinsky*. Hearing that David, the young yeshiva student, wishes to go to America the rabbi exclaims, "Lord of the universe, one becomes a gentile there." In an ironic twist Singer, by having Yadwiga convert to Judaism, argues that only someone from Eastern Europe can be(come) a Jew. Americans lack the cultural, and religious sensitivities necessary to inhabit a covenant world.

Singer's third option consists of two parts: either a return to Israel or embracing a skewed kabbalistic interpretation of cosmic events. But Herman cannot dismiss completely either the God idea or Jewish rites. Masha, for her part, when speaking of German cruelty to the Jews, "would run to the mezuzah on the door and spit on it." The attempt to live as *apikorsim* (unbelievers) proves finally to be unbearable for Herman and Masha. Those who do manage to achieve a qualified form of transcendence do so by clinging to *ahavat Yisrael*, love of and dedication to the Jewish people, thereby adhering to Hillel's ancient admonition, "separate yourself not from the community." Herman Broder violated this precept. Certain characters in *Enemies* who otherwise possess little or no moral stature, such as Rabbi Lampert and Leon Tortshiner (Masha's first husband), share Tamara's commitment to *ahavat Yisrael*. Quarreling with, or even denying, God does not grant license for hedonism or for ignoring one's communal obligations. The classical triad of God, Torah, and community may have been, as Rubenstein argues, irrevocably truncated by the Holocaust. But an absent God leaves Jews who wish to remain Jewish with the compelling necessity of embracing their tradition of study and community.

Singer shares with Wiesel and Nissenson the belief that the Holocaust makes two simultaneous and conflicting demands: the need to bear witness and the impossibility of accurately conveying its meaning. For example, Tamara, Masha, and Shifra Puah continually tell their Holocaust tales with ritual intensity. But Herman knows that ultimately nothing can be revealed. "They were all silent: God, the stars, the dead" (p. 115). Moreover, those who speak of the immensity of evil failed to convey their meaning. "The creatures who did speak," thought Herman, "revealed nothing." Holocaust survivors are for Nissenson, Wiesel, and Singer, unspeakably different from those who did not undergo the camp experience; they exist on a different plane of being than others. Broder observes to Rabbi Lampert that "anyone who's gone through all that I have, is no longer part of this world." Unlike Wiesel's Bontchek in *The Fifth Son*, Singer's survivors do not fuel their listener's imagination

Singer's manifest pessimism may, however, mask his true purpose. His Nobel lecture contends that the pessimism of the creative person is not decadence, but a mighty passion for the redemption of man. Mysticism and skepticism are not mutually exclusive. No better description of Singer's role has emerged than that offered by Alfred Kazin.

> Singer became the fictional historian of the whole Jewish experience in Eastern Europe because his extraordinary intelligence and detached point of view turned the heart of the tradition—acceptance of God's law, God's will, even God's slaughter of his own—into story, legend, fantasy.[54]

Equally at home citing the Talmud and Nietzsche, Singer nevertheless views the artist's role as being invested with crucial civilizational implications. Like Cohen and Wiesel, he perceives the novelists' task as being akin to that of the theologian, noting that in ancient Jewish literature there was no basic difference between the poet and the prophet. Singer's stories provide the metaphysical maps whereby man can chart his course in the continuing struggle against the powers of evil unleashed so devastatingly by the Holocaust.

Conclusion

Despite the profound and real differences in culture, experience, language, access to classical sources, and traditional upbringing, there are strong bonds linking the Holocaust works of Cohen, Nissenson, and Ozick with that of Wiesel and Singer. For example, the Americans and the Europeans both view the Holocaust as an orienting event which forces Jews consciously to decide to be Jews. This decision is more a mental than a physical phenomenon. No set ritual pattern or specified action is involved. Consequently, the decisive moments in the works of these authors revolve around theological discussion, parable, and metaphysical reflection. These events are, moreover, part of everyday moments. In this sense the works are hasidic in their striving for salvation amidst the chaos of the ordinary. Cerebral engagement is akin to studying a page of Talmud. It transforms the individual while simultaneously strengthening the community. The persistent theme of this fiction is that the Holocaust has worked in a double sense. On the one hand, the catastrophe has thrown into sharpest possible relief the question of the viability of the covenant and its assumption of a special relationship between God and the Jewish people. On the other hand, these writers call for a return to the norms of Hebrew and Yiddish culture, while demonstrating a renewed intensity of concern for Jewish religious and mystical symbolism as the mode for self-expression in an age of catastrophe.

Taken collectively, Holocaust responses in Act II share the following elements: 1) the call for religious authenticity which involves a reinterpretation of Jewish mystical and messianic themes; 2) an inward journey whose goal is salvific; 3) an emphasis on the necessity of community for Jewish identity and continuity; 4) a recognition of the reality of evil and its ambivalent relationship to good; 5) an affirmation of a Lord of History so as to invest the universe with meaning; and 6) the realization that as God becomes less accessible man's efforts to locate the divine element within human existence must become correspondingly greater. All of the authors embrace—in varying degree—Wiesel's neohasidic evaluation of the theological potential of midrash, stories, and tales as vehicles for transmitting, shaping, and creating authentic Jewish expression.

Serious writers of fiction, this group asserts, are those whose works are midrashically anchored in the tradition and who view their vocation in salvific terms. Survivors serve in their works as links to a past which has been brutally obliterated. Therefore, novelists are responsible for preserving a civilization which is able to live in the dialectical tension between history and covenant. The contemporary task of the American Jewish novelist as theologian of culture is a struggle against a majority and alien society, recognizing that Jewish-Christian encounter has a dismal historical record and must be avoided. These writers seek instead a rootedness in Jewish experience and expression, believing that only the world of Jewish myth and religious symbols can provide authenticity for those living in the aftershocks of the Holocaust.

We now turn our attention to a group of writers whose Holocaust fiction, while remaining in contact with the midrashic framework, testifies to the increasing pressures of secularization on Judaism.

Chapter 4

Holocaust Responses II: Judaism As A Secular Value System

The religious-secular distinction in Judaism is, as we have seen, a complex and paradoxical phenomenon. The sociologist Peter Berger reminds us that secularization and its derivative, secularism, refer less to a coherent philosophical position, and more to a process whereby increasing areas of culture are lived outside the domain of religious symbols and institutions. Consequently, secularism is not so much a systematic interpretive category as it is reflective of the mood of an age or historical period. When applied to the normative but flexible notion of covenant, the concept appears even more ambivalent. Lacking a centralized hierarchical church and without confessional utterances, Jews have neither ecclesiastical authority nor sacred locutions which, if forsworn, would signify termination of Jewishness. Jewishness is determined on a fundamental level biologically. Not faith but birth comprises Jewish identification. This identification is, moreover, conferred both internally by the community of those calling themselves Jews and, in Sartre's sense, by the outside, Christian, world. It is no accident, therefore, that Heinrich Heine observed "Jewishness was an incurable malady." Nazis, in a terrible and murderous parody of *halaka*, similarly defined Jews according to descent in the infamous Aryan paragraph of the 1935 Nuremberg Laws, which made grand-children of Jewish grandparents eligible for extermination. However, Europe's Jews were sent to their death not because of their faith, although many were pious and observant, but because of their birth. The exterminators were not interested in religion, although in overwhelming numbers they were members of the church in good standing.

The paradox of secularism in modernity for Judaism lay in its appeal for Jews who embraced it as a means of attaining civic freedoms and cultural pluralism. Secularism seriously undermined the Jewish ideology of tradition. Jacob Katz observes that a break with tradition means "it is re-evaluated and no longer serves as the basis for justifying the changes that take place, but becomes the point of departure for reservations and criticism."[1] Modern Jews had, notes Fackenheim, stepped outside of the midrashic framework. Jews were, however, unable to achieve the stated Enlightenment goal of a neutral society, that is, neither Jewish nor Christian in orientation but a grouping based on fellowship in reason. At best there appeared what Katz terms the "semineutral society" where the inferior status of Jews was consciously ignored rather than eliminated. Despite Western European Jewish willingness to forego the ancestral faith in order to achieve civic integration, the dominant secularism was neither able nor willing to accommodate this goal. While abandoning the formal religious element of Christianity, Enlightenment Europe, as we have seen, retained the Christian teaching of contempt toward Jews. "The era of Western history that began with the French Revolution," writes Arthur Hertzberg, "ended in Auschwitz."[2] Neither assimilationist tendencies nor traditional ties were sufficient to preserve Jewish lives.

Specifically concerning Judaism's experience of modernity in America, Nathan Glazer observes the peculiar relationship which exists between Jews of recent times and the Jewish past. Each generation of Jews has selected out a different aspect of the Jewish past as normative. Simultaneously, this selection included a rejection of those elements which were deemed irrelevant. Reform Judaism is the institutional epitome of this process. But at no point, Glazer notes, "has everything been rejected at once."[3] The secular faith of Jewish modernity focuses on the concept of peoplehood. S. Niger, the Yiddish writer, contended in fact that "Jewish identity is not a screen of Jewish theology, but the truth of Jewish history."[4] Mordecai Kaplan's emphasis on Judaism as a civilization is based on his comprehension of the special situation of Jews in America who wished to be Jewish even if not religious in the formal sense.[5] Thus, Fackenheim's contention that modern Jews have stepped outside the midrashic framework is not wholly accurate.[6] For many secular novelists this framework has been stretched but not broken.

The novelists whose Holocaust fiction is analyzed in this chapter view the *Shoah* as an orienting event. Their centrally Jewish characters, while having no formal theological training, demonstrate a concern for the continuity of Jewish existence, and a realization that the Jewish presence in history defies all attempts at merely rational explanation. The covenant and the midrashic framework are juxtaposed with modern secularism in an attempt to indicate the outlines of post-Holocaust Jewish identity. Only two novelists, Saul Bellow and Susan Schaeffer, write directly of the Holocaust. Their work is complemented by Cynthia Ozick who depicts the continuing impact of the *Shoah* on survivors. Hugh Nissenson and Robert Kotlowitz distance the *Shoah* by writing of antecedent times; Nissenson's *My Own Ground* is set in the early teens of twentieth-century America, while Kotlowitz's *The Boardwalk* tells of events during a two-week period in 1939 America. Their conscious omission of the catastrophe makes it loom even larger. They depend on their readers' knowledge of the Holocaust to provide an essential part of the reading experience. Both Nissenson and Kotlowitz focus the readers' attention on the naïveté of American Judaism's dissipation of its spiritual energies.[7] Two of Bernard Malamud's short stories, "The German Refugee" and "The Lady of the Lake," testify to the centrality of the Holocaust for Jewish identity.

Like the novelists in chapter three, secular authors portray survivors as having been metaphysically changed by their experience. For example, Bellow's Mr. Sammler, having escaped death, represents an oasis of moral stability amidst the chaotic and amoral desert of New York City. But Sammler is human only "in some altered way." He wonders if he has "a place among other people." Reacting to the wartime memory of omnipresent hunger, Sammler in New York sees food displayed and thinks: "Things edible would always be respected by a man who had nearly starved to death." Sammler's attitude is reminiscent of Singer's Shifra Puah who viewed a piece of bread as a sacred object. Survivors are described as embracing their Jewishness even though unable to articulate its contents.

Abandoning *halakic* and—to a large extent—ritual aspects of Jewish religious life, they nonetheless cling to Judaism. Susan Schaeffer's Anya is, for example, a survivor who, although "not a religious woman," remains "traditional in my own way." Her position speaks for the condition of much post-Holocaust secular Judaism. Ozick's Rosa Lublin, a pre-Holocaust assimilationist, bears grudging witness that affirming links of Jewish kinship is the only option for survivors. Hester Lilt, Ozick's mysterious European nonwitness, stubbornly embraces the midrashic method in asserting the continuity of Jewish redemptive hope even after the Holocaust. Malamud's survivor, Isabella del Dongo, stands in stark contrast to her would-be lover Henry Levin/Freeman. Imprisoned at Buchenwald, Isabella values the Jewish identity for which she suffered, while Levin changed his name and asked "with ancient history why bother?"

Responding to the Jewish specificity of the *Shoah*, authentic secular Jewish novelists treat the catastrophe's impact on the community of Israel and its ramifications for all who live in an Auschwitz universe. The death camps have radically called into question the very continuity of the human species. Having once occurred, the Holocaust has set the stage for further assaults against human endurance. One thinks here of Wiesel's cogent observation that Auschwitz made Hiroshima possible. Is it perhaps already too late? The broken strands of covenant faith and the eradication of Europe's Jews have not destroyed the American Jewish writers' quest for identity and meaning, but have increased immeasurably the difficulty and pain of achieving these goals. More at ease in a mental universe of Jewish covenant than in geographic America, secularist fiction seeks to demonstrate that for post-Holocaust American Jews covenantal claims, however modified, are prior to, and often in conflict with, the American experience. The America of Artur Sammler, Anya, Rosa, Hester, Nissenson's Jake Brody, and Kotlowitz's Teddy Levin is inhospitable to the notion of Jewish specificity and covenantal demands. These literary figures are pessimists concerning the possibility of creative Jewish expression in America. Nevertheless, the writers in chapter four utilize classical religious exemplars, such as the *lamed-vov zaddik* as moral teachers, while underscoring the spiritual and physical perils of assimilation.

Considering the Evidence

Bernard Malamud

Bernard Malamud's short story "The Lady of the Lake"[8] graphically portrays the difference between those Jews who orient by the Holocaust and those who do not. Henry Levin comes into a small inheritance, quits his job, and travels to Europe seeking romance. In Paris Levin begins calling himself Freeman; symbolically identifying with the French Revolution he thereby renounces his Jewish identity, seeking instead an illusory universal citizenship. Traveling to Italy— it was August near the time of *Tisha b'Av* (the fast day commemorating the two destructions of the Temple)—Freeman meets and falls in love with a beautiful Italian girl named Isabella del Dongo. Freeman thought that Isabella's face held "the mark of history, the beauty of a people and civilization" (p. 105). Freeman was simultaneously mesmerized by and totally ignorant of European culture. Isabella unexpectedly asks him if he is a Jew. Freeman denies his Jewish identity. Revealing himself as a Jewish self-hater, Freeman mused that being Jewish had brought him only "headaches, inferiorities, and unhappy memories" (p. 117). Besides, he was convinced "that a man's past was, it could safely be said, expendable" (p. 117).

On the verge of proposing to Isabella, Freeman is again asked if he is Jewish, and again he denies his identity. She exposes her breasts revealing "on the soft and tender flesh" the tatooed numbers placed there by the Nazis at Buchenwald. Isabella is Jewish. "I can't marry you. We are Jews. My past is meaningful to me. I treasure what I suffered for" (p. 123). Levin/Freeman attempts to reply but is tongue-tied. Isabella disappears into the darkness. After the *Shoah*, Malamud is saying, authentic American Jewish existence, even for the secularist, requires coming to terms with the specifics of Jewish identity and history. This new specificity is forever linked with the Holocaust.

"The German Refugee,"[9] is the second of Malamud's two stories dealing directly with the Holocaust. Here the time is immediately prior to the catastrophe. Oskar Gassner, who managed to leave Germany six months after *Kristallnacht*, lives in New York City, one of several middle-class intelligentsia who are being tutored in English. A writer who now could neither write nor speak—"to many of these people . . . the great loss was the loss of language . . . they could not say what was in them to say" (p. 200)—Gassner was scheduled to give a series of public lectures on the literature of the Weimar Republic. Gassner commits suicide, by gassing, upon discovering that his wife—a convert to Judaism—had, despite the frenzied protests of her antisemitic mother, been murdered by the Nazis. "The German Refugee" is an attempt to bring the Holocaust to American shores while simultaneously distancing the event.

Oskar Gassner had, like many of his Jewish countrymen, been first attracted by, and then blamed for, the Weimar experiment in democracy. The loss of speaking ability is Malamud's way of indicating that the terrors of National Socialism are, literally, unspeakable. The collapse of political and religious freedom, the rise of government sponsored murder programs, and the apathy of the nations had revealed the extent of Jewish vulnerability. Both Gassner and Isabella del Dongo are secularists whose Jewish identity is brought into sharp relief by the Holocaust. The sufferings of these characters underscore the naïveté of any American Jewishness which feels itself untouched by the Nazi horror.

Saul Bellow

Mr. Sammler's Planet (1978) is Saul Bellow's most direct engagement with the Holocaust.[10] Unlike Joseph's dream of the slaughtered in *Dangling Man* or Moses Herzog's rueful lament about European Jews who "depart in a black cloud of faces, souls," Artur Sammler's reactions are those of a survivor. A seventy-two-year old Polish Jew, Sammler has twice escaped death. He crawled from a bloody pit whose victims included his wife Antonina and he had hidden in a mausoleum to elude not the Germans but Polish partisans who shared the Nazi goal of a *Judenrein* (Jewfree) world. The most Jewish of Bellow's fiction, *Mr. Sammler's Planet* is a meditation on the meaning of history and the task of being Jewish and human amidst the scarred contemporary landscape. Sammler reflects on the persistence of antisemitism (even Cieslakiewicz, the Polish caretaker of the cemetery, who fed and clothed Sammler, lapsed into post-Holocaust antisemitic sentiment), the reality of evil and suffering, the contemporary fascination with apocalypse, and the unalterable, frequently fatal, impact of the outside world's definition of Jewishness.

The novel is above all an indictment of secular humanism. Liberation of the self from binding ethical, moral, and religious values has ended in the disaster of Holocaust. "Individualism," observes Sammler, "is of no interest whatever if it does not extend truth" (p. 214). *Mr. Sammler's Planet* is a literary expression of the results of what theologians term the "collapse of the secular absolute." Irving Greenberg notes that secular humanity lives in "a world closed off from any transcendence or divine incursion." This resulted in:

> transferring allegiance from the Lord of history and revelation to the Lord of science and humanism. Yet, in so many ways, the Holocaust is the direct fruit of this alternative. Modernity fostered the excessive rationalism and utilitarian relations which created the need for and susceptibility to totalitarian mass movements and the surrender of moral judgment. There is the shock of recognition that the humanistic revolt, celebrated as the liberation of humankind in freeing humans from centuries of dependence upon God and nature, is now revealed—at the very heart of the enterprise—to sustain a capacity for death and demonic evil.[11]

Sammler has a twofold task; revelation of the errors of unfettered humanism, and advocacy of a secular Jewish alternative.

The story line treats Sammler's attempt during an event-filled three days to say goodbye to Doctor Arnold Elya Gruner, his patron and nephew who is hospitalized with an inoperable aneurysm which may burst at any moment. Bellow compares the fragile state of civilization to the seige of an aneurysm. America is staggering if not breaking up; "New York," says Sammler, "makes one think about the collapse of civilization, about Sodom and Gemorrah, about the end of the world" (p. 277). Between hospital visits Sammler interacts with both survivors and nonwitnesses. His most sustained encounters are with Shula-Slawa, his somewhat unhinged half-Jewish half-Catholic daughter who had been raised in a convent during the war, and with Dr. Govinda Lal. Lal's manuscript "The Future of the Moon," a treatise on moon colonization, was stolen by Shula-Slawa and given to her father. Sammler has long discussions with Gruner's two grown children, Angela and Wallace, concerning their relationship to the dying physician, observes a black pickpocket at work and is subsequently sexually victimized by the man, discovers that Gruner has performed abortions for Mafia friends, and discourses about the lessons of the Holocaust.

In terms of structure, *Mr. Sammler's Planet* is a subtype, along with *Anya* and *The Pawnbroker*, of what Sidra Ezrahi terms the survivalist genre. This category is distinguishable by three major characteristics: a description of the *ancien régime*, a descent into the *anus mundi*, and postliberation existence.[12] Bellow, like Schaeffer and Wallant, distances the Holocaust by utilizing a non-American survivor in an American setting and by underscoring the difference between those who went through the experience and those who did not. Mr. Sammler differs from Anya and Sol Nazerman by the fact that he was not in a death camp but fought with partisans, killing a German soldier in the Zamosht forest. This act had filled the corpse-like Sammler with bliss, although the German had begged for his life. Consequently, Sammler dwells more than Schaeffer on the ambiguity between victim and victimizer; an ambiguity heightened by his trip to Israel during the Six Day War.

Drawing on Hebrew and humanist traditions, Bellow advocates a reverence for the sacredness of life and rejects apocalypticism. Sammler espouses three principles which simultaneously put him at odds with American Jewry and make him a sought after source of moral authority. He speaks of the duty of fulfilling human obligation in order for history to cease being Hegel's slaughter bench; the value of compassion; and the need for ethical behavior. Sammler's temporal values are modifications of traditional Jewish concepts and practices. Although abstaining from an explicit covenantal reference, Sammler's "longing for sacredness" is testimony to covenant persistence, as is his condemnation of licentiousness. Eschewing ritual, temple, and laws of *kashrut*, Sammler has nonetheless his own form of prayer and does address God. Sammler's peculiar form of Judaism (like that of Moses Herzog) emerges from the opposition between intellect and emotion. Emotion signifies a revolt against the oppressive rationalism of modernity; its Jewish component is revealed in a concern for Israel and the centrality of the Holocaust for succeeding generations. Intellectualism is, on the other hand, the curse of modernity. Explaining everything, man ends by understanding nothing; victim of his own *hubris*. Operating on the rationalistic premise that man alone is the measure of all things, modernity breached the moral and religious barriers to mass murder. The Holocaust in this view is a logical outcome of modernity.[13]

Sammler's encounters with death cause him to wonder "what besides the spirit should a man care for who has come back from the grave?" (p. 109). His spiritual concern is, however, a cerebral reinterpretation of the Jewish vocation. He views his triumph over death as signifying that he has been "assigned to figure out certain things," after having "been sent back again to the end of the line" (p. 250). Sammler's mission is to condense his life experience into a testament for American Jews in whose midst he has been living for twenty years. Not unlike the prophets of antiquity, he resists this calling, but his "friends and family had made him a judge and a priest" (p. 86) who was much in demand "often visited, often consulted and confessed to." He is both a warning and example to American Jews whose covenantal amnesia draws them into a vortex of spiritual destruction and physical excess.

Bellow's portrayal of the saved remnant is, like that of Isaac Bashevis Singer, an unsentimental one. Sammler is one-eyed, suffers from tachycardia, and reflects that "his onetime human, onetime precious, life had been burnt away" (p. 205). Eisen is Shula-Slawa's handsome but mad Israeli ex-husband who—during the war—had been thrown out of a moving train by Russians after they discovered that he was a Jew. Walter Bruch, the only character in the novel who actually survived a death camp, endlessly recounts his Buchenwald experiences to Sammler. Bruch tells of a fellow prisoner who drowned in human excrement while the others watched helplessly. His own survival is marked by his sexual fetish for Puerto Rican women's arms.

Released from death's grip, he remains in death's orbit. Bruch and a fellow survivor hold mock funerals during which Bruch loves to play corpse. These survivors have been shattered by their experience. Nevertheless, they are committed to a prophetic view of the world in spite of the Holocaust.

The psychic deformity of the survivors is mirrored by the spiritual bankruptcy of American Jewry. Dr. Gruner's children are studies in contrast to their father's *ahavat Yisrael*. Angela and Wallace Gruner are narcissists who engage in sexual libertinism and mindless intellectualism, oblivious to the Jewish tradition and to human commitment. The doctor describes his daughter as having "fucked out eyes" while Wallace is a "high-IQ moron" (p. 249). Sammler mentally compares Angela's sexual paganism to the orthodoxy of her murdered European grandparents, both of whom he had known. Angela's promiscuity marks the distance traveled by tradition from the boundaries of *halaka* to the chaos of modernity. Sammler:

> doubted the fitness of these Jews for this erotic Roman voodoo primitivism. He questioned whether release from long Jewish mental discipline, hereditary training in lawful control, was obtainable upon individual application (p. 69).

Wallace's rejection of Judaism is more cerebral than that of his sister. Jewish attention to continuity with the past smacks of peasantries' concern for roots and this attitude is, attests Wallace, about to disappear from the historical scene. He is also opposed to his father's Zionism. Bellow's depiction of American Judaism's covenant betrayal is rounded out by the character of Lionel Feffer, a slick, self-promoting huckster, and graduate student at Columbia University who takes financial advantage of Sammler. These representative American Jews express neither a commitment to the Jewish community nor an awareness of the dimensions of evil. They do, on the other hand, seek out Sammler, desiring absolution for their aberrant behavior.

Early on in the novel Sammler penetrates beneath the layers of obfuscation with which certain intellectuals have overlaid the Holocaust. Margotte Arkin, Sammler's widowed niece, herself a refugee from pre-Holocaust Germany, is fascinated by Hannah Arendt's "Banality of Evil" thesis. Sammler has no use for Margotte's perpetual wrong-headedness and silences her with the uncharacteristic passion of his response, insisting on calling murder, murder. Unlike intellectuals, Sammler does not engage in avoiding the obvious. Arendt contended that Aldolph Eichmann, master bureaucrat of murder, was an average citizen who represented everyman. She indicated that even such a person can become, under particular historical conditions, a murderer. She goes so far as to call Eichmann "the truth-revealer for generations to come." The truth referred to concerns the banality of evil. One unfortunate implication of Arendt's position is, of course, that if everyone is potentially guilty then no one is actually guilty. Sammler is having none of this theoretical exoneration. There is, he contends, nothing banal about murder. "The best and purest human beings," he mused, knew from the very beginning "that life is sacred" (p. 21). The banality was camouflage, a device to get the curse out of murder.[14]

Sammler was, himself, well acquainted with the deceits of camouflage. Prior to the catastrophe, his family had been "almost free-thinkers" (p. 79), and Sammler had believed that "there was no judge but himself" (p. 130), and had had no use for Judaism. An intellectual and a man of high culture, Sammler's espousal of universalism led him to conclude that as an heir of the Enlightenment he had outgrown Jewish parochialism. And he was correct. Friend of H. G. Wells, participant in the Bloomsbury ambience, Sammler viewed his rejection of Jewish specificity as a passport to Western citizenship. Bellow corrects the assimilationist's self-delusion by accurately portraying the Nazis's intention concerning the total destruction of Jews and Judaism. The act was viewed in terms of cosmic hygiene, ridding the world of poisoners of Aryan blood. The aging Sammler knows that if the war had lasted only a few more months, "he would have died like the rest. Not a Jew would have avoided death" (p. 249).

The Holocaust is Sammler's point of entry into Jewish history and human awareness. His relationship to the tradition in fact undergoes three distinct phases. Born a Jew, initially he is indifferent to religion and hostile toward Judaism; Sammler is named after the antisemitic philosopher Schopenhauer. About this stage of his life Sammler later reflected that until forty he had been a man of culture, "relatively useless." Samler enters, is forced into would be more accurate, the second stage by historical events. Like Anya, Rosa, and other assimilated Polish Jews enmeshed in the murderous Nazi web, Sammler discovers the binding reality of the *others* definition. He is a Jew because the Nazis have so defined him. Regardless of his own orientation to the tradition, he is singled out for murder. Sammler achieves the third stage of his Jewish identity when he willingly self-identifies as part of the Jewish people; concerned for the well-being of the world and anxious about the fate of Israel. Bellow, with Schaeffer, Nissenson, and Kotlowitz, contends that being born of a Jewish mother is a necessary but insufficient ingredient of Jewish identity. Biology is subservient to Jewish commitment.

Rushing to a final visit with Gruner, Sammler is reminded again of the relationship between the madness of the past and the violence of the present. Witnessing the black pickpocket choking Feffer because the latter had photographed him in action, Sammler initially attempts to persuade some of the onlookers to intervene. No one moved, apathy continues now as it did during the Holocaust. Spotting Eisen (iron man) in the crowd, Sammler calls on him to separate the two men. Eisen hits the black man with iron objects which he carries in a leather bag hung from his wrist. The metal cuts deeply and Eisen keeps swinging, although the criminal is on his hands and knees bleeding heavily. Speaking in Russian to his former son-in-law, Sammler commands him to stop. Eisen responds as one survivor to another:

> You can't hit a man like this just once. When you hit him you must really hit him. Otherwise he'll kill you. You had a gun. So don't you know? (p. 266).

Eisen's message "sank Sammler's heart completely," for the Polish survivor knew its truth and realized that the Holocaust had changed nothing.

Arriving at the hospital too late, Sammler insists on being taken to the hospital's morgue where, uncovering Gruner's face, he recites a secular *kaddish*.

> Remember, God, the soul of Elya Gruner, who, as willingly as possible and as well as he was able, and even to an intolerable point, and even in suffocation and even as death was coming was eager, even childishly perhaps (may I be forgiven for this), even with a certain servility, to do what was required of him. At his best this man was much kinder than at my very best I have ever been or could ever be. He was aware that he must meet, and he did meet—through all the confusion and degraded clowning of this life through which we are speeding—he did meet the terms of his contract—the terms which, in his inmost heart, each man knows. As I know mine. As all know—For that is the truth of it—that we all know, God, that we know, that we know, we know, we know (pp. 285–86).

Sammler's *kaddish* differs from the traditional recitation in important and revealing ways. The Aramaic prayer extols God, and not man; it expresses the hope that God's kingdom may soon prevail in the lifetime of the mourner "and within the life of the entire house of Israel, speedily and soon;" and it petitions for the blessing of peace and life for the congregation and for all Israel. There is no explicit mention of either the dead or of the covenant. Gruner's body is, moreover, to be cremated after the autopsy. Both of these practices violate *halaka*. Nevertheless, Sammler's insistence on ritual utterance, however modified, is an important measure of his own post-Holocaust Jewish awareness. The need to address God, affirm the covenant (the contract), and uphold ethical standards is very strong in Sammler. Moreover, the absence of Gruner's own children at the eulogy serves to heighten the difference between European and American Jewry. Self-absorbed and Jewishly illiterate, the actions of Angela and Wallace do not bode well for Jewish continuity in America.

Mr. Sammler ponders the meaning of three planets; Earth, Moon, and Planet Auschwitz. He rejects the moon because man, even if able to escape earth, cannot flee from himself. Planet Auschwitz has, on the other hand, a message for all the inhabitants of planet Earth. Sammler's testament concerns the meaning of being human in an inhuman age. Posed as a question, Sammler wonders how one can prevent the world from again collapsing. He is, however, under no illusion concerning man. Echoing the rabbinic contention that man has two impulses, the *yetzer tov* and the *yetzer ha-ra*, a good and an evil drive, Sammler realizes that man is by nature both moral and a killer (pp. 180–81). It is, however, man's moral duty to prevail over his killer instincts; this is the Holocaust's universal lesson.

Sammler's own moral authority stems from his Holocaust experience. He acknowledges to Lal that his earlier seduction by Enlightenment promises and by H. G. Well's theories was a past thing. "Of course," utters Sammler, "since Poland, nineteen thirty-nine, my judgments are different. Altered. Like my eyesight" (p. 192). Yet his visual impairment allows Sammler to see things unavailable to the physically sighted. Like Cohen's blind Nathan, Simon Stern's scribe, Artur Sammler is a seer whose perceptions are keener, more profound; having to do with salvation itself. Rejecting Lal's scheme, for example, Sammler refers to himself as a "depth man rather than a height man" (p. 168). He prefers the ocean to the moon because however deep the sea, it has a top and a bottom. Sammler's quest for meaning on the post-Auschwitz planet is an inward journey rather than an escape from earth; a reflective examination of the human and the cosmic condition.

Sammler's self-referential use of "depth man" is a transmutation of the earliest expression of Jewish esoteric speculation. Practitioners of *Merkabah* mysticism were called *Yorde Merkabah* (descenders into the chariot). The goal of these protomystics was to behold the realm of the divine throne, but to accomplish this they first had to descend into themselves. Mystics in the Jewish tradition also interpreted God's command to Abraham, *lech lecha*—get thee to a far country—as referring to an inner descent. Sammler, with these earlier "depth men," realizes that the curing of souls, the most urgent task confronting those living after the catastrophe, begins within. This perception is entirely consistent with Sammler's postwar turn to religion.

Sammler's basic insight concerns the folly of anthropocentric salvation. Contrary to modernity's assumptions, the world cannot function in a condition of spiritual disenchantment. Sammler is a survivor in a double sense; he lived through the Holocaust, and he is one of the few who continue to long for sacredness while realizing that this sensitivity has been conceptually banished, suffocated by a rationalism which measured the worth of individuals in a purely instrumental fashion. It is, therefore, no accident that Sammler abandons his earlier reading of social theorists and historians of civilization preferring instead the Bible, and Meister Eckhart in Latin. Sacredness has been murdered along with the Jews. "Yes," Sammler reflects, "go and find it when everyone is murdering everyone" (p. 86).

Sammler the Jew and the Hindu Lal express contrasting views of the human condition. Lal, a scientist, contends that "there is no duty in biology," no implicit morality in the will-to-live. "Duty," attests the Hindu, "is pain,—hateful-misery, oppressive." Sammler responds utilizing a rabbinic debate concerning whether it would have been better not to have been born. Found in the Babylonian Talmud (Erubin 13b), the rabbis agree on two things: it would have been better not to have been born and, once here, man must make the best of things.[15] Cohen's Simon Stern also raises a talmudic controversy concerning whether it was good or bad that God had created the universe. Simon disagrees with the sages—and with Sammler—who conclude that the universe is faulty. Instead Simon Stern argues, as we have noted, that creation is complexity; all men do evil but desire the good.

Sammler then challenges Lal's interpretation of duty on two grounds. "The pain of duty makes a creature upright," attests the Polish survivor. In and of itself this is an important discovery. But Sammler, in addition, stands firmly by his conviction that "there is also an instinct against leaping into kingdom come" (p. 201). Sammler's is the prophetic and not the apocalyptic voice.

Despite their disagreement, Sammler and Lal share an experience which unites them and distinguishes their perceptions of reality from those of native-born Americans. Both have first-hand acquaintance with mass slaughter; European extermination for Sammler, while Lal has witnessed Asian homicidal maniacs in the great Calcutta killing. In a somewhat ironic reversal, it is the man of Eastern culture who advocates a technological rather than a meditative solution to the problems of being earthbound. Moon settlement represents the best future for mankind. Sammler, the European, rejects technological panaceas in favor of facing the obligations of being human. A human being, muses Sammler, must have "the internal parts" in order. The moon simply is not metaphysically advantageous for us.

Mr. Sammler's Planet is Bellow's refutation of Enlightenment assumptions.[16] Taking a cue from his own main character, Bellow subsequently wrote that the authenticity of any truths about the human condition need to be measured against the raw mass of the Holocaust.

> The Holocaust may even be seen as a deliberate lesson or project in philosophical redefinition: "You religious and enlightened people, you Christians, Jews, and Humanists, you believers in freedom, dignity, and enlightenment—you think you know what a human being is. We will show you what he is, and what you are. Look at our camps and crematoria and see if you can bring your hearts to care about these millions."[17]

The Bellow/Sammler view is a literary form of Greenberg's admonition that "no statement, theological or otherwise, should be made that would not be credible in the presence of burning children." Sammler's encounters with death serve to distill the essential from the irrelevant. He recalls that the times when things had seemed most real and true to him were when he was confronting death.[18] "Asking basic questions like, 'Will I kill him? Will he kill me? If I sleep, will I ever wake? Am I really alive, or is there nothing left but an illusion of life?' " (p. 210), has forced Sammler to realize the shallowness of culture.

That the Holocaust is a Jewish problem is clear. But Sammler wishes to draw out its universal implications. While hiding in the Mezvinski family tomb, Sammler recalls that "there was a yellow tinge to everything" including a yellow light in the sky. This parlous illumination was "bad news for Sammler, bad news for humankind, bad information about the very essence of being" (p. 35). The yellow tinge may be Bellow's reminder of the yellow armband which Jews were compelled to wear while the majority stood idly by. If so, Sammler recalls the old truism which is nonetheless true for its antiquity that a society's treatment of its Jews is a bellwether of its own spiritual and political health. The Holocaust is, in any case, a civilizational cautionary sign. The world is radically altered not only because of the slaughter, but because of the massive apathy which accompanied it. Sammler notes, for example, the refusal of Churchill and Roosevelt to bomb Auschwitz. His own immersion in the Bible and in Eckhart's mysticism indicate that the Holocaust, perpetrated by those calling themselves religious, radically challenged the original teachings of Judaism and Christianity.

Sammler's postwar mental habit is in fact to juxtapose modern schemes and ancient texts. Responding, for example, to the opening sentence of Lal's manuscript—"How long will this earth remain the only home of man?"—Sammler echoes the psalmist's question "How long? Oh Lord." Drawing upon the Book of Ecclesiastes, he reiterates the preacher's feeling that "for every purpose under heaven there is a time. A time to gather stones together, a time to cast away stones." Bellow's conjoining of the two texts is meant to demonstrate the eternal relevance of the Bible as a guide for grappling with fundamental problems of existence. Lal's technological salvation pales beside the ancient wisdom. Sammler's attitude at this point calls to mind Herman Broder's observation in *Enemies* that in times of trouble Jews always returned to the Bible whose "sentences fitted all circumstances, all ages, all moods, while secular literature, no matter how well written, in time lost its pertinence." Sammler, although no scholar of the Bible or of Jewish texts, is nonetheless struck by biblical authenticity.

Sammler outlines his philosophy of history to Lal, Margotte, and Shula-Slawa. The awesome failure of modernity consists in its liberation into individuality. Antiquity and the medieval world accepted models or societal norms for human behavior. Modern man has rejected this criterion and strives instead for uniqueness. Commendable in principle, the quest had resulted in mere theatricality. By way of illustration Sammler relates the bizarre but true tale of Mordecai Chaim Rumkowski, the mad Jewish King of the Lodz Ghetto. Rumkowski, the Jews of Lodz, Sammler, and Shula-Slawa all belonged, says Sammler, to the category "written off."

Rumkowski is a controversial figure in Holocaust historiography. Yet Bellow's description of him as a "failed businessman, a noisy individual, corrupt, director of an orphanage, a fund-raiser, a bad actor, a distasteful fun-figure in the Jewish community" (p. 210), is accurate. As Lal had never heard of Rumkowski, Sammler provides details. The Nazis made Rumkowski *Judenältester* (head of the Jewish council) of Lodz, an important prewar industrial center. After walling off the Jewish section, Lodz became a Jewish ghetto and Rumkowski its king. Stamps and money were printed bearing his picture, he appeared at ceremonies wearing royal robes, and traveled about the corpse-strewn streets in an ornate coach pulled by a dying horse. His reign was one of terror, although he evidently had two moments of dignity. Once he protested the murder of his first council members. He was then beaten and thrown into the streets. When the ghetto was liquidated he is said to have voluntarily gotten into a freight car for the trip to extermination at Auschwitz. Sammler's use of Rumkowski to illustrate the "antics of failed individuality" is questionable. Interpretations of the *Judenräte* phenomenon range from those scholars who view the councils as actively cooperating in the destruction process (Arendt and Rubenstein) to interpreters who contend that the councils acted in hopes of saving at least a remnant of the Jewish people (Dawidowicz and Robinson). Interpretations of Rumkowski's own role mirror the controversy.[19] He apparently hoped that by making the Lodz ghetto economically vital to the Third Reich, Jewish lives could be saved, and it is true that Lodz lasted the longest of all the Jewish ghettos. However, what is true without a doubt is Sammler's observation that Nazis took pleasure at degrading the Jews, having "a predilection for such *Ubu Roi* murder farces."

Sammler then introduces the biblical Job as an exemplar of the task of being human. Bemoaning God's excessive demands on man, Job had committed the sin of self-sufficiency. What God requires of us, according to Sammler's rendition of Job is twofold; a moral demand, and "the demand upon the imagination to produce a human figure of adequate stature." Did Rumkowski, "King of rags and shit,— ruler of corpses," possess adequate stature? Sammler argues that the misery of Rumkowski and the protest of Job illustrate how difficult it is to be human. A life which is ethically unanchored—as is the case with Angela, Wallace, and Feffer—is one in which "everything is poured so barbarously and recklessly into personal gesture." Against the concern for body and ego, Sammler counterposes the life of the spirit "which knows that its growth is the real aim of existence" (p. 215).

Theologically, Sammler's position is a type of Greenbergian compromise. The Polish survivor rejects, on the one hand, "the implicit local orthodoxy . . . that reality was a terrible thing, and that the final truth about mankind was overwhelming and crushing" (p. 255). Yet Sammler agrees with Greenberg's contention that there should be no final solutions after the Holocaust. Sammler has lived in history, is a member of the people who have been its principal victims, but he remains hopeful about the possibility of redemption. Sammler's

prophetic tone is a refutation of Rubenstein's "Death of God" position. In place of a fatal eschatological resignation Sammler advocates
the covenantal metaphor of struggle. Writing to Lal, Sammler notes,
"everyone grapples, each in his awkward muffled way, with a power,
a Jacob's angel, to get a final satisfaction or glory that is withheld"
(p. 119). Bellow's intentional reference to Jacob's angel is reminiscent
of Nissenson's epigraphical use of Genesis 32, and it underscores the
dialectical nature of covenant reality: elusive yet omnipresent. Sammler urges that the struggle not be abandoned to despair. Unlike
his refugee friends, Sammler did not view a second collapse of the
world as inevitable.

Sammler's God is neither the living God of Abraham, Isaac, and
Jacob nor the God of the philosophers. While during the war Sammler
confesses that he had no belief—"God was not impressed by death.
Hell was his indifference," yet after the Holocaust he has a sense of
God. Inability to explain, opines Sammler, is no ground for disbelief.
Sammler's argument is in fact similar to Herman Broder's contention
that even if one could not prove the existence of oxygen one would
continue breathing. The sense of God persists and brings with it
painful contradictions. Sammler finds it difficult to live in a world in
which God appears indifferent. Job-like, he inquires of God "No concern for justice? Nothing of pity?" (p. 215). Yet, Sammler has "strong
impressions of eternity" and yearns for his "God adumbrations in
the many daily forms." Sammler's dialectic—not unlike that of Greenberg's—moves between a knowledge of divine indifference as man-
ifested by the Holocaust and intimations of divine presence in everyday
existence. The tension is made bearable for Sammler, as it was for
Job, in the realization that "all is not flatly knowable."

Sammler's Planet is one in which the choices are sainthood or
madness. Only a few comprehend, observes Sammler, "that it is the
strength to do one's duty daily and promptly that makes saints and
heroes." In fact most people fantasize about "vaulting into higher
states, feeling just mad enough to qualify" (p. 87). He confides to
Angela that being human is not a natural gift at all. "Only the capacity
is natural." As with the 613 commandments which consist of more
negative than positive strictures, there are for Sammler far more "thou
shalt nots" which act as moral brakes for a civilization careening
apparently out of control. His Holocaust experience has proven to
Sammler that ethically neutral individualism can lead to the worst
excesses of human behavior.

Elya Gruner is a Jew from Eastern Europe who has lived in America for over fifty years. Elya is the diminutive form of Elijah ("Yah[weh]

is [my] God." Although not religious, Gruner is a *lamed-vov zaddik* absorbed by Jewish history and concerned for the survival of Israel. The *lamed-vov* is one whose righteous acts, charity, and communal concern elevate the life of all mankind, although the *zaddik*'s true identity may be concealed not only from his contemporaries but from himself as well. Elya has always accepted what Sammler termed his assignments, doing what he disliked and accepting the pain of duty. Bellow masterfully portrays the ambiguity of Gruner's role. As a physician, he symbolizes responsibility and compassion. Yet Wallace insists that Gruner had hidden huge sums of cash from performing Mafia abortions. Shula-Slawa, a habitual scavenger—frequently rummaging through garbage cans—does in fact find the money.

Elya was one in a great chain of individuals stretching across history and through time whose presence and behavior provided meaning amidst the welter of chaos and immorality which threaten to engulf man. "He knew," said Sammler of the dying Gruner, "there had been good men before him, that there were good men to come, and he wanted to be one of them. I think he did all right" (p. 276). Elya is a philanthropist who prefers helping anonymously, adhering to the highest Jewish ideal of *zedakah* (charity). The norms which Gruner embodied—feeling, outgoingness, expressiveness, kindness, heart—Samler interprets as distinctively Jewish and paradigmatic for post-Auschwitz humanity.

There exists a special bond between Gruner and Sammler which goes far beyond the doctor's benevolence. Gruner viewed Sammler as a link with the destroyed Jews of Europe whose numbers included the doctor's own relatives, although Sammler did not remember many of them and had not shared their spirituality. By having Sammler return from the dead, Bellow emphasizes the underlying mystery of millennial Jewish survival. This strategy also differentiates covenantally based Eastern European Judaism from the covenant abandonment which Bellow perceives as a root problem of American Jewry's ethical and moral shortcomings. Gruner's obsession with the Jewish past is revealed in the fact that he spent long hours doing genealogies. His wife Hilda, a German Jewess—above him socially—disapproved of such activities. Elya's one eccentricity consisted of flying to Israel on a moment's notice and strolling into the King David Hotel without any luggage. His is the classical attitude of *ahavat Yisrael* displayed so magnificently by Tamara in Singer's *Enemies*.

Sammler's own espousal of *ahavat Yisrael* is seen in his response to the Six Day War. Although not a Zionist, Sammler is irresistibly drawn to Israel, refusing to remain in New York passively watching events on television. He goes, as a reporter for a Polish newspaper, because for the second time in twenty-five years, the Jews are threatened with extermination, and again the West is apathetic.

Two events reveal Bellow's perception of Israel's post-Holocaust role for world Jewry. Stranded for a time in Athens, Sammler finally resumes his El Al flight to the besieged nation. Bellow describes the effect which Israel's plight has elicited amongst young Jewish hippies. Having once spent time in Israel, these international youth wished now to return. Recognizing no government, they were "responding to a primary event." Bellow argues that Jewish identification with Israel is a necessary and irreversible effect of the Holocaust. Israel is the only country to which Jews may go for refuge. Linking this fact to the Holocaust, Sammler observes that Israel is a haven for physical and emotional cripples such as Eisen.

Victim of Jewish powerlessness, Sammler has mixed feelings when confronted with the results of Israeli power used in self-defense. Visiting the battlefields, Sammler discovers that the Israelis have used napalm. Sammler then goes to El Arish and stands in the waters of the Mediterranean where he sees and smells and tastes the omnipresent battlefield dead, although it is curious that he sees only Egyptian and not Israeli corpses. Sammler remains torn between his understanding of powers' necessity and his revulsion at its use. He despairs of a world which has made Israel act militarily in order to survive the continued attacks of those interested in destroying her. Bellow has rightly seen that even Jewish power has not negated Jewish vulnerability.

Bellow has created in Sammler an ambiguously Jewish character far removed from the tradition's classical sources, more at home in the library than in the synagogue. Nonetheless, Sammler's message is etched with Jewish specificity. Gruner, for example, respected Sammler's *"experiences*; the war-Holocaust-Suffering." Even the self-hating American Jews seek out Sammler. Angela, who sends her father's money to a defense fund for black rapists; Wallace, who, ignorant of Hebrew, asks "why does God speak such a funny language?" and Feffer all see in Sammler a moral beacon. This stands in sharp contrast to Sammler's self-description as "only an old Jew whom they had hacked at, shot at, but missed killing somehow, murdering everyone else with their blasts."

Sammler differs markedly, however, from those who actually survived the death camps or who are themselves refugees. Unlike Wiesel's Eliezer and Reuven, Sammler does not think of himself as a messenger of the dead. Nor does he share Herman Broder's obsession, in Singer's *Enemies*, that there is going to be an imminent Nazi invasion of New York. Sammler, we read, did not "practice the arts of hiding and escape in New York" (p. 48).

Sammler, unlike Gruner, is a man whose musings prevent him from acting. He had, for example, written only two articles over the years; one on Rumkowski and the other on the Six Day War. Sammler had also been invited to testify at the Eichmann trial but did not feel up to it. Action for Sammler, as for Eliezer and Herman Broder, is cerebral in nature. Sammler is, like Tamara Broder, a guide for those wishing to traverse the moral wilderness of modernity. Unlike Tamara, however, Sammler's teachings lack a specifically Jewish base. His communing is largely a self-conversation. Artur Sammler knows, however, that a convenantally based ethic does not confuse modernity's claim of the autonomous self with antiquity's norm of the accountable self.

Sammler is pessimistic concerning the future of Jews and Judaism in America. Authentic Jews, such as Gruner, are either dead or dying and have unmarried Jewishly indifferent children. Sammler himself has an unmarried daughter whose matrimonial prospects are dim. What can Judaism's future be without Jews? On the other hand, young Jews traveled to Israel when the country appeared to be on the brink of destruction. The Jewish future has, for Bellow, a much better chance at surviving in Israel than in America, although it remains clouded. Bellow underscores a fact of Jewish existence which even the State of Israel has not been able to alter:

> there is one fact of Jewish life unchanged by the creation of a Jewish state: you cannot take your right to live for granted. Others can; you cannot. This is not to say that everyone else is living pleasantly and well under a decent regime. No, it means only that the Jews, because they are Jews, have never been able to take the right to live as a natural right.[20]

The Holocaust and Israel remain for Sammler twin pillars of Jewish authenticity. America's Jews, in order to remain Jewish, must somehow incorporate the lessons of the Holocaust while simultaneously defending Israel's right to exist. Israel is neither the response to nor the reward for the Holocaust, but it embodies the preciousness of Jewish continuity, which itself is more than mere physical endurance.

Susan F. Schaeffer

Susan Fromberg Schaeffer, born during the Holocaust, is a third-generation American Jew. Her family is Russian-Jewish in origin, but evidently sheltered their daughter from learning about the *Shoah*. Schaeffer is a professor and a writer who has had a very productive literary career, having written poetry and short stories as well as several novels. Her novels are concerned with history and reveal a painstaking attention to details of social, temporal, and spatial interest. *Falling, Anya*, and the more recent *Love* are her most widely acclaimed novels; each being a chronicle of the Jewish historical experience in modernity. Schaeffer's Jewish concerns may be seen in her attention to parent-child relationships, the conflict between individual destiny and historical forces, and an emphasis on family sagas. Schaeffer reports becoming interested in the Holocaust from meetings with survivors. These encounters, in fact, proved to be the origin of *Anya*.[21]

Anya (1974)[22] treats the prewar, Holocaust, and post-Holocaust existence of Anya Savikin an acculturated Polish Jewess whose once idyllic life is forever shattered by Hitler's war of extermination. Prior to the catastrophe Anya is admitted to medical school despite being a Jew and a woman, marries, and has a daughter, Ninka, to whom she is devoted. The Holocaust, however, sweeps everything away. Having given Ninka to a Christian family before being deported to a labor camp, Anya is kept alive by the need to be reunited with her daughter. Physically and psychically scarred by her experiences, Anya is broken in confidence and vocationally disoriented. At the novel's conclusion, in America, she is unable to work even as a nurse and instead owns an antique shop. Unlike Artur Sammler, Anya's interpretation of the Jewish vocation is not intellectually sophisticated. She rejects the notion that any meaning can be extracted from the disaster of European Jewry: "I do not understand today, any more than I did thirty years ago, why all that had to happen to us" (p. 595).

Although theologically naïve, Anya does believe that she survived her many ordeals because a superpower—variously identified with a nontraditional God or fate—wished her to. *Anya* provides the reader with much to ponder concerning post-Holocaust Jewish identity and religion: the image of God, the purpose of chosenness, the meaning of suffering, the complexity of Jewish-Christian relationships, and the Holocaust's continuing impact on survivors and their children.

The novel is structured in a manner similar to Cohen's *In the Days of Simon Stern*. *Anya* consists of a prologue, an epilogue, and three books each of which is separately titled—"In History," "Biblical Times," and "The Lion's Jaws." A fable, poem, proverb, or quotation precedes each section, establishing a mythic framework for succeeding events. *Anya* differs from Cohen's novel, however, in terms of its setting—

only the last forty pages deal with Anya's experience in America and, because it is based on interviews with a survivor, the novel reveals a wealth of detail concerning prewar family life in Poland and conveys a sense of realism rarely found in the literature of other Jewish-American writers. *Anya* begins and ends with a dream, and employs dreams and fairy tales to blur the lines between reality and fantasy, thereby emphasizing that the unimaginable but real Holocaust universe far exceeds the limits of the imaginal world. Before the war Anya read *Mein Kampf* and described it to her mother as a fairy tale. After the war Ninka heard stories about the crematoria and told Anya that their friend Max "was telling someone a fairy tale about cooking people in ovens" (p. 567).

Anya displays the ambivalence toward tradition characteristic of Jewish modernity. The Savikin family has abandoned *halakic* Judaism, but their lives give secular expression to Jewish values: an intense passion for reading, storytelling and study, a love of languages, and a deep and abiding humanism. A silver Noah's Ark bread basket is displayed next to two silver candlesticks in the Savikin's dining room. A wedding present which Mrs. Savikin received from her father, the basket plays an important symbolic role in *Anya*. The novel spares no details when describing the ideological fission between the Savikins and the Levinskys, an orthodox family whose son Stajoe is to marry Anya. The Levinskys from Warsaw ("a little Paris"), are hasidic Jews. The Savikins are from Vilno, seat of traditional opposition to hasidic fervor, and have great reservations about hasidism. Yet *Anya* also reveals the truth of Katz's observation about the persistence of tradition in modernity. Anya, for example, despite her indifference to Jewish religious and ritual practice would not marry a non-Jew. She is, therefore, different both from Artur Sammler and from Ozick's Rosa Lublin in her positive pre-Holocaust Jewish self-identity.

"In History" portrays the Savikins as a family whose lives are almost unbelievably rich in texture and human relationships, confirming Edward Alexander's astute observation that *Anya* is "as much about memory as about the Holocaust."[23] Anya's parents are saintly people and gifted tellers of tales. Rebecca Savikin, a former schoolteacher, endlessly recites the family's history to her daughters thereby establishing a link with the pious Jews who, while living in the past, continue to exercise influence in the present. Anya, herself, provides a measure by which the reader can begin to understand the enormity of what was lost in the Holocaust when she observes of those halcyon days "comfort, always comfort."

The question of why the Jews are chosen, which subtly runs

throughout the novel, is focused in the views of the elder Savikins. Mrs. Savikin frequently observed that "the Jews are chosen, but they are unlucky." Fate contends with human responsibility. Anya, herself, begins to come to terms with these questions in the wake of an ugly pogrom at her university. The male students deface Jewish girls with iron nails, killing some of their classmates. Mr. Savikin's frantic telephone call saved Anya from this danger. She also learns that asylum inmates have thrown one of her medical school professors into a pot of boiling soup. The first incident is historical, the second symbolizes the activities of the Holocaust universe. Mr. Savikin states a type of kabbalistic aphorism concerning the relationship between good and evil, reminiscent of Cohen's Dr. Fisher Klay who insisted that even their redeemer, Simon Stern, is both good and evil. "Get used to the fact," Mr. Savikin tells Anya, that "good and bad insist on sharing a room" (p. 97).

Much later—in America—Anya reflects on the episode of the iron nails. Her belief in a suprahuman force to whom she could speak began then. She remembers sitting with her mother thinking:

> What for, the chosen people, what for? Chosen for what? For this, to be endlessly persecuted, just because we are Jewish? (p. 596).

Anya believes that even the "endless persecution was a form of being chosen." Although far removed from a *halakic* base, Anya's willingness to accept—inability to resist is more accurate—the burden of Jewish identity is her way of witnessing to the mystery of Jewish survival which in the post-Holocaust era, as Fackenheim argues, grips even the secularist Jew.

"Biblical Times" derives its title from Mrs. Savikin's recollection of her grandfather's saying: "When you are living through biblical times, the living will come to envy the dead." Echoing Ecclesiastes, this inversion of the normal order of existence—like Wiesel's observation that the cemeteries are all in the sky—underscores the immensity of the Holocaust and the lack of Jewish (or any other) preparedness to cope with the exterminators' zeal. This section provides a vivid and depressing account of the step-by-step destruction of Polish Jewry: restricting Jewish access to public places, random murder for the crime of appearing in public (Anya's father was beaten to death for being outside—he was on his way to borrow a book), mass murder, ghettoization, and resettlement in the East.

Anya reveals the depth of despair felt by secularist Jews at the onslaught of the Holocaust by introducing the figure of mystic and

scholar as link with the tradition. Anya, for example, turns to suprarational means of guidance seeking out a Vilno yeshiva student
who read kabbalah, knew all the mysteries, and practiced chiromancy.
Anya journeys to the mystic in order to ask whether she should give
Ninka to a Christian family. The kabbalist first verifies his own authenticity for the outsider, much in the manner of Ozick's rebbe in
"Bloodshed." Identifying Anya's place in her familial structure, and
knowing her age, the mystic advises Anya to keep Ninka unless there
is an order that children should be killed. He concludes by accurately
predicting that while he himself will not survive, Anya and Ninka
will.

The introduction of the mystic as revealer of the future and pos-
sessor of truth opens the way for a guarded optimism about Jewish
destiny. Wiesel utilizes this strategy throughout his fiction. Hugh
Nissenson, as we shall see, also employs a fortune-telling kabbalist
in his novel *My Own Ground*. Nissenson, however, views this vocation
as indicating the perversion of mystical authenticity. Seeking advice
from, or asking a question of, rabbinic or mystic authorities is a well-
established practice among the orthodox and other believers. For example, Saul Bellow's Isaac Braun in "The Old System" has a rebbe
in Williamsburg to whom he turns for advice on crucial matters. But
one would hardly expect this type of behavior from an acculturated
Jew in so-called normal times.

Anya dialectically justaposes the bleakness of the Jewish historical
situation with symbols of hope which intermittently appear. Mr. Ler-
monsky, the family's attorney, callously refuses Anya's entreaty to
help her husband, imprisoned by the Gestapo. Momma, for her part,
predicts the worst: the living will have no time for the dead, she sees
nothing good ahead for the Jews. In fact, she does not see anything
ahead for the Jews of Europe, (pp. 201, 202). Christian antisemitism
and personal feelings of dread are real and powerful Holocaust facts.
On the other hand, Mrs. Savikin provides some measure of hope that
a "remnant shall remain" when she hides jewelry and a watch above
the stove in their apartment. After the war, Anya will retrieve these
items. More pointedly, Mrs. Savikin repeatedly emphasizes that Anya
will live because she has Ninka to live for. Mrs. Savikin also gives
Anya practical advice which saves her daughter's life on several occasions: in the death camps, hiding in the forest, and as a postwar
refugee. "A woman," Momma admonishes, "must always look her
best, especially in the worst circumstances." Primo Levi relates an
insight from his Auschwitz experience which confirms the importance
of self-esteem for survival.

precisely because the Lager was a great machine to reduce us to beasts, we must not become beasts; that even in this place one can survive, and therefore one must want to survive, to tell the story, to bear witness; and that to survive we must force ourselves to save at least the skeleton, the scaffolding, the form of civilization. We are slaves, deprived of every right, exposed to every insult, condemned to certain death, but we still possess one power, and we must defend it with all our strength for it is the last—the power to refuse our consent. So we must certainly wash our faces without soap in dirty water and dry ourselves on our jackets. We must polish our shoes, not because the regulation states it, but for dignity and propriety. We must walk erect without dragging our feet, not in homage to Prussian discipline, but to remain alive, not to begin to die.[24]

The meaning of Jewish history, the continued existence of the *lamed-vov zaddik*, and the complexity of Jewish-Christian relationships form the matrix of "The Lion's Jaws," the novel's longest book—actually a self-contained novella. Anya is plunged into the depths of the concentrationary universe where gratuitous but normalized violence and sadism combine with unexpected heroic acts. The usually unphilosophical Anya, herded out of a cattle car, reflects on the different motivations for killing in the world of nature and among humans. She longed

to feed the pigs and the cows and the chickens, the little things that never hurt anyone and who were killed for a reason, or who killed like the bears, without pretending to have a higher nature (p. 273).

However, Anya survives her many ensuing ordeals, not through philosophical means, but by exceptional resourcefulness.

At Kaiserwald, a Nazi camp, Anya sharpens her belief in a superpower. "But," she adds in kabbalistic fashion, "it needs help" (p. 295). Part of this help is provided by Erdmann, a bizarre figure whose introduction adds to the novel's underlying sense of the miraculous amidst even the murderous evil of the mundane, and who functions as a secular *lamed-vov zaddik*. Erdmann wears a Nazi uniform, lives in the camp commander's house, writes stories and songs, and frequently intervenes in Anya's behalf, feeding her and eventually helping her to escape. It is he who arranges for Anya to hide with the Rutkauskus family who had taken in Ninka. Erdmann confesses that he is a Jew whose family had been murdered, but whose own life had been spared by switching identity papers with a dying

Christian friend. Historically, the existence of Jews in Nazi uniform is a bizarre assertion, although certain high-ranking Nazis followed the dictum of Karl Lueger, the Jew-hating mayor of Vienna who, in the 1920s, contended: "I decide who is Jewish."[25] In terms of plot and structure, however, Erdmann's presence opens the possibility of Anya's continued existence and her ultimate freedom from Holocaust assault. Erdmann's actions make possible a kind of moment faith which clings to the possibility of redemption in the midst of despair.

Escaping from Kaiserwald, Anya realizes the precariousness of Jewish existence. Hiding in a stove in the Rutkauskus kitchen—as her mother had done in the ghetto—she engages in a soliloquy which is a meditation on the Holocaust's historical meaning. Agreeing with the theological views discussed in chapter 2, Anya affirms that the Holocaust has forever changed the world. She recalls the globe on her father's desk and sees him slice an inch from both halves and press it together again. The globe was solid but not the same, "something important had been taken out." Anya's murdered father incinerates the globe which goes "up like newspaper."

Anya describes the depth of Christian Jew-hatred while simultaneously revealing the existence of sparks of moral light. Antisemitism is presented—much in the manner of Bellow, Ozick, and Nissenson—as a deep and abiding presence in the European mind. Disguised as a Christian and wearing a cross, Anya hears the antisemitic voice of the people. A laundry worker reports that a friend unknowingly took in a Jewish child: "imagine it, taking it in, you think it's normal, you know, and it turns out to be a Jew; the war is messing everything up" (p. 393). German officers speak of the necessity of extending the final solution to American Jewry. By repetition of ancient canards—the Jews have too much influence and too much money—this scene emphasizes the popular resonance of Hitler's insane extermination scheme. *Anya* is, however, distinguishable from other American Jewish Holocaust fiction in noting the existence of a special group of people—*hasidei ummot ha-olam* (the pious ones of the nations of the world)—righteous gentiles who saved Jewish lives at the risk of their own. Rutkauskus and his wife Onucia are Lithuanians who not only raise Ninka but shelter other Jews. Queried as to his motive, the drunkard Rutkauskus responds, "Jesus would do the same."[26] The Nazis murder the Rutkauskus's for this crime, leaving their baby to starve in his parents' sealed apartment.

Anya's postwar reflections center on the Holocaust and its relationship to Judaism. Visiting Kaiserwald and noting the difference between the way Jewish inmates had been brutalized and the benign treatment given its current German prisoners, Anya realizes that the Holocaust is, to use Greenberg's term, an orienting event.

> I would be forever attached to this camp by an invisible umbilical cord, infinitely elastic and infinitely strong, one that could never be cut; I would forever be one of its inmates (p. 459).

More passionate and intense than Sammler, Anya shares her fictional countryman's perception that the *Shoah* has radically altered Jewish existence.

Anya's post-Holocaust meeting with Anzia, the Savikin's former servant, in a Warsaw suburb provides both a link with the past and a measure of hope for the future. For Anya, Anzia is "a cord, a thread, a telephone wire going back into the old rooms where the old voices still spoke; her memory went back further than mine" (p. 490). Anzia returns the Noah's ark basket (which she had taken from the Savikin's house). It is to be used as a wedding present for Ninka. The symbolism of the ark is pertinent, if somewhat overdone. God's covenant with Noah, as we have seen, is a universal one and represents a divine promise never again to destroy the world. Man and not God, testifies the Noachide covenant, is responsible for evil. *Anya's* use of religious symbolism draws on both Jewish and Christian icons. Anya firmly believes that the cross she had received from Onucia saved her life, and she is powerfully drawn by the Lithuanian woman's contention that to exchange crosses is to exchange fates (pp. 362–63). This notion had in fact been introduced earlier when Mrs. Savikin told Anya that her father's grandmother had prayed that she die in order that her critically ill grandson might live (p. 38). The repetition of this theme underscores the importance of fate for Anya.

Prior to leaving Europe, Anya has two experiences which continue the novel's dialectic of history and hope. She accidentally encounters a Berlin seamstress who is the wife of the Gestapo man who had taken Ninka from the Rutkauskus home. The woman is upset because the war ended before her husband could return with the child. "It's a tragedy," she laments, "that the war ended so fast." Anya is unable to go to Palestine because only those with family already there are receiving visas. Anya learns, however, that she has an aunt in America and this kinship tie seals her decision to go to the United States. At this point in the novel Schaeffer introduces a second *lamed-vov zaddik* figure, Joseph Brodsky, chief of the refugee relief association who befriends Anya and takes both mother and daughter under his protective wing. Anya is beset by bureaucratic obstacles; she and Ninka are refused visas, and Ninka is declared medically unfit to sail. Brodsky threatens to resign unless mother and daughter receive first-class accommodations on the next boat to America. Brodsky's action provides counterevidence to a prominent Holocaust characteristic, acquiescence in bureaucratically administered decisions. Like Erdmann, he functions to assure Anya's future at a time when great forces are arrayed against her.

In America, Anya begins to come to full awareness of the contradictions of post-Holocaust Jewish existence. Echoing Wiesel and Herman Broder, she testifies that survivors are different from others, their lives have been amputated. Anya fears the police, worries about her possessions being confiscated, and has nightmares about the Gestapo. Although she frequently thinks of God and affirms the existence of an Almighty power, by war's end she confesses that "the dead were more real to me than the living" (p. 468). Anya's position is allied much more with the Wieselian messenger of the dead, rather than Artur Sammler's modified humanism. Anya, however, thinks that survivors can serve as exemplars, believing that "God wanted someone to live to become more experienced, to live longer, to have certain influences" (p. 595). There is a great irony in her position because remarkably little interaction occurs between Anya and American Jews who are portrayed as talking much about but knowing little of the Holocaust. On the other hand, Anya, at age fifty-two, is depressed and defeated. She still has hope, but no longer believes that Jews make their own choices—"Hitler chose for us" (p. 594).

Anya is the only novel in this study which scrutinizes the relationship between survivor and child during and after the Holocaust. From the time Ninka was an infant Anya synchronized her breathing with that of her daughter. Unlike Sammler, Anya's one constant thought during the Holocaust was for her child. In America, the relationship between mother and daughter displays many of the clinical characteristics described in children of survivor literature: overprotection, obsession with health and eating, and overidentification with children. These same traits characterized Anya's relationship to her own mother. Ninka's behavior reflects the difference between being a Jewish teenager in secular prewar Vilno and in secular postwar America. Ninka's life is touched by what the psychiatrist Robert Jay Lifton terms "the imprint of death," although Lifton's term refers specifically to children of survivors, rather than child survivors like Ninka. Ninka initially rejects her mother's experience and her own identity by dating a Gentile. By story's end, however, she has begun to affirm her own Jewishness. Reluctantly she visits Israel, a trip Anya paid for by pawning some of her mother's jewelry. Consequently Ninka marries an Israeli, thereby symbolizing Jewish continuity and authenticity.

The epilogue focuses on Anya's post-Holocaust confusion. She poses, but cannot answer, questions about the meaning of suffering, why she had survived and the others had not, and what life is for. Overwhelmed by the theodical question, Anya can only wonder: "What is any life for? But these are questions I cannot answer" (p. 596). The meaning of chosenness continues to elude Anya. While admitting that normal suffering has some purpose, Anya contends that Jewish suffering during the Holocaust was perversion and without meaning; although at an earlier point she recalls thinking that the war was a punishment for all the intermarriages or perhaps a payment for Israel.

Anya, more intimately than Sammler, knows about man's capacity for evil which the Holocaust revealed. She remembers what happened when the Nazis came for Jewish children.

> A Gestapo officer picked up a little boy and swung him by the feet into a tree. His skull shattered like an egg; his brains shone down the tree and dropped onto the sidewalk (p. 596).

It had taken Anya ten years to remember this, although these things were the rule. "I do not believe," Anya comments, "that anyone is as happy about the human animal as they were before." Anya herself is absolutely changed. Her prewar love of children has become an obsession with Ninka and her grandchildren. She now views children as a false treasure, electing to have an abortion. She agrees with the position of her second husband—also a survivor—"after what we've been through we should not be parents" (p. 585). Singer's Herman Broder espoused a similar view of post-Auschwitz life. These views contrast sharply with the messianic hope Wiesel's *The Fifth Son* attributes to the second generation.

Anya is continually plagued by the massiveness of holocaustal evil. She recalls the two women who had been in her camp and had hidden when the Gestapo men—holding their children—came looking for mothers. The women lived and the children were murdered. But Anya does not judge the women, even thinks—briefly—that she might visit them in California. Instead, she concludes that during the war there were no ethical lives. This naïve assertion overlooks her own remarkable acts, as well as those of Rutkauskus. Unable to live with the constant pain of Holocaust memories, Anya tries to escape her Jewish experience. She visits a psychiatrist in hope that he will ease her burden, even praying that hypnosis would work. But the doctor was himself a survivor who refused to erase her past because "the Jews get fewer . . . and what will you have left?" (p. 611). Jewish continuity is here upheld by the secular psychiatrist. But the man, who had had two children before the war, shared Anya's fear of having any more.

Anya's contradictory feelings testify to her belief in fate. She had always felt a hand over her, believing that she was the lucky one and she knew that there was no rational explanation for all of this. She decides, therefore, to commit her feelings to paper. Echoing Anne Frank's diary sentiments, Anya observes that "paper has patience." Anya's view of theodicy provides a capsule summary of her post-Holocaust Jewish identity. The God whom she addresses and in whom she believes is a diminished but real deity who, along with dreams of her murdered family, sustains her as she ponders the future. Anya contends "we are all ruled by death. It is always coming" (p. 598). This Rubenstein-like assertion of the sovereignty of holy nothingness does not, however, convey the depth of Anya's Jewish self-under-standing. When, for example, Ninka began dating a Greek-Orthodox boy, Anya undertook extraordinary measures—including disguising herself as a Christian woman and convincing a parish priest to send the boy to Greece for one year—to insure that her daughter not marry a non-Jew. Like Malamud's Isabella del Dongo, Anya treasures what she suffered for. Anya reflects the position of post-Holocaust secular Judaism that the burden of modern Jewish history is both overwhelming and inescapable. Having been subjected to the worst excesses of history, Anya, who at her wedding to Stajoe, had felt like "a Christian woman, an Irishwoman," clings to hope for post-Holocaust redemption in the form of Jewish continuity.

Cynthia Ozick

Ozick's "Rosa" (1983) and *The Cannibal Galaxy* (1983) are a shift from her earlier focus on the religious efficacy of survivors' testimony. These later works explore the trauma of survival, elevate the role of women and, in the novel, emphasize the necessity of the midrashic method for authentic post-Holocaust Jewish existence. "Rosa," animated by the twin themes of witnessing and the omnipresence of the dead,[27] chronologically fills in all the omitted biographical details of "The Shawl." Rosa's pre-Holocaust biography shares several features displayed by both Mr. Sammler and Anya. She was, for example, born into an assimilated Warsaw family. Her own mother despised the Yiddish lullaby which her grandmother crooned to the sleeping Rosa. Rosa remembers her prewar home being laden with books in many languages; her father was an avid reader and her mother a published poetess.

Ghettoized and not realizing their own destiny, the Lublin family resented being incarcerated with religious Jews:

> old Jew peasants worn out from their rituals and superstitions, phylac- teries on their foreheads sticking up so stupidly, like unicorn horns, every morning (p. 66).

Ozick, like Schaeffer, depicts the very real rifts which existed among Polish Jewry. Rosa discovers, however, that the Nazis were uncon- cerned about her religious attitudes. Ozick, in fact, adroitly links the fate of religious and assimilationist Jews in giving Rosa the family name of Lublin and Warsaw as a birthplace; two major ghettos of Polish Jewry. Refraining from any explicit theologizing, Rosa none- theless exemplifies a specifically Jewish determination to survive and to testify. Consequently, she—like Sammler and Anya—espouses her own form of the voluntary covenant.

The story centers on Rosa's experiences in Florida where she lived in a broken-down Miami hotel room while recovering from a nervous breakdown. Much in the manner of Shula-Slawa, Rosa is described as a "madwoman and a scavenger," who had owned an antique/junk shop in Brooklyn. Rosa "tells" the long dead Magda, via the child's shawl, that she had frequently attempted to relate to her non-Jewish customers—innocent of any Holocaust knowledge— stories of the Warsaw ghetto. Rosa confides that she still could not cope with the indifference displayed by Poles who took the tramcar which ran through the heart of the ghetto. Starving, wretched, and diseased Jews could be seen from the vehicle's windows, but there were no displays of sympathy, no sharing of precious food, no po- litical outcry, no recognition that Poland's Jews were either fellow citizens or even human beings. Rosa's confessions express a twofold problem. On the one hand, people do not remember because they do not know what happened even such a short time ago. There is, however, a more serious issue here. Rosa's customers are described as deaf, they—like the Polish women who sat in the tramcar carrying their groceries, including precious heads of lettuce which Rosa once spied and for which her salivary glands ached, and like many good German citizens—did not know, because they did not want to know.

Ignored once, Rosa refused to be abandoned twice. She demolished her store with a hammer. In order to spare the distraught woman a jail term, Stella agrees to pay for her aunt's Florida recuperation. Rosa is ambivalent toward Stella, whom she calls "the Angel of Death" owing to the niece's insistence on facing the truth that Magda is dead, and to her uncompromising stance on what really happened in the past. While in Florida, Rosa meets Simon Persky, a fellow Warsaw Jew who had left Europe in 1920 and whose wife is in a private mental hospital.

Ozick invites her readers to contrast the clinical madness of Mrs. Persky to Rosa Lublin's Wieselian moral madness, wisely choosing an act of destruction to protest indifference. Well anchored in the prophetic strain of Judaism, this type of protest frequently occurred in the face of Israelite covenant abandonment. Jeremiah, to cite but one example, publicly broke a clay flask in the Valley of Hinnom (Jer.19:10–11) symbolizing that Jerusalem would, like the clay vessel, be broken into fragments. Concerning the *Shoah*, Rosa Lublin's action makes her a literary descendant of Shmuel Zygelboym. Zygelboym, one of two Jewish members of the Polish National Council (parliament-in-exile) in London, committed suicide in the British capital on 12 May 1943. His suicide note spoke of a final protest against the passivity of a world which permitted the extermination of the Jews. Against this background, one begins to see the wisdom of Robert Alter's observation that if the world is Auschwitz, moral madness is preferable to "sanity."

"Rosa" captures the isolation and the determination of Holocaust survivors. Ozick's tale is in fact both an attack on psychologistic trivializing of survivors, and a sensitive portrayal of their pain and suffering. Dr. Tree, a clinical social psychologist, bombards Rosa with requests to take part in studies on the metaphysical implications of repressed animation among camp inmates. The academic wishes to study her, but at no point is he protrayed either as wishing to learn anything about the Holocaust itself, or as being able to see Rosa as a human being. Instead, as an earnest of his good intentions, he sends her a chapter entitled "Defensive Group Formation: The Way of the Baboons." Ozick's description conveys two important messages. First, survivors are not damaged people to be swept under the societal carpet; they are people from whom one can learn a great deal about survival and human coping strategies. Secondly, the Holocaust will continue to elude the grasp of those who fail to realize the universal implications of the *Shoah* which is an orienting event for all peoples.

One example of profound psychological folly is provided by Dr.

Tree's theory of the metaphysical side of repressed animation applied to certain camp inmates. His interpretation rests on the assumption that selected prisoners became Buddhist-like; they ceased craving and attempted to overcome pain while aiming for nonattachment which, attested the Buddha, can be attained through following the noble Eightfold Path. Tree's foolish and naïve interpretation is actually a description of the *Muselmänner*. Primo Levi contends that the *Muselmänner* is the single image of all the evil of our time. Levi's description bears repetition.

> Their life is short, but their number is endless; they, the Muselmänner, the drowned, form the backbone of the camp, an anonymous mass, continually renewed and always identical, of non-men who march and labour in silence, the divine spark dead within them, already too empty to really suffer. One hesitates to call them living. One hesitates to call their death death, in the face of which they have no fear, as they are too tired to understand.[28]

Rosa, wiser by far than Dr. Tree, calls him a bloodsucker—repeated twice for emphasis—and utters an oath (again twice) "drop in a hole."

Ozick effectively employs the use of doubling in order to delineate Holocaust uniqueness. Unlike Nissenson's Willi and Heinz (both German Jews) or her own Joseph Brill and Hester Lilt (see pp. 130–136), Ozick's Rosa Lublin and Simon Persky come from the same city, but survivors are different from refugees. "My Warsaw," Rosa tells Persky, "is not your Warsaw" (p. 39). Although both Rosa and the other Florida Jews are described as having left their real lives behind, there is an abyss between survivors and American Jews. Rosa notes that the American Jews only care for the human race and naïvely continue embracing Enlightenment universalism. The tension between particularism and universalism has not even been recognized as a problem. Rosa's otherness is also indicated linguistically. Her English is crude and a syntactical disaster: "Why should I learn English?" she asks Persky. "I didn't ask for it, I got nothing to do with it" (p. 41).

It is the Holocaust itself, however, which indelibly stamps Rosa Lublin's life. Rosa offers a survivor's philosophy of history, telling Persky that her life is divisible into three periods: the life before (which is "our *real* life, at home, where we was born"), the life after (which is a "joke"), and the life during. The latter refers to her Holocaust experiences. "Only during stays," says Rosa, "and to call it a life is a lie" (p. 61). Rosa's life had stopped with the *Shoah*; repeatedly she contends that "thieves stole her life." Rosa knows that she has shamed her older but not wiser countryman. Long ago Rosa realized that she had "this power to shame."

Following in the footsteps of Anya's post-Holocaust career, Rosa, too, was unable to continue with her earlier love of science. She turned instead to the past, antique mirrors were her speciality. The metaphor of the survivor holding up mirrors of the past for contemporary Jews is a powerful one. Glancing into this looking glass, for Ozick, is the way to learn not only of the past and one's identity, but to avoid a repetition of the European Jewish destiny. Rosa is especially agitated at American Jews' indifference to the Jewish tragedy. At one point Rosa finds herself temporarily trapped on a homosexual beach where she notes that Jews were among the participants in what she refers to as "sexual mockery," and "Sodom!" Seeing barbed wire around the beach's perimeter, Rosa finds the hotel lobby where she accuses the Jewish manager of being a Nazi, and an S.S. man. She is certain that "only Nazi's catch innocent people behind barbed wire." This scene of contemporary sexual perversion is juxtaposed against the background of Rosa's own memories of sexual and emotional rape at the hands of the Nazis:

> Darkened cities, tombstones, colorless garlands, a black fire in a gray field, brutes forcing the innocent, women with their mouths stretched and their arms wild, her mother's voice calling (p. 51).

These "pitiless tableaux" went on for hours.

Against Rosa's idealized memory of Magda's father and her daughter's Holocaust fate, stands the relentless verity of her own dreams and Stella's testimony; Magda's father had been a German (in "The Shawl" Magda was described as looking like one of theirs). Stella contended that Rosa was making a "relic" of Magda. Rosa, unable to cope with the terrible truth of her daughter's fate, invents three different careers for Magda: a physician, a professor of philosophy, and a sixteen-year-old youth full of potential. These imaginings represent only a small fraction of what Magda and the one and a half million other murdered Jewish children might have become. By having both Stella and Persky insist that Rosa cannot live in the past, Ozick underscores not only the difference between survivors and refugees, but points out varying orientations amongst survivors themselves.

"Rosa" ends with a bittersweet mixture of the past and the present. Rosa allows Persky to see Magda's shawl and then, alone, she wraps the shawl around the telephone receiver where it springs into life when Stella says "long distance." Rosa then begins to tell her daughter of the Warsaw ghetto. Symbolically, Ozick has achieved the goal of having Holocaust Jews tell their children of the suffering, the heroism, and the history of the *Shoah*. She tells the hotel operator to send Persky up to her room, thinking: "He's used to crazy women." Prior to Persky's arrival, Rosa removes the shawl from the phone causing the wraith's disappearance: "Shy, she ran from Persky. Magda was away" (p. 71). Rosa has taken the first step toward reentering the post-Holocaust world, "the life after." To do so, however, she must, like Wiesel's Eliezer in *The Accident*, triumph over the past. This means transforming Magda's memory into a creative means of witnessing. Rosa's willingness to see Persky indicates that she also wishes to speak to the living on behalf of the dead.

Ozick's tale is like post-Holocaust Jewish existence itself, an admixture of despair and hope. The shawl has, for example, become transformed from a symbolic tallit to an icon, which serves as a link to the brutally murdered past. There are, moreover, no sweet-smelling spices with which Rosa might fortify herself against the vicissitudes of history. On the personal level, things appear equally bleak. Rosa has no children and is beyond childbearing age. Her life has, in Wiesel's terminology, been amputated. Stella is, for her part, unmarried and unmarriageable. There is, in addition, no positive mention of Israel. Quite the contrary, Rosa confesses to Magda's ghost her pique at Stella whom, after the war, she had saved from being sent to Palestine where she would have become a "field worker jabbering Hebrew." The sheer overwhelmingness of holocaustal loss is borne out in Rosa's unwanted burden of Jewish history.

There are, on the other hand, signs of Rosa's voluntary assumption of a modified covenantal Judaism. She is attracted by the Yiddish headlines of Persky's newspaper, and by his kinship ties both to Israel (he is a third cousin of Shimon Peres) and to America (Lauren Bacall—Humphrey Bogart's wife—is also a distant cousin). Rosa's post-Holocaust attraction to Jewishness stands in sharp contrast to her pre-Holocaust assimilationist tendencies. Like Sammler and Anya, Rosa's Holocaust experience has forever marked her as a Jew. On the historical level, Rosa bears Jewish witness to the disaster of Holocaust. She seeks some mode by which to remind the world of the collapse of its articulated ethical, moral, and religious standards. Witnessing to the horrors of the past, Rosa—however unwittingly—assumes the prophetic role in Western history. Her solidarity with the murdered is also simultaneously an expression of Rosa's Jewish identity. On the personal level, she rejects American sexual libertinism and makes a conscious decision to continue seeing Persky, thereby indicating that Jewish life will persevere, and that only European Jews are able to speak about the Holocaust and truly know what it means. The mysterious and irresistable appeal of Jewish peoplehood is decisive for Ozick's authentic Jewish figures. Consequently, while the results of history are oppressive and unrelenting, the impulse to bear witness to Jewish endurance symbolizes that covenant may prevail over history.

The Cannibal Galaxy,[29] Ozick's second novel, is an exquisitely written book which differs significantly from her earlier Holocaust fiction in two respects; a survivor does not serve as moral exemplar, and the novel emphasizes her growing concerns over the status of women[30] in Judaism by employing a female *lamed-vov* figure who—while a nonwitness and a secularist—demonstrates the post-Holocaust validity of the midrashic method. In less than two hundred pages, Ozick deftly portrays the life of Paris-born Joseph Brill who survived the *Shoah* in hiding and is now headmaster of the Edmond Fleg Primary School whose dual curriculum is taught to mediocre Jewish children somewhere in middle America. Brill serves as the foil for Ozick's central contention that the demands of covenant are superior to, and irreconcilable with, the allure of foreign culture. While Brill proudly and naïvely announces that he has been nurtured by his Talmud *tante* (aunt) and his Paris *tante*, he remains blind to the fact that the Holocaust is radical countertestimony to assertions of cultural unity. Ozick views the dissolution of covenant Judaism through the prism of pedagogy thereby combining both biblical and rabbinic aspects of the tradition. But Judaism's position is so precarious that Ozick feels compelled for the first time to utilize a variety of historical figures, such as Rabbi Akiba, Edmond Fleg, and André Neher—all of whom live after a great historical upheaval—as models of authentic Jewish response to disaster.

The novel can, like a talmudic text, be read on a variety of levels. It is a biting satire on the mediocrity of American Judaism—confirming her earlier view in "Levitation"—and the inadequacy of day school education. The cultural assault is so great that even a survivor may succumb to covenantal numbness. Unlike Bellow's Shula-Slawa, Schaeffer's Anya, and her own Rosa, Brill has erred in arriving at an answer to the *Shoah*. His reliance on the dual curriculum as a utopian/messianic reaction to the Jewish disaster is a secular version of "forcing the end." Brill's two worlds, "scholarly Europe and burnished Jerusalem," were in fact worlds apart. In this sense the dual curriculum can be understood as a metaphor of post-Enlightenment Jewish aspirations. Ozick means to identify and eradicate this Jewish disease—"Enlightenment syndrome." She writes that Brill's curriculum "could be done and yet it could not be done. Rather, it could be done only in imagination; in reality, it was all America, the children America, the teachers America, the very walls . . . America" (p. 61).

Joseph Brill is a complex figure living precariously between memory and forgetfulness. As a Talmud student he had learned from his mentor Rabbi Pult the depth of European antisemitism. "The Enlightenment," asserted Pult, "engendered a new slogan: There is no God, and the Jews killed him" (p. 16). Paris was, in Pult's words, "catching up eighteen centuries late . . . to the postulates and civilities of Hillel and Akiba" (p. 7). In America, Brill's Holocaust melancholia is rendered in a variety of ways; he believes in the prevalence of ash, thinks that Fleg may be shorthand for Phlegethon (the fiery river of Hades), and is reminded—by the school's architecture—of boxcars which, rolling eastward, had taken away his family and "released their souls into a field of ash." Moving a considerable distance from "The Shawl," Ozick's novel only indirectly invokes holocaustal fear and violence. She describes Brill's feelings during the roundup of Parisian Jews, a time when

> fire and steam had transformed the world: the glass of the *boucherie* (vernacular use of this word implies slaughter, carnage, or massacre) below Rabbi Pult's flat was smashed. It became more and more urgent to cry out that his family had disappeared (but he did not understand what he was doing or why) (pp. 23–24).

Joseph's disorientation reflects the collapse of the Jewish world. Describing Rabbi Pult's desecrated apartment with its bonfire of books, she employs adjectives which powerfully convey both the assault on Joseph's senses, and the fate which awaited Europe's Jews; "dead," "ruin," "reek," "flame," and "fetid." In keeping with her basic dichotomy between pagan nature and Jewish history, Ozick describes Parisian non-Jews in terms of nature; they had become a herd, "creatures like centaurs scuttled and scrabbled, flinging their rods, sticks, rocks, poles." All about him, Joseph witnessed "fangs, hoofs, strange hairinesses."

Ozick's insistence on the normative quality of rabbinic Judaism manifests itself in her utilization of the talmudic treatise *Ta'anit* as a connection between the Jewish past, the murderous present, and a possible future. The *Ta'anit* deals with reasons for fast days (to appease God), bids its readers not to despair, and contains many *aggadot* (legends) dealing with miracles and the redemption of Jerusalem.

Rabbi Pult had received an ancient copy of the treatise—printed in Venice—from his own teacher, and had given it to Joseph the evening before deportation. Forcing himself to walk slowly away from his parents' now empty apartment, Brill:

> swung the *Ta'anit* upward—mother! With the next mercilessly slow step, downward—father! Brothers! Sisters! (p. 24).

Ozick skillfully captures the cohesiveness of Jewish family ties and the authority of traditional Judaism in contrast to the civilizational madness which confronted European Jewry at every turn.

Like Israel of old, Brill wanders through forty years of turbulent Jewish existence. Unlike his ancestors, however, he neither enters the promised land nor does he deepen his covenant faith. Prior to the *Shoah*, Brill literally set his sights on the stars, matriculating as a Sorbonne student of astronomy. Thrown out of the observatory by his collaborationist professor, Brill's life was saved by four nuns who hid him in their convent cellar where he read voraciously the works of Edmond Fleg. In the blackness of the cellar/Holocaust which Joseph termed—in Wieselian fashion—his perpetual night, the Jewish student vows that if the war ends he will marry, have children, and found a school based on Fleg's dual curriculum. Spirited out of the convent, Joseph—like Singer's Herman Broder—spends the remainder of the war in a hayloft. Unlike Broder, Joseph ceases all intellectual activity, living as a beast of the field. After the war, Joseph is reunited with his three surviving older sisters, abandons the study of astronomy (although retaining the motto *ad astra*), comes to America where he is hopelessly mired in mediocrity—"brilliance gone to seed"—finds a rich benefactress for his school, engages in verbal duels with parents whom he detests, becomes a father late in life, and is made exceedingly uncomfortable by the presence of a European Jewess whom he can neither charm nor ignore and whose questions compel his realization that he has abandoned the Jewish vocation. Brill's American experience is succinctly described by Ozick who writes "for all that time, and more, he lived, in fact, in a hayloft" (p. 35).

Ozick's choice of astronomy as that which attracts Joseph away from Enlightenment aestheticism is profoundly revealing. Unlike Feingold, who in "Levitation" must literally leave the earth, Brill remains earthbound but reaches for the heights. In this sense, he represents the simultaneously held Jewish notions of rootedness in history (earth) and yearning for redemption (heights). Stars are synonomous with the covenant idea. God promises that Abraham's descendants will be as numerous as the stars of heaven (Gen. 15:5). The patriarch does not literally see the stars, however, but has a vision and places his faith in God. Advanced in years and without children, Abraham's condition jeopardizes the divine promise. Later, when the idea of covenant was altered to include the notion of kingship, the image of the star is again employed; this time as a royal symbol referring to David's empire (Num. 24:17).

Abandoning pursuit of the stars (astronomy) is tantamount to covenant abandonment. Joseph's post-Holocaust musing prior to leaving Europe for America confirms this observation.

> He was discovering himself not to be a discoverer—both too shabby and too cunning for the stars, so he abandoned his life to the chances and devisings of another continent (p. 34).

There is great irony in Brill's enrolling as a university student of astronomy. He had—without realizing it—been studying stars—covenant—with Rabbi Pult. Hiding in the cellar, Joseph had even imagined an encounter between Pult and his university professor on the subject of the heavens: "How unschooled each would think the other!"

Ozick's novel moves beyond the level of *peshat*, or plain meaning, in being one of the few post-Holocaust works which takes seriously the classical tradition's linking of teaching and salvation. That she intended to underscore the differences between inauthentic and authentic pedagogy can be seen from an earlier version of the novel, "The Laughter of Akiva,"[31] where the headmaster is English, and no mention is made of the Holocaust. Both versions, however, portray the main character as thinking of himself not so much as the schoolmaster but as a man of sacral power. Brill's character is, however, flawed. Thinking of his sacral task, Brill recalls a fragment of the Babylonian Talmud: "The world rests on the breath of the children in the schoolhouses" (Shabbat 119b). But he views his charges in less than cosmic terms; "We grow pygmies here," he tells his head teacher. Ozick implicitly asks what and how Jewish teachers are teaching in the post-Holocaust world.[32] Brill's teachers, who never mention the Holocaust to their students, are pale reflections or, better, parodies of the authentic Jewish teacher. Mrs. Seelenhohl (hollow soul) wants "no answers at all, only tactics and guesswork." Mr. Gorchak, whose name may be a play on the German *Gör*, small child or brat, or an allusive reference to Janosz Korczak, saintly martyr of the Warsaw orphanage—to whom he stands in the sharpest possible contrast—is the school's best teacher; he "wanted only right answers exactly memorized." Gorchak's stress on rote memory conflicts with Rabbi Akiba's insistence on mental facileness. According to Louis Finkelstein, Akiba was fond of citing the Babylonian Talmud: "Not he who answers quickly is worthy of praise, but he who can support his views" (Pesahim, 109a). Inauthentic post-Holocaust teaching or witnessing consists precisely in continuing to teach or profess as if the *Shoah* had never occurred.[33]

Ozick reacts to the malaise of post-Holocaust Judaism by reaffirming covenantal response to catastrophe, utilizing a type of Fackenheim's mad midrash. Midrash—as noted—has proved the ideal vehicle for Jews who, cut off from temporal power, have sought to continue to exist in a world where the divine presence and promise were seen as increasingly problematic when measured against historical onslaughts. It is, observes Fackenheim, "the profoundest and most authentic theology ever produced within Judaism."[34] Its profundity lies precisely in the fact that it refrains from systematizing, thereby not foreclosing the new or the unanticipated from being placed within a specifically Judaic understanding of the relationship between covenant and history.

At this point Ozick introduces Hester Lilt, a contemporary fictional descendant of both Akiba and Pult. Brill attempts to identify the woman etymologically, comparing her name to the Hebrew *leyl* (night) or to the night demoness Lilith. Hester plays a prophetic role; she is the theological interlocutor and troubler of Joseph's tiny pedagogic kingdom. Lilt's mediocre daughter Beulah is a student at Brill's school, although having tested below average according to the school psychologist. Initially, Brill and Lilt seem literary doubles; European Jews scarred by the Holocaust—she had been saved on a children's transport—both are intellectuals and both teach. He erroneously thinks that Hester is a "looking glass" for him, and that they were "unfailingly alike, members of the same broken band, behind whose dumbshow certain knowings pace and pitch." But Hester differentiates herself from Brill, and from American Jews, admonishing him for giving up the stars. To his protest that for him it was either the heights or nothing, Hester adamantly exclaims "but it might have been the heights. You stopped too soon" (p. 63). Stopping too soon is Hester's often repeated term for being mired in the snares of history as opposed to adopting the open-ended response of midrash in the face of calamity.

The novel's Judaic pivot innocently appears in the form of Hester's invitation to a university symposium "An interpretation of Pedagogy." Ozick prepares the reader for this turning point in two ways. Hester had utilized the word desmesne—"I intrude on your desmesne—she recognized his narrow reality, his tiny kingdom, his scepter the width of a thread, his diminutive sovereignty" (p. 65). Secondly, Joseph's trip to the university was a long and confusing journey. The institution was on the far side of the city and, in a fitting metaphor of Joseph Brill's own life, Ozick writes "though he had set out in sunlight, night overtook him" (p. 65). Brill is an auditor at the lecture, "summoned to squat there, penitent" much like "Bloodshed" 's Bleilip seated in the rebbe's schoolroom.

Hester's pedagogical key is "the unsurprise of surprise" which, like all of what she says, has multilayered meanings. On the one hand, Hester critiques both art and psychology's tendency to predict the future based on the present. Mechanistic thinking is "the hoax of pedagogy." Brill is uncomfortable with this reference to his school's reliance on screening tests for all prospective students. Having shaken the underpinnings of Brill's sham pedagogy, Lilt now embarks on a midrashic *tour de force*, based on three apparently random sources: midrash, natural science, and outer space. Ozick retells the midrash "There Ran the Little Fox" centering on Rabbi Akiba's laughter in reaction to the destruction of the Temple (Makkot 24b), a story of the entelechy of the bee in its relationship to the flower, and cannibal galaxies, "Megalosaurian colonies of primordial gases that devour smaller brother-galaxies." The book's title implies not only galactic phenomena, however, but refers also to history; Europe's cannibalizing of the Jews, and to Hester's relationship to her daughter (according to an angry Joseph Brill). Akiba is the centerpiece of Hester's response.

Akiba and his three rabbinic companions—Gamaliel, Elazar ben Azariah, and Joshua—display very different reactions when encountering the results of historical defeat. Watching Babylonian idolators rejoice while the Jewish Temple lay in ruins, "All began to weep, but R. Akiba smiled." Arriving at the Temple mount, they saw a fox coming out of the Holy of Holies. Again, there was a similar response. Asked why he laughed, Akiba responded "Why do you weep?" In the first instance Akiba contends that if the Babylonians are rewarded for acting against God's will, the Jews will someday be rewarded even more for obeying God. In the second tale, Akiba's friends weep because they assume the correctness of the prophecy (Lam. 5:18) "for Mount Zion which lies desolate; jackals prowl over it."

Akiba, on the other hand, refuses the tyranny of history. His joy is based on Isaiah 8:2 "And I will take unto me faithful witnesses to record, Uriah, the priest, and Zechariah." Akiba finds significance in the joining of Uriah and Zechariah because the former was at the first

Temple and the latter at the second. The prophecy of Zechariah is thus dependent on Uriah's prediction. Uriah interpreted Micah 3:12 and envisioned the destruction of Zion and Jerusalem. Zechariah's prophecy foretold of Jerusalem's rebuilding. Akiba feared that if Uriah's prophecy was unfulfilled, then Zechariah's vision might be false. The accuracy of Uriah's prophecy convinced Akiba that Zechariah's dream would come to fruition in the near future. His companions respond "Akiba thou hast consoled us, thou has consoled us" (Makkot 24b). Dreamers, concludes Hester Lilt, are taken for blockheads by pedagogues who stop too soon; "to stop at Uriah without the expectation of Zechariah is to stop too soon" (p. 68).

After the Temple's destruction Akiba had a momentous decision to make between fidelity to or abandonment of covenantal Judaism. The choice for post-Holocaust Jews is no less profound. Fackenheim notes that,

> for Jewish thought in our time to *situate* rabbinic Judaism *historically*—as an epoch-making response to an historic challenge—is no light matter. It is a fateful step.[35]

Akiba's laughter is a laughter in spite of and pointing beyond the merely historical or, in Ozick's words, "the laughter of Akiva outfoxes the fox."

Ozick underscores a profound difference between second and twentieth century Judaism noting that Brill "did not . . . believe that midrash was *min hashamayim*," a "celestial anecdote." The oral law (*Torah b'al peh*), was not equal to the written law (*Torah b'ktav*). The distinction between these two types of learning is historically significant. Sadducees, the Temple party in Palestine, affirmed only the legitimacy of the written law. Lacking flexibility, and the Temple, Sadducean Judaism disappeared as an historical force. Pharisees, predecessors of rabbinic Judaism, of course accepted the written law but added—as an interpretive method and an attempt to account for the tradition's changed historical circumstances—the oral law. Whatever the rabbis discovered in the Torah, providing they did so according to accepted means, was viewed as having been revealed at Mt. Sinai. For Brill, midrashim were only "little stories made up to color a moral lesson."

The difference between Brill and Lilt lay in their sensitivity to decoding hidden meanings in, and connections between, events. Brill knew "the separate pieces" of Lilt's midrash; the bee, the fox, Akiba's laughter, and the Cannibal Galaxy, but was unable—independently—

to see "how the pinwheel cosmos interprets pedagogy." Although he always wore a yarmulke, he was a theological skeptic. He had become not unlike the idols referred to by the psalmist: "They have mouths, but do not speak; eyes, but do not see. They have ears, but do not hear" (Psalm 115:5–6). Opposed to this Judaic incomprehensibility, Hester—although not formally religious—understands the cosmos as "a long finger tapping." This felicitous image retains the dialectic between covenant and history.

Hester, in contrast to Joseph Brill, does what authentic Jews have always done following a catastrophe: seek meaning by immersion in traditional methods which affirm the possibility of surprise. Brill's dual curriculum, on the other hand, implies—like the position of Rubenstein—that all is known and final answers can be given. Brill's method sharply contrasts with that of Akiba whose laughter symbolically transforms destruction into an occasion of rebirth. Brill's pedagogical/covenantal sin lies, according to Hester, in wanting to know "how to manage fate." Having been saved in the convent, Brill thinks he has "earned salvation forever." Hester's rebuke reveals Brill's lack of sensitivity to the necessity of continual covenant struggle.

Brill has an ambivalent Jewish identity. His associations and memories, while clearly differentiating him from nonwitnessing American Jews, do not necessarily link him to the Jews of Europe. He recalls but does not understand Pult's admonition: "Always negate. Negate, negate." Hester knows that Pult meant something less frivolous than keeping away from what the crowd likes. The rabbi was in effect testifying to the meaning and mission of Israel in the world. To be holy (*kodesh*) means both separation—a separating of that which requires apartness—and wholeness or completeness. In the context of post-Holocaust Jewish expression, Pult's warning can be translated as a plea for steadfastness against the temptations of both nihilism and assimilation.

Brill comes to America as an orphan in both the biological and symbolic sense of the word.[36] The status of orphan means being denied access to and nurture by one's sources. Although plagued by the meaning of his surviving, Joseph lacks the spiritual and religious tenacity to endure as a post-Holocaust covenant witness. His infatuation was instead with normality and is expressed literarily by marrying the school's secretary, Iris Garson, a divorcée with an uncertain religious orientation and minimum Jewish knowledge. Brill's actions are in sharp contrast to the observation of Lucy Feingold in "Levitation" who wondered if Jewish intensity was a condition of being chosen. Brill has, for his part, ironically chosen *not* to be chosen.

There is, however, another side to Brill's post-Holocaust Jewish identity. He experiences moments of covenant awareness. "He feared for himself, because he was of the elect, the fearful elect who are swallowed up by a look at immortality. The look flashed in him often and often. He saw how he had not died in the middle of the time of dying" (p. 45).

This burden is at odds with several other of the novel's characters. His wife resents Brill's speaking French, telling him "it's creepy . . . "and that "it feels as if you're talking to somebody else; somebody you knew a long time ago; somebody in history." Iris correctly observes, "I'm not in history!" (p. 116). Brill is torn between the Hebrew command to rememberr (*zachor*), and the contemporary attitude of covenant amnesia. In a similar vein, Brill—alone with his elderly sister—is overcome by survivor guilt.

> Memory burned in his kidney . . . Gabriel and Loup, *maman* and *papa*, Michelle, Leah-Louise, Rabbi Pult, Ruth's little fingernails—it struck him that Ruth would have been a woman in her forties now (p. 128).

His sister had fallen asleep, "old, exhausted, far from history." Similarly, he imagined the four nuns who had hidden him during the war were retired: "aged, severe, fatigued, themselves by now far from history; silent; dead." Away or far from history is Ozick's metaphor for those who either no longer, or never did, live on the edge between covenant and history.

This usage is confirmed by the reaction of the daughters of the long deceased benefactress to retaining the elderly Brill as headmaster. They argue that what had happened to Brill (the Holocaust) was a long time ago. There is no reason for Brill's "history to become an idol, and the school its shrine." Their position is a literary embodiment of the argument that too much attention is paid to the *Shoah*, and it reveals American naïveté concerning the effects of the disaster. Ozick's characters, who are away from history, thus represent two types; American nonwitnesses (Iris and the rich daughters) who cannot either know about or be bothered with the Holocaust, and Europeans (Anne and the four nuns) who are either fatigued or defeated by Holocaust history.

Brill's post-Holocaust Jewish confusion contrasts sharply with the lives of the authentic Jews—both real and fictional—portrayed in *The Cannibal Galaxy*. The historical figure with whom Brill has the most in common is Edmond Fleg, an intellectual whose reconversion to Judaism began with the Dreyfus affair. Fleg's *Pourquoi je suis Juif* (Why

I am a Jew, [1929])[37] tells of his Jewish odyssey, and contains an epigraph whose concluding lines reveal Fleg's deeply covenantal and mystical orientation: "We are God's people, for we will it so, the stars our quest and truth our watchword still." Fleg's quest for the stars, unlike Brill's, did not stop too soon. Even after the Holocaust, Fleg wrote of a specifically Jewish hope which, in André Neher's words, is "gathered in the depths of disaster." It would be difficult to find a better description of the covenant-history dialectic. Neher's own book, *The Exile of the Word*,[38] is a phenomenological analysis of the role of silence in Jewish theology from the Bible to Auschwitz. Hester Lilt's essay "On Structure in Silence" observes that "silence is not random but shaping. It is like the empty air around the wing, that delineates the wing" (p. 101). There are times when silence is creative and theologically necessary. Silence is crucial in the Judaic theological tradition and, as we have seen, plays an important role in Wiesel's work. Silence in the face of Auschwitz is certainly a more appropriate and potentially meaningful response than Brill's dual curriculum.

Brill differs from both Fleg and Neher. The headmaster in fact reversed Fleg's Jewish sojourn, beginning as a student of Talmud and ending by limiting his vision to the merely earthly; he has stepped outside the midrashic framework. In contrast to Neher, Brill is unable to decisively declare that he belongs to the Jewish world; he is himself in exile from the Word.

Brill is a flawed example of the biblical Joseph and Abraham. Unlike his namesake of antiquity, he succumbs to a foreign (American) culture even while attempting to impose upon it an order. Like Abraham of old, Brill had a son when already advanced in years. Naphtali, named for Brill's exterminated father, is a gifted child (*yeled peleh*) who, like Brill, expresses an early interest in the stars. The boy ends, however, by studying business administration and aspiring to become secretary of transportation in which capacity he would "resuscitate cross-country land mobility" (p. 159). Far from siring a patriarch, Joseph has begotten his own image; one who gives up seeking the heights (covenant) and who sets his sights on terrestrial goals. This index of covenant abandonment is in line with Ozick's earlier portrayals of the phenomenon—Bleilip's empty secularism and Feingold's mixed marriage. Brill does not, however, like his literary predecessors, respond to the Holocaust with an increased awareness of the intricacies of covenant faith.

Brill's anger at Hester Lilt—"Aesopian woman! The fox, the bee, the cannibal galaxies, Akiba laughing! Thief of Pult!"—is in fact an admission of his own confusion. At novel's end, Brill is convinced that Hester had "plundered" him. "In hindsight he knew he had been ambushed by Hester Lilt" (p. 162). Brill is crushed when, in a television interview, Beulah Lilt—who had become the leader of an *avant garde* artistic movement—mentioned neither the school nor his beloved dual curriculum. Earlier, Gorchak—who replaced Brill as headmaster upon the latter's forced retirement—wrote that the school's name had been changed because the young parents neither knew nor cared about Edmund Fleg. Nor did they view the European experience as relevant. Brill's monument to the Holocaust has, therefore, not outlived even its founder much less being able to impart the catastrophe's meaning or message to subsequent generations.

The Cannibal Galaxy is Ozick's most polished piece of Holocaust fiction, but admits to no easy classification. Consequently, it leaves the reader sensitive to both problems and possibilities of post-Holocaust Judaism. Her Jewish Jews are stringently Jewish in order to accentuate the difference between American Judaism, which is metaphorized as middle and earth, and authentic or covenantal Judaism, whose metaphor is greatness and stars. Bona fide Jewish expression is, for Ozick—as for Isaac Bashevis Singer—associated with Europe. At novel's end Lilt returns to Paris in order to accept a teaching post, while Brill retires to Florida, leaving behind Pult's Ta'anit. There is, moreover, no tale of conversion or reconversion to Judaism as with Bleilip, Jimmy Feingold, and Rosa. Lilt's separation from the American mothers—she was an imagistic logician, a "Brahmin among untouchables"—is Ozick's literary device for revealing the vast gulf between post-Holocaust Jewish genuineness and American Judaism. The novel is concerned with the demise of midrashic promise in America. Hester's method, unlike the survivor testimony in "Bloodshed" and "Levitation," persuades no one.

Ozick's portrayal of the Jewish future is not, however, without a glimmer of hope. Wherever there are Jews some amongst them will reveal Jewish authenticity. Hester Lilt is the wandering Jew who has lived all over the world. Her contribution to Jewish continuity is biological (her daughter), and historical—she models the midrashic way wherever she lives. Rabbi Sheskin, a young American whom Brill accused of believing in sacred texts, possessing a kind of "holy ardor," and turning scripture into story, symbolizes Jewish verity. In the post-Shoah world, a midrashic stance differentiates authentic from inauthentic Jewish response to history. The distinction between the two types has, as Fackenheim attests, nothing to do with and in fact collapses the traditional separation between secular and religious. A secular event such as a symposium on teaching may be fraught with salvific import.

Since Akiba plays so central a role in *The Cannibal Galaxy*, it is appropriate to conclude this analysis with his parable of the wise fish; a parable told, incidentally, by Wiesel's Rabbi Aharon-Asher to Reuven in *The Fifth Son*. Asked by Pappias, his rabbinic opponent, why he continued to teach publicly when to do so risked death, Akiba responded as follows. A fox asks some fish why they are fleeing. They answer, we flee from the fishermen's nets. The fox then invites the fish to join him on dry land so that they all may dwell together. The fish outfox the fox by replying that if they are afraid in the water, their life-element, how much more fearful would they be on the land, "a place which is our death-element!" Akiba analogizes this to the Jewish situation under Roman domination. "If now, while we sit and study Torah, in which it is written, For that is thy life, and the length of thy days (Deut. 30:20), we are in such a plight, how much more so, if we neglect it" (Berakot 61b). Bona fide Jews must live by their tradition if they are to survive. The Holocaust was a terrible repudiation of secular humanist promises and should serve as a warning both against stopping too soon and the adoption of any illusory cultural panaceas.

Ozick, in this phase of her Holocaust fiction, refrains from actual encounters with the *Shoah* while at the same time portaying the variety of Holocaust victims; survivors of death camps, those who survived by hiding, and those who were fortunate enough to escape Europe before the full fury of Nazi murder was unleashed. She steadfastly contends that the Holocaust must touch the lives of all Jews, and is concerned because the catastrophe is apparently being forgotten. Ozick's Holocaust fiction is, moreover, now linked to her concern for the contribution of women to Judaism. "The Shawl," "Rosa," and *The Cannibal Galaxy* all stress women as keepers and/or teachers of the tradition.

PRE-HOLOCAUST AMERICA: JEWISH EXISTENCE AND COVENANT DIMINISHMENT

Hugh Nissenson

My Own Ground (1976), Nissenson's first novel, departs from the Jewish covenantal hope of his earlier characters.[39] Although depicting pre-Holocaust Judaism, the novel underscores the Holocaust problematic of Jews who appear overwhelmed by their historical burden, portraying a tradition whose divine covenantal partner appears striking by His absence.[40] The novel's epigraph reflects this shift in tone from Nissenson's earlier Holocaust fiction. His two collections of short stories are inscribed with biblical (Gen. 32) and rabbinic (talmudic messianic speculation) themes. These themes reflect a covenantal understanding which provides hope for the future as well as the possibility of a continuing divine-human encounter. *My Own Ground* is, on the other hand, prefaced by a sentence taken from the "Epic of Gilgamesh"; a Babylonian work essentially secular in theme which tells of Gilgamesh's unsuccessful attempt, after a long and dangerous journey, to achieve immortality. The future of man is, in the Babylonian epic, clouded by the caprice of divinity. Nissenson's own theological anguish is evident when he states: "We made the covenant with ourselves and there is nothing else but that."

The narrator of *My Own Ground* is Jake Brody who, two decades after the Holocaust and from the security of upstate New York, relates his experiences as an "innocent abroad" in early twentieth-century New York City. Brody's tale reveals the intense religious and political upheavals of European Jews in America. The plot centers on the struggle for the soul of Hannah Isaacs, daughter of Rabbi Isaacs, a pious mystic. The major characters embody various orientations to modernity: Schlifka, the pimp, the Marxist, Roman Osipovich Kagan, and Rabbi Isaacs, a kabbalist and Hebrew teacher. Their Jewish experiences in Europe pervades the lives of the pimp, the Marxist, the rabbi's daughter, and Miriam Tauber, the landlady. Hannah must choose between her father's mystical God intoxication, which she simultaneously detests and understands; her father's eccentricities which, for example, forbade him from going near her because she has irregular periods; Kagan's Marxist utopianism; and Schlifka's sexual perversion. Hannah fantasizes herself a sexual slave of Bodgan Chmielnicki, the seventeenth-century persecutor of Polish Jewry. Schlifka and Chmielnicki are, in fact, comparable in their sexual perversion, their passion for violence, and their degradation of the Jewish people. Unable to bear the conflict, Hannah admits there are times she loves Schlifka's sexual abuse. Hannah's choice is suicide by gassing.

Nissenson utilizes his earlier emphasis on the ambivalent relationship between good and evil. Jake and Schlifka are approximately the same age, both are orphans from Russia, where they had gone to shul on Shabbos and studied Gemara, each spoke Yiddish, and both knew the Jewish mystical tradition. Schlifka confided to Jake that he had discovered the "root of his soul" which was the mythical Og, alleged to have had a thousand wives.[41] Nissenson's portrayal is,

however, tinged with ambiguity. In an obvious break from *shtetl* men-
tality, Schlifka advises Jake to Americanize himself. The pimp is linguistically facile, feeds Hannah nonkosher (*trayf*) food and wine,
prostitutes her, and bribes the neighborhood policeman. On the other
hand, Schlifka contends that sex is not so great for guys like Jake and
himself who have access to higher, spiritual things (p. 80). A drunken
Schlifka relates in Yiddish the tale of his uncle Nachman, a pious but
unlearned Jew who had raised him. Kagan and Rabbi Isaacs are both
portrayed as "forcers of the end." Each attempts to hasten the messianic era, although having vastly different understandings of the
meaning of messianism. Kagan believes that he helps "move history
along," identifying himself as "a Russian social democrat," who believes that "from the perspective of history the individual doesn't
mean a damn thing" (p. 91).[42] Hannah Isaacs compares Kagan's Marxist utopianism to her father's mystical beliefs on grounds of intensity
and because "they're both convinced they know some secret" (p.
115).

Most earlier critics have stressed the novel's illustration of evil's
persistence, its Freudianism, its moral, or its mystical aspects. Ruth
Wisse correctly interprets the novel as an antidote to the false nostalgia
surrounding Eastern European Jewish immigrants, while underscoring the moral dilemmas of a Judaism pushed somewhat reluctantly
into early twentieth-century America.[43] Alvin Rosenfeld analyzes the
work as a contemporary midrash on the Sabbatian notion that plung-
ing into chaos is a necessary prelude to redemption. In Rosenfeld's
words, "*My Own Ground* is meant to disabuse us once and for all of
both the normative secular and religious options for a better world."[44]

My Own Ground should, however, be read as a Holocaust novel.
Unlike Bernard Malamud's *The Fixer*, a fictionalized account of the
Mendel Beiliss trial and limited to a precise historical moment (1911–
1913), and which concentrates on personal and antecedent disasters
as harbingers of the Jewish catastrophe (see this volume, chapter 5),
Nissenson's memoirs are dated 1965.[45] Concerning the *Shoah*'s specificity, *My Own Ground* reveals themes from the Jewish disaster, for
example, by choosing which child shall live and which shall die.
Tofetsky, a character in *My Own Ground*, and Moscowitz, a Jew in
Nissenson's short story "The American," are both forced to leave a
sick daughter in Europe while the rest of the family emigrates. Tofetsky commits suicide after receiving news that his daughter had
disappeared.[46] Nazis gave ghetto Jews yellow work permits enabling
the bearer to live another day. But the murderers gave each family
fewer passes than there were family members, thus in effect forcing

the parents to choose which children would die immediately and which would live until tomorrow. Deceit also played an enormous part in the *Shoah*, the most infamous example being the macabre sign stenciled in iron over the portals of various death camps—*Arbeit Macht Frei* (work will make you free). Tofetsky was deceived by a man who falsely promised that for a fee he would care for his sick daughter until she was well enough to come to America. Nissenson portrays modernity's indifference to Jewish fate by employing the American setting. *My Own Ground* also includes death by gassing, in the case of Hannah Isaacs as well as Tofetsky.

Themes which define modernity's challenge to covenantal Judaism and illuminate Holocaust portents characterize the novel. The problematic of Jewish-Christian relations and the murderous strain of peasant antisemitism are portrayed in the graphic tale of Uncle Nachman's encounter with a drunken peasant. The drunkard views all Jews as "Christ-killing sons of bitches" who, postmortem, are to be "jammed together up to their chins in a lake of green snot" where they will be fried alive, "over and over again, forever" (p. 85). Holocaustal events are encapsulated in this description. The persistence of the deicide charge, religious in nature and itself a vile lie, can be seen in the behavior of secular nation-states; and it continued to affect the popular perception of Jews as untrustworthy and deceitful. This negative image of Judaism provided grist for the killers' propaganda mill. Nissenson claims he is only being realistic about the world's attitude toward the Jews, especially after Auschwitz. "It seems," he told an interviewer, "that they can't swallow us and they can't puke us out! We're stuck in their craw."[47] Physical torment and psychic humiliation of Jews, prior to their inevitable physical extermination, were an essential part of the Nazi Final Solution. The peasant's depiction of Jewish fate was a foretaste of the excremental assault and other death camp horrors visited upon Jews. *My Own Ground*'s depictions of oral and anal sodomy are literary modes for describing Jewish destiny in the Holocaust. Nissenson also underscores the futility and self-deception of universalistic alternatives to the specifics of covenant adherence, *viz.*, Marxist socialism and sexual libertinism.

Covenantal Judaism's capitulation to the overwhelmingness of history is personified in Nissenson's portrayal of Rabbi Isaac's spiritual career. When Jewish secularists and atheists decide to abandon or ignore covenantal existence, we are neither surprised nor dismayed. Their failure to hear authentic prophecy is a personal and not an historical defect. The transformation of pious Jews is, however, a more serious matter. Rabbi Isaacs is a kabbalist who reads from the

Zohar. Each midnight, the rabbi removes his shoes and socks, symbolically dresses in sackcloth and ashes, and prostrates himself while performing the mystical rites for Rachel and Leah which kabbalists employed in memory of the destruction of the Temple and the subsequent exile of the *Shekhinah*.[48] But Rabbi Isaac's piety is anachronistic in America. Brought to America by a congregation of old world Jews who preceded him, the rabbi and his former congregants discover they no longer inhabit the same Jewish universe. Distressed by the rabbi's singular Jewish appearance, Applebaum, the president, advises the holy man to Americanize himself; much in the manner of Schlifka's advice to Jake. Isaacs immediately resigns and devotes himself to study while working gratis for the Podol Burial Society (*Hevra Kaddishah*) of East Broadway.

Nissenson's Rabbi Isaacs is a seer who combines *halaka*, mysticism, and folkloristic expressions of Judaism. Messianic signs are omnipresent. He recalls that during the Kishinev pogrom (1905) nails were hammered into the heads of Jewish children. When asked by Jake if this were a sign, the rabbi, citing Amos 3:6, answers in Hebrew "Shall there be evil in a city and the Lord hath not done it?" Rabbi Isaacs contends, in addition, that "this is the time—when the face of the Shekhinah is dark; when she tastes the other side." Redemption will occur only when Israel has sunk to the lowest level. Explaining this statement to Jake, Rabbi Isaacs explicitly prophesies the Holocaust.

> It means—and, God help you, you'll live to see this—that the mirror you hold up in your hand will reflect someone else's face. That Esau, covered with the hair of a goat, will unsheathe his sword, and Israel . . . Yes, it's true. The war of Gog and Magog is coming, and the soldiers in the field on his left. . . . No, a mound of earth, a fresh grave, filled with Jews, some living, some dead . . . the earth will move. . . . The footprints, all the footprints of the soldiers' boots, in the soft earth, will fill up with Jewish blood (p. 109).

The interchanges between Rabbi Isaacs and Jake—theological in tone—reveal the rabbi's transformation from a practitioner of religious mysticism, one who engages in *kabbalah iyyunit*, to a devotee of the occult, a sorcerer captivated by *kabbalah ma'asit*. Isaac's reactions to two suicides illustrate his despair at achieving covenant fidelity. The rabbi refuses Jake's entreaty to bury Tofetsky according to *halaka*. This burial would "break our holy law." And the law is all we have. Jake's understated interrogative response, "Is it?" powerfully emphasizes the chasm between believing and nonbelieving Jews. Earlier Jake had confessed that, although he would like to believe in God, in the coming of Messiah, and the triumph over death, these notions—for him—no longer had validity. Rabbi Isaacs replied that he could see in Jake's eyes his wish to believe. Jake, no less than Hannah, is caught in the struggle between old world covenant religion and modern ideology.

Hannah Isaacs' suicide moves her father to respond in a vastly different manner. Rabbi Isaacs prepares his daughter's body for burial, but in a way which violates *halakic* norms. For in addition to the orthodox rites of *taharah*, ritual washing of the corpse, Isaacs' burial preparation violates the injunction concerning modesty. He leaves her body naked, and washes the corpse himself rather than allowing it to be washed by people of the same sex. This infraction constitutes a dishonoring of the dead (*hillul ha-met*). The rabbi adds to this transgression by utilizing magical practices such as clipping and saving Hannah's fingernail parings and mixing a wine and egg preparation to bathe his daughter's head. Reproached for his actions by the knowledgeable but unobservant Jake, Isaacs responds; "The time has come for us, at last, to break all of our holy Laws, one by one."

Rabbi Isaacs then repeats that Israel's redemption will occur only when she has sunk to the lowest level, concluding that in order to bring Messiah man must "force the end." This kabbalistic notion is associated with disaster. Sabbatai Zvi (seventeenth century), Simon Stern, Cohen's contemporary Messiah, Wiesel's Simha-the-Dark, and Ozick's Joseph Brill are also guilty of this breach. Forcers of the end are those who falsely confuse human action and divine prerogative. For Isaacs, following Sabbatai Zvi's example, this meant descending into and breaking open the *kelipot* (shells of matter or evil) which cover the fallen sparks of divinity. Radically confronting evil in order to restore cosmic harmony, such individuals in Jewish religious history end by precipitating a double disaster; they intensify evil, and they cut themselves off from the possibility of redemption. At this point, Isaacs, like Anya's kabbalistic Yeshiva student, turns his efforts to fortune telling. He predicts that Jake will live a long time and, if lucky, will dance at the wedding of God and the *Shekhinah*. Kagan, the Marxist, will be murdered by his socialist brothers in Russia. The rabbi's deviation from *halakic* Judaism is also revealed when he agrees to perform the wedding ceremony for Mrs. Tauber and Feibush, a Jewish atheist.

Overwhelmed by the course of events, Jake travels upstate where he is fortified by contacts with other Jews. In Binghamton he is employed by Borowitz, the Jewish owner of a dry-goods store who had come to America after a pogrom in Russia. Jake's sole qualification for employment was his ability to speak Yiddish. Leaving Binghamton, Jake goes to Elmira, arriving just prior to Rosh Hashanah. This time Weiss, the coalyard operator from Latvia, hires Jake. Jake explains to Weiss's daughter the reasons for blowing the Shofar on Rosh Hashanah but hastily adds that he personally did not believe either in a redemptive future or in the mercy of the human heart. When asked what is wrong with the human heart, Jake can only respond with a cryptic "I wish I knew."

Jake returns to New York City for the last time, to visit the pregnant Mrs. Tauber and Feibush. While in their apartment he has a dream, which epitomizes the covenantal dialectic with history. Jake sees Mrs. Tauber giving birth. First suckling her newborn, she then began devouring him, biting off his thumb which she chewed and swallowed, and then proceeding to his second and third fingers. Running wildly from the room, Jake finds himself outside the Russian steam bath where Rabbi Isaacs stands barefooted amidst shards of glass from a broken bottle of bourbon. Isaacs tells Jake to take off his shoes and socks because the ground on which he stands is holy. All the ground is sacred as is everything on it, including the cigarette pack which the rabbi has tossed away. Worried that he will cut his feet, Jake nonetheless balances on one foot and begins unlacing his right shoe. He awakens and is found sobbing by the still pregnant Mrs. Tauber who comforts him.

My Own Ground is Nissenson's most pessimistic literary treatment of the possibility of covenant renewal. Authentic religious piety deteriorates into pseudoreligious attempts to force the divine out of concealment. Exposing human illusions and divine inscrutability in both stages of his writing, Nissenson offers little consolation in this novel. His Jewish atheists and secularists are unable to hear the prophetic voice. They have abandoned God and do not trust man. Mrs. Tauber's cannibalism symbolizes the fate of Jewish children thrown alive into burning pits. The Holocaust, much in the manner of Rubenstein's analysis, is portrayed as the logical outcome of Jewish modernity. Nissenson, however, unlike Rubenstein is not writing about power or psychology. Instead, he asks the covenantal question: Can a people insensitive to its own redemptive demands expect to be redeemed? Rabbi Isaacs looks at broken glass and sees holiness. He is a visionary. Jake looks at the same sight and trembles; the orphan cries out against the raw mass of a history which threatens to engulf the Jews. *My Own Ground* takes a dim view of Jewish-Christian relationships as well. Reenforcing his earlier "The Law" and "The Crazy

Old Man," Nissenson argues that Jews and Christians live in two incompatible worlds.[49]

There are, however, possibilities of recovering a dimension of covenant Judaism in *My Own Ground*. For example, Brody refuses to draw apocalyptic conclusions from his renunciation of a redemptive future. He seeks, but does not describe, his own ground. Jake's affirmation of Jewish kinship, or *k'lal Yisrael*, carries overtones of Wiesel's additional covenant in requiring an ethical dimension which is expressed in mutual Jewish assistance. The hidden convenantal deity may, as Greenberg argues, actually be revealed by human acts of compassion. This is not to state that the covenant tradition emerges unscathed. Quite the opposite is true. Tradition is increasingly experienced as discontinuity in the age of modernity. But *My Own Ground* is a window on the terrible ambiguity of post-Holocaust Judaism, and the diminishment of its covenantal framework.

Robert Kotlowitz

Robert Kotlowitz is the son of a cantor and was raised in a Jewishly observant home. Kotlowitz, a public television executive, as well as a novelist, recalls that four themes dominated his home: Judaism, Zionism, culture, and his and his sister's future.[50] His European-born parents received letters and pictures as well as occasional visitors from Warsaw. Remarking on the prewar existence of American Judaism, Kotlowitz writes:

> And all the time history crept up on us, not quietly but with constant reverberations, echoes, signals, subtle warnings, and the sight and sound of noisy, sad events unrolling in grimy black-and-white on the newsreel screen (p. 247).

His own Jewish self-consciousness markedly distinguished Kotlowitz's attitude toward World War II from that of his non-Jewish teenaged friends. Kotlowitz is the author of two novels, *Somewhere Else* and *The Boardwalk*. *Somewhere Else* (1972) describes the journey of a rabbi's son from a Polish *shtetl* to pre-World War I London. Kotlowitz received wide acclaim for his realistic portrayal of the *shtetl* atmosphere. Both works deal with the dissolution of covenantal bonds which resulted from Judaism's encounter with modernity.

The Boardwalk (1977) portrays the conflict between covenant and history in terms of the struggle for the allegiance of fourteen-year old

Teddy Lewin (born Levin).[51] Late in the summer of 1939 Teddy arrives from Baltimore for a two week Atlantic City vacation. During this time he grows increasingly restive over the alarming news from Europe while simultaneously discovering his parents' marital infidelity. Like Nissenson's Jake Brody, Teddy seeks his own Jewish ground but the difficulty of finding it has increased immeasurably since the early teens of the twentieth century; now, for example, there is little direct contact with European Jewry. Those European-born Jews who are in America are either physically impaired (Teddy's grandfather Sandler is in an old-age home) or behaviorally exotic (his grandfather Levin's sexual appetite appears insatiable). Teddy's guide to Jewish identity is Gustav Levi, veteran of World War I, a Palestinian pioneer, an expert on Jewish history, a lover of culture, and well versed in Hebrew.

The novel is composed of three prologues, vignettes of important preceding events, and three parts; the second of which is central in focusing the distinction between authentic and acculturated Jews. The news from Europe is frightening, Hitler is ready to march and the allies appear paralyzed. Teddy's father denies that there will be a war and his mother does not even speak of world events. They are concerned instead about Teddy's music. His own near virtuosity on the piano, viewed by his parents as a ticket of admission to Gentile culture, is counterposed by Teddy's concern over the danger faced by his Warsaw cousins whose peril underscores Jewish weakness everywhere. An opera singer, staying at Sloans, reminds those assembled that opera would be the first casualty of the war because art always suffered in totalitarian regimes. The major action of the novel occurs in the form of dialogues held in the dining room of Sloan's (formerly Solomon's) kosher hotel.

As a critique of American Jewry on the eve of the Holocaust, *The Boardwalk* lays bare the community's religious and social rifts. Sloan's hotel is, for example, not as elegant as the Shelburne where wealthy Jews, such as Teddy's Aunt Celia, stay. The two Jewish country clubs in Baltimore reflect ideological and geographical differences between the Jews who originated in Eastern and those from Western Europe. Jewish infatuation with universalism is presented in the person of Ben Lewin, Teddy's older brother, whose concerns about mankind are not matched by an affirmation of his Jewish identity. Moreover, the antisemitic strain in American life itself is represented by Christian guests at the Cotswald hotel who sit on their veranda staring at Sloan's Jews. The sight of Jews praying at a Friday night service was "the other side of the moon, an insistent, foreign, harassing mystery which would never quite reveal itself fully, orbiting darkly in the reflected light of the Atlantic City sun" (p. 53). Kotlowitz, in addition, adroitly brings into focus the collision course of American and authentic Jewish culture by introducing the theme of Jewish antisemitism. Teddy is an ardent listener to the Ford Sunday Evening Hour, which features "W. J. Cameron spilling anti-Semitic intermission bilge all over the living rooms of America." Teddy is also overly critical of the Jewish amateur performers at an Atlantic City night club, prompting Gus Levi to claim that American Jewish kids are "thin as paste, have no blood, and cannot even imagine an anti-Semitic Jew" (p. 76).

Kotlowitz stresses the Holocaust's threat to American Jewry in several ways; Teddy's Warsaw cousins whose lives were much like his; the introduction of Erich Kessler, a boy Teddy's age from Frankfurt am Main whose mother is stranded in Germany without a visa; and by noting that Levin's Polish relatives—against the exhortations of Celia to leave Poland—stay in Warsaw thinking themselves safe because they are all assimilated. "They were trying to put the old Yiddish behind them, anyway. They were all new Jews, Western liberals and assimilated Europeans, had absolute faith in their world" (p. 205).

Nowhere had the illusions of modernity been embraced more enthusiastically than by the Jews of Germany. Frederick Kessler, Erich's father, is proud to be a citizen of Frankfurt am Main which he describes as a city of great culture, the birthplace of Goethe, as well as having been the capital of the Holy Roman Empire and the home of the first Rothschild bank. However, Kessler admits there are no Jews left in the city's orchestra. On the other hand, on hearing that Hitler's army had invaded Poland, he contends that it will all be over in a week because the German army cannot be defeated. He remains a convinced German who was, quite secondarily, a Jew. Frederick Kessler spends his time reading Franz Werfel's historical novel of the Armenian genocide *The Forty Days of Musa Degh*, unable to see the historical analogy between Armenians in the Turkish Empire and Jews under German domination.

Gus Levi functions as a secular *lamed-vov zaddik* in the novel. Alone amongst the novel's Jews, it is he who articulates the dilemma facing the West—"all moral authority was gone, all authority as he recognized it, the West was done with" (p. 54). Gus is a teacher with a twofold task: to help Teddy think historically, which means "being able to think about the world—with the authentic conviction that it didn't just begin the day you were born" (p. 32), and to guide Teddy to an appreciation of the importance of Jewish kinship ties.

Appalled by the Jewish illiteracy and covenantal ignorance of

Sloan's Jewish guests, Gus unexpectedly asks Teddy whether he had ever thought about the revolutionary events leading to the destruction of the Second Temple, thereby symbolically establishing a parallel between ancient and contemporary catastrophes. It is, however, Levi's philological excursus on the Hebrew root *lwh* which serves as a reminder of Jewish kinship and destiny. Seated at dinner, Gus establishes that Levi, Levin, and Lewin are all derived from the Hebrew name Lewy. *Lwh* can mean whirling like a dervish, achieving ecstasy while worshipping God; it can mean attachment or faithfulness, the Levites who had specifically ordained religious duties; and, finally, the root word implies pledging one's self, being vowed to God. Gus is impressed by Ben Lewin's suggestion to reverse the order thereby making a logical progression from outward to inward commitment. But the Jewish veteran specifically interprets the purpose of his linguistic exercise. "It comes," says Gus, "to a way of connecting." Against the amorphous and alluring culture of America, study of Hebrew "adds up to a way of learning how to link your life with others, now and then" (p. 129).

Gus, like Artur Sammler and Hester Lilt, is a moral center of gravity and therefore appears as an eccentric. Unlike Sammler, however, he is familiar with the language, history, and culture of Judaism. Gus "knew how to hold fast to the nature of ordinary things, he knew where everything belonged, in what place, at what level, and what it was all worth" (p. 260). He is, at the same time, described—like Hester—as a total stranger to the conventional world who, when he finally did step outside the hotel, looked like a kind of fugitive. Gershom Scholem's studies of Jewish mysticism reveal that kabbalistic definitions of the *zaddik* (righteous man) apply to Gustav Levi. Scholem writes "the man who gives each thing its due, who puts each thing in its proper place, is the Righteous Man to whom the Kabbalists relate the verse from Proverbs (10:25): 'The righteous is the foundation of the world.'"[52] That Gus Levi is unrecognized may be adduced as further proof that the *lamed-vov* is anonymous owing to the unworthiness of his generation. Levi argues against Jews who adopt Gentile culture, noting the Christian animus against Jewish existence. Jews, contends Gus Levi, "are not even supposed to be alive, not even supposed to be here. Not if the *goyim* had their way all these years" (p. 273). Kotlowitz's Gus Levi shares with Cohen's Simon Stern, Ozick's survivors, Nissenson's Willi Levy, and Singer's Herman Broder an intense distrust of Christians and Christian culture. The task of the post-Holocaust Jew is to remain Jewish and apart from American (Christian) norms.

Kotlowitz utilizes Gustav Levi, who had lived in Palestine and had faced death in the Great War, as an exemplar of healthy Jewish consciousness in contrast to the identity crisis experienced by American Jewry. Levi, and not Jack Lewin, will teach the tradition to Teddy. The boy has a concern for his Jewishness but is unable to articulate his feelings. The naïveté of American Jewry on the brink of the Holocaust is suggested in Kotlowitz's description of Teddy who, while obviously concerned about the fate of his Warsaw cousins, was not even sure of Poland's location. Yet it is important that Jews learn that only their kinship ties will provide some measure of comfort. Gus is, for example, pleased that Teddy and Erich Kessler have become friends. Friends, attests Gus, are the only protection against the steady chill of daily life. Levi wonders if Teddy has yet developed a sense of how cold the world can be.

What is the status of the covenant, and what is the future of American Jewry for Kotlowitz? *The Boardwalk* underscores the point made by Cohen's Simon Stern. American Jews need consciously to choose between American culture and Jewish history. Many of the Jews at Sloan's Hotel are interested only in material matters and display little or no concern for the war and for Jewish destiny. In fact the bridge games, daily prayers, dirty stories, seductions, and war profiteering all come together in a grand mosaic of indifference. The very ordinariness of events—which Kotlowitz describes in exquisite detail—serves to heighten the sense of tragedy which will soon engulf world Jewry. The time for sermons is, observes Gus Levi, too late. In their place he advocates a quasihasidic alternative: holding fast to the nature of ordinary things.

> That's what will console us. A determination not to give up essential matters. Not to let go. No matter how banal they seem, how commonplace. Reject the phenomenal! (p. 257).

Gus's appeal is, in short, for a prophetic response to history. In terms of the categories set forth in chapter 2, Kotlowitz's novel attempts to demonstrate that modernity and its Holocaust intimations have stirred the souls of secularist Jews such as Gus Levi, prompting them to espouse their Jewish identity with even greater vigor while simultaneously teaching the tradition to the new generation. While not a survivor, Gus possesses two survivor qualities: he willingly affirms his Jewish identity, and he views himself as a link in the great Jewish chain of being. Levi's contribution to Teddy's development of Jewish identity comes in his admonition to think historically, which means putting each successive assault on the covenantal framework within the perspective of Jewish existence thereby seeking to ensure Jewish continuity.

Conclusion

Collectively speaking, the common themes which emerge from the secular writers may be grouped around a movement from belief in an intervening deity to an emphasis on the moral obligations imposed by Jewish life. In other words, while religion and its themes of transcendence and an omnipotent deity seem to have lost their compelling force, the secular novelists insist that their bona fide Jewish characters remain Jews, committed but observant in modes of their own making. Rejecting institutional religion and its rabbinic custodians, secular fiction of the Holocaust transforms classical religious types: Bellow's Elya Gruner, Schaeffer's Erdmann and Joseph Brodsky, Ozick's Hester Lilt, and Kotlowitz's Gustav Levi are secular *lamed-vov zaddikim* whose actions provide a glimpse of light in a very dark world while testifying to the truth of Greenberg's assertion that in the post-Holocaust universe deeds speak louder than words. Jewish continuity, these works attest, rests on their central Jewish characters voluntarily (in Greenberg's notion) assuming the covenant. Jewish-Christian interchange has been profoundly disappointing and, with the exception of Sammler, Anya, and Joseph Brill, there is nothing positive to report about Christianity's attitude toward Judaism.

There is, moreover, an inescapable political aspect to these novels. One need not accept Fackenheim's contention that a contemporary Jew affirming his Jewish existence is simultaneously accepting his singled-out condition. But after the extermination of European Jewry and the indifference of Western nations, one must take seriously the political implications which Fackenheim draws from his premise. Absolutely opposing the demons of Auschwitz, the secularist, argues Fackenheim, stakes "on that absolute opposition nothing less than his life and the lives of his children and the lives of his children's children."[53] Jewish survival for the secularist novelists is tinged with a sense of mystery and awe. The difference, after all, between Jews and other minority groups in history is that the Jews have survived. An essential linkage is implied between the Jewish past and Jewish destiny. This linkage celebrates continuity, and takes seriously the persistence of antisemitism and the epoch-making nature of the Holocaust. The dialectical relationship between history and covenant is viewed as seriously imperiled by historical events, and the image of God is one of diminished deity. However, these novelists provide either a moral teacher to guide the new generation of Jews to an understanding of their identity and destiny (Hester and Gus), or centrally Jewish characters who reconvert to their tradition (Sammler, Anya and Rosa), or authentic Jews who continue to embrace a prophetic view of existence despite the evidence of history (Jake Brody and Isabella del Dongo).

We now turn to a group of novelists whose Holocaust fiction reflects a shattering of the midrashic framework.

Chapter 5

Holocaust Responses III: Symbolic Judaism

Symbolic Judaism is a subtype of secular Jewish expression, but with a crucial difference which has become a characteristic feature of the tradition's experience of modernity. Moving beyond the secularist view that the covenant-history dialectic is imperiled, symbolic Judaism assumes that this relationship has been completely disrupted. Consequently, Judaism is interpreted not in theological or moral terms, but rather is viewed in psychological and sociological perspectives which tend to be ahistorical. God is seen as a *deus absconditus* or so far removed from the course of history as to be irrelevant to man. Little or no concern is shown for *halaka* or for Judaism as a coherent set of teachings which can offer guidelines for behavior and belief. Novelists who write Holocaust fiction based on a symbolic interpretation of Judaism have abandoned the midrashic framework and advocate the interchangeability of Jews and Christians, while viewing Jewish specificity more as a problem to be solved than as a divinely ordained vocation. It is, therefore, not surprising that symbolic Judaism has transformed *k'lal Yisrael* from its role as a holy community. In its place there has arisen a religiously amorphous people; lacking communal, ritual, or theological warrant. Symbolic Judaism emphasizes the individual divorced from both history and covenant; and portrays the salvific quest as occurring beyond the borders of institutional religion.

Novelists discussed in this chapter have, however, felt compelled to somehow address the Holocaust. They treat the *Shoah* indirectly,

151

emphasizing the painful and complicated relationship between Jews and Christians. Edward Lewis Wallant, Philip Roth, and Norma Rosen write of this relationship in an American context; Richard Elman and Bernard Malamud have written works which treat the problematic in its European and Russian settings. While only Wallant includes particular events in the death camps, all of the novelists in this chapter are concerned with drawing what they perceive to be appropriate societal lessons from the Jewish catastrophe. Deemphasis of Jewish specificity has, however, resulted in two types of universalizing of the Holocaust, which this author terms genuine and spurious. Rosen's *Touching Evil* suggests how holocaustal lessons authentically involve all post-Holocaust Christians. Wallant's *The Pawnbroker*, and Elman's Holocaust trilogy advocate, on the other hand, spurious types of universalizing which reduce religion to the interpretive values of social psychology. This is especially true in the case of Elman whose character Alex Yagodah seems much more shaped by Jewish self-hate than by covenantal awareness. Malamud's *The Fixer* treats pre-Holocaust Judaism and is more than any of his other works historically based, but ends by being only symbolically Jewish; Yakov Bok's covenant is an anthropomorphic one. The Holocaust writings of Philip Roth represent yet another aspect of symbolic Judaism by utilizing tokens of Jewish piety—the four-fringed garment and a hasidic ethos—against which to evaluate the depth of assimilationist American Jews' insecurity and their covenant revolt. It is the assimilationists, and not the religious Jews, however, whose existence Roth has most skillfully analyzed. He captures the nervousness of Jewishly tenuous Americans whose main concern is with what Christians will think of them.

Each of the novelists whose works deal at any length with Holocaust survivors portrays them in a negative manner. Wallant and Elman are unsparing in their criticism. Roth employs survivors as merely emblematic and does not deal with their inner lives. Differing from the secular novelists, not all the writers in this chapter view the *Shoah* as an epoch-making event. Although the world is indeed a perilous place, there do exist moral and principled individuals who are noble in spite of, rather than because of, their religion. Symbolic novelists employ neither moral exemplar nor *lamed-vov zaddik* as guarantors of Jewish continuity. On the other hand, these novelists, while embracing a variety of orientations to Judaism, all seem to share two features: the unwillingness or inability to take Judaism seriously as a covenant tradition (this is less clear in Rosen's case), and a persistence in writing about Jews and Judaism although in nontraditional and idiosyncratic terms.

Considering The Evidence

Philip Roth

Philip Roth is the most controversial of the American Jewish literary triumverate—Bellow, Malamud, and Roth. His portrayals of Jewish life in America have provoked a veritable eruption of reaction, mostly negative and rabbinically authored, among those about whom he purportedly writes. His own orientation to Judaism is ambivalent. Roth has stated in the past that he was a writer who happened to be Jewish and that he neither wants, intends, nor is he able to speak for American Jews. He has no wish to do public relations for the Jewish community, nor should that be a writer's task. More recently, Roth began acknowledging his Jewish identity. Visiting Prague in 1976, looking for Kafka's landmarks, Roth confesses surprise at having "come upon some that felt to me like my own."[1] But Roth's portrayal of Judaism in America is actually a satire of middle-class values which the author inexplicably equates with Jewishness. Nonetheless, Roth's evaluation of American Jewish expression is symbolically measured against covenantal and communal norms derived from his understanding of Eastern European Judaism.

What happens when a satirist addresses the Holocaust? Roth has written two works which are literary responses to the *Shoah*, "Eli, the Fanatic," and *The Ghost Writer*, both of which appear seriously to question any expression of Judaism which is unable or unwilling to confront the Holocaust and its implications. Roth's literary use of the Holocaust reflects, however, his equivocal relationship to Judaism. On the one hand, he is expressing agreement with Greenberg's view that the *Shoah* is an orienting event. On the other hand, Roth appears more interested in employing the Holocaust in a triumphalistic manner to underscore the moral and religious bankruptcy of assimilationists than he is in discerning a way in which post-Holocaust Jews can express themselves in an authentically Jewish manner.

"Eli, the Fanatic," is the most important of the stories comprising Roth's first published book, *Goodbye Columbus* (1959).[2] The tale deals with the relationship between authentic (Holocaust survivors) and spurious (American Jews) Judaism. The assimilated Jews of Woodenton (Wooden Town) panic when a yeshiva, composed of eighteen children and two adults (all survivors), is established on a hill overlooking the town. Fearing that the yeshiva and its strangely garbed residents will offend Woodenton's Protestants, the city's Jews are concerned that the Gentiles will be reminded that Woodenton's Jews are, after all, Jewish. This pattern of assimilationist Jewish nervousness over the arrival of nonintegrationist Jews has precedence in modern Jewish history. Integrationist German Jews who emigrated to America in the nineteenth century were initially embarrassed when their more visibly Jewish Eastern European brethen began arriving in America. Ironically, the German Jews began assisting those from Eastern Europe because of fears that the latter would become a public burden thus reflecting badly on the former. Following the first World War, Eastern European Jews—refugees from Ukranian pogroms— first arrived in vast numbers in Germany. Because of their idiosyncratic appearance and behavior, German Jews thought that the new arrivals would fuel and provoke antisemitic feeling among German Christians. Consequently, Jews were put in the ironic but typical situation of being blamed for antisemitism.

Eli Peck, a secularist attorney with a history of nervous breakdowns, is hired by his fellow Jews to close down the yeshiva because its existence violates an obscure zoning ordinance. In the space of forty-nine pages, Eli progresses from being an emissary of the assimilationists to embracing hasidic Judaism. His reconversion, so to speak, is accomplished with the assistance of two people: Leo Tzuref (Tsouris = trouble), the yeshiva's headmaster who engages Eli in talmudic-like exchanges whose effect dramatizes the religious ignorance of Woodenton Jewry; and the greenie, a hasidic Jew whose family, friends, town, and synagogue had been destroyed by the Nazis. Emasculated by a Nazi medical experiment, the greenie is unable to speak, but, being the same age and size as Eli, symbolizes the connection between American Jewry and the Holocaust. Eli and the greenie will ultimately exchange not fates—as Anya and Onucia had done— but clothes.

Roth's tale sharply distinguishes Jewish from American culture, ascribing moral superiority to the former. Eli claims merely to be obeying the law when he attempts to evict Tzuref. The headmaster sardonically queries, "When is the law that is the law not the law? And vice versa" (p. 251), impressing on Eli an important distinction between Gentile and Jewish history. For the goyim, contends Tzuref, it is the twentieth century—"For me the Fifty-eighth." Tzuref also distinguishes between impersonal ordinances which are man made, and the obligations of being Jewish and human. "The heart, Mr. Peck," he says, "the heart is law! God" (p. 266).[3] The struggle for Eli's soul is pursued in the form of laconic and provocative dialogues between the headmaster and the attorney. Queried by Tzuref concerning his own position regarding the yeshiva, Eli replies "I am them (Woodenton Jewry), they are me." Tzuref, however, asserts that Eli has a prior identity claim: "Aach!" the principal exclaims, "You are us, we are you" (p. 265).

Woodenton Jewry, for its part, has abandoned the covenant and ignored history. Ted Heller, Eli's friend and instigator of the eviction process, contends that hasidim are "goddamn fanatics." The biblical *Akedah* (the parable of Abraham and Isaac) shows, Ted argues, that Abraham was psychologically sick, and anybody doing that today would be locked up. Equating Jewish religion with superstition, Ted's model of piety is Unitarianism. The twin aspects of the covenant deity, *mysterium tremendum* and living God of the patriarchs, has given way to a domesticated God and an antiseptic view of religion as a social activity whose sacred text is the *Atlantic Monthly*.

Symbolically the story utilizes two epoch-making events—the Holocaust and the proclamation of Israeli statehood—as a counter to the aspirations of Woodenton's Jews, which are set forth in Eli's letter to Tzuref:

> Woodenton, as you may not know, has long been the home of well-to-do Protestants. It is only since the war that Jews have been able to buy property here, and for Jews and Gentiles to live beside each other in amity. For this adjustment to be made, both Jews and Gentiles alike have had to give up some of their more extreme practices in order not to threaten or offend the other. Certainly such amity is to be desired. Perhaps if such conditions had existed in prewar Europe, the persecution of the Jewish people, of which you and those 18 children have been victims, could not have been carried out with such success—in fact, might not have been carried out at all (p. 262).

The letter reflects a complete failure to comprehend the Holocaust's uniqueness. The amity of which Eli speaks had in fact existed in much of prewar Europe—Czechoslovakia and France are but two examples—and had proved illusory during the time of testing. The Jewish people of Europe were, moreover, not merely persecuted; they were systematically exterminated. The eighteen yeshiva children are the numerical equivalent of *chai* (life). They represent continuity with the European Jewish past and hope for an authentic Jewish future in America, which Woodenton Jewry is threatening to foreclose.

Roth reacts to the post-Holocaust Jewish condition by employing both initiatory symbolism and the theme of birth and rebirth. Mysteriously attracted by the hasidic ambience, Eli proposes an unauthorized compromise. The survivors can stay if all of their activities are confined to the yeshiva grounds, and yeshiva personnel are welcome in Woodenton if they dress as Americans. Eli himself makes four trips to the Yeshiva; the first two are on business, the third is to deliver his Brooks Brothers suit to the greenie, and on the fourth he comes as a convert. Dressed in hasidic clothes, Eli sees the greenie painting a pillar on the yeshiva porch. The pillar glowed like white fire, much in the same fashion no doubt as the pillars of fire and cloud which led the Israelites in the wilderness (Ex. 40:34–38). Eli's initiation consists not only of an outward change—clothes, speech (he says shalom rather than hello—but in his willing acceptance of Jewishness. Receiving a wordless revelation from the greenie, Eli understands that he must return to Woodenton in order to publicly proclaim his new/old Jewish identity, which prompts his friends and neighbors to think he is having another nervous breakdown. But Eli, wiser than they, knew that he had chosen to be crazy and "if you chose to be crazy, then you weren't crazy" (p. 295). Roth here suggests a type of Wieselian "moral madness" as the only appropriate stance in face of widespread covenant abandonment.

Birth and rebirth are presented on both a personal and a historic level. Eli's wife, Miriam, is having a baby. A new generation will have to affirm the covenant and confront the Holocaust. Miriam, whose dependence on her analyst symbolizes society's reliance on psychologistic explanations—much in the manner of Ozick's school psychologist—is portrayed as understanding (but not loving) Eli. Eli contrasts one of Miriam's frequent notes to "scribblings on bits of paper [which] had made history this past week." He refers to the proclamation of Israeli statehood, the significance of which had escaped Woodenton Jewry. Eli's new son will share his birthdate with the rebirth of the Jewish state.

Roth does provide a measure of optimism concerning post-Holocaust American Jewry. Dressed in his newly acquired hasidic garb, Eli speaks to his son through the nursery glass, admonishing him always to remember his Jewish identity by wearing a hasidic suit in May, the anniversary of Israel's independence. Immediately prior to being tranquilized by hospital attendants who think him overwrought by the birth, Eli calls out to his son what the heroes, martyrs, and victims of the Holocaust asked of those of us who follow: "Remember" (zachor). Eli is in fact observing the basic obligation of a Jewish father— to pass on the tradition: "Tell your children of it, and let your children tell their children, and their children another generation" (Joel 1:3). The drug which he received calmed Eli's soul, "but did not touch it down where the blackness had reached" (p. 298).

"Eli, the Fanatic," contends that the American experience has so anaesthetized Judaism that Jewish sensitivity and identity have been overwhelmed, swept away in an antiseptic sea of Protestant culture. Not even the murder of six million Jews will be permitted to cause a ripple on the apparently placid surface of Jewish-Christian relations. Roth's resolution of the situation is, however, artificial. Eli's transformation from a *maskil* to a hasid is only a symbolic one, sustained by a hasidic outfit that included the fringed garment (*arba kanfot*) which he initially assumed to be some kind of special BVDs. The crucial difference between Eli and the greenie was not clothes, but the Holocaust. Roth's use of the double, Eli and the greenie, differs from the usage of Cohen and Nissenson. The latter two novelists employ the double in terms of good and evil residing in the same person (Cohen's Simon Stern and Janos Baltar) or victim and victimizer coming from the same culture and being the same age (Nissenson's Willi Levy and Heinz Berger). For Roth, as for Ozick, the double represents two types of orientation within Judaism; the believer and the agnostic for Ozick, while in Roth's case it is European and American Jewry. Putting on the greenie's suit Eli had the notion that he was two people. The whole metaphor of putting on and taking off is superficial. Confronting the Holocaust is not something which one can turn on and off like a faucet. Either one has, to use Fackenheim's phrase, confronted the demons of Auschwitz, or one has not. But once having done so, one can never cease doing so. There is a similar problem with Roth's understanding of Jewishness. Judaism is not akin to a club to which one applies or from which one resigns. If the Holocaust teaches anything, it is that Judaism is a matter of descent rather than preference.

Roth, like Ozick in "Bloodshed," symbolizes Jewish authenticity by linking the figure of hasid and survivor. Both novelists stress the courage, moral superiority, and determination of Jewish as opposed to American culture. Ozick isolates and insulates her authentic Jews. Roth's bona fide Jews underscore the frailty of American Judaism by moving near their assimilated kinsmen. But Roth has written a more realistic story than Ozick. He accurately assesses the impact an exotically dressed group of European survivors is likely to have on Jewishly insecure suburban Jews, posing the question that is still central: What will the *goyim* think? Whereas Bleilip and the rebbe in "Bloodshed" discuss faith and doubt—*the* issue for post-Holocaust covenantal Judaism—Roth's tale refrains from examining post-Holocaust theology focusing instead on social psychology.

The Ghost Writer (1979) moves a considerable distance from "Eli, the Fanatic," in addressing the relationship between the Holocaust and American Jewry.[4] Nathan Zuckerman is a young and promising

Jewish writer (Roth himself in the late fifties) whose story depicting a bitter family feud caused considerable parental anguish. Proud of their son, the Zuckermans were nonetheless scandalized by his story—thus far, it seems a continuation of Roth's relentless attack on the insecurity of suburban American Jewry overly sensitive to Gentile reactions. But this time the protagonist recognizes his need for a Jewish mentor, whom he finds in the aging novelist E. I. Lonoff. While visiting Lonoff, Zuckerman encounters Amy Bellette, an exotic young woman with a foreign accent who may have been Anne Frank miraculously saved from the Holocaust. The novel unfolds this bizarre plot in four sections, the first two describe Zuckerman's relationship to his family and to Lonoff. Parts three and four deal with Nathan's discovery of Anne/Amy's story.

Lonoff's writings are a vehicle for Zuckerman's Jewish identity. Himself a Jew, Lonoff writes solely about Jews and their burden of exclusion. His tales attract Zuckerman because they aroused "feelings of kinship" with his own family heritage, a kinship which he discovers only when reading literature in college as opposed to the Jewishly negative experience of growing up in his parents' house. While a guest of Lonoff, Nathan fantasizes that marrying Anne Frank would bring him unquestioned acceptance by the American Jewish community. Despite the total implausibility of the plot, Roth makes several important points about American Jewry's relationship to the Holocaust and about writers of fiction utilizing the *Shoah* in their works.

Roth employs two models of authentic Judaism, the Russian-born Lonoff, raised in "primitive Palestine," and the Holocaust victim Anne Frank, whose diary provided the world with a record of Jewish innocence, faith, and courage. The weakness of American Judaism is seen in its reaction to these figures. Lonoff is criticized by the New York Jewish literary establishment as a "quaint remnant of an Old World Ghetto" and as "an out-of-step folklorist" (p. 10). Anne Frank's diary was, for many years, unavailable in English thus symbolizing the fact that the Holocaust experience remained beyond the reach of Americans, Jews, and others. In fact Anne/Amy, brought to America in the author's imagination, must write to the Amsterdam publisher for a copy of her own diary.

Anne's diary is the novel's focal point, serving as a link between American Jewry and their slaughtered European brethren, as well as pointing up the enormous difficulties of dealing with the Holocaust. In postwar America, Anne does not recall writing her diary, but does remember the experiences, thereby underscoring the inadequacy of language in confronting the Holocaust. A letter of reprimand to the errant Nathan, written by a prominent Newark judge, admonishes him to see the play based on Anne's diary. If Nathan would do this, the judge is certain that the young writer would refrain from writing anything potentially harmful to the Jews. The irony here is that the Broadway production of Anne's diary presented a dejudaized and artifically universalized version of the young Jewish girl; something which was not too Jewish and therefore more readily acceptable to a Gentile audience.[5]

Anne/Amy relates her odyssey to Lonoff, providing guidelines for those who wish seriously to approach the Holocaust. Her reflections about Westerbork, Auschwitz, and Belsen, are brief, comprising about one page of the novel. In that short space the reader is reminded that anyone who survived the camps did so for inexplicable reasons. Somehow surviving, Anne/Amy took a vow of silence, but in England her foster parents and her teachers were insensitive to Jewish suffering. Her Uncle David told everyone about Anne's Holocaust history. Here Roth is reflecting the truth of Wiesel's observation that the Holocaust, having been robbed of its sacred aspect, "became a fashionable subject: good to impress or shock."[6] People speak without knowledge and without feeling. Anne's teacher, Miss Giddings, was full of compassion but asks her why over the centuries people have hated Jews, thereby requiring the victim to account for the behavior of the victimizer. Miss Giddings' query is the forerunner of another spurious question; why did the Jews not fight back? Both questions blame the victim for the crime and Roth's message to the careful reader is to resist this type of cavalier approach to the massiveness of the Holocaust problematic.

Roth's uncertain relationship to the Holocaust is, however, never far from the surface of this story. Anne/Amy moves from one foster family to another. In order to avoid sensationalism and the pain of prying strangers, she began telling people that she had been evacuated from Holland with a group of Jewish school children a week before the Nazi invasion; occasionally she refrained from identifying the school children as Jewish. This omission would bring rebuke from the Jewish families with whom she stayed. At this point Anne/Amy articulates a truth worth telling.

> But she could not bear them all laying their helpful hands upon her shoulders because of Auschwitz and Belsen. If she was going to be thought exceptional, it would not be because of Auschwitz and Belsen but because of what she had made of herself since (p. 132).

It is true, as Greenberg and others have pointed out, that the Holocaust should not be used triumphalistically by anyone, especially by those Jews who were not there.[7] The Holocaust should never be substituted for the personal struggle required to stand in the dialectic between covenant and history. Roth's thinly veiled admonition is correct. But one wonders about the overall theme of *The Ghost Writer* itself. Is Roth not utilizing the Holocaust to give himself legitimacy in the Jewish community? Zuckerman mentally composes scenarios in which he introduces his bride Anne Frank to various family members thereby compelling them to admit how wrong they had been about Nathan. Thus, familial revenge rather than Jewish maturity seems to be the motivating force behind Roth's literary ploy.

Roth's title *The Ghost Writer* is, however, quite significant. It can be understood on two different levels: on the level of *peshat*, or literal meaning, Roth has constructed a tale in which an artistically gifted young woman—Amy Bellette—receives the inspiration for her writing from the ghost of Anne Frank. But penetrating further, if not to the *sod* (mystical), at least to the *derash* (homiletic) level, it is arguable that Roth wants to contend that Anne Frank and the Holocaust are the ghosts behind all authentic post-Holocaust Jewish literary effort. Jews, in this reading, cannot merely pick up and subsequently discard the Holocaust as a literary motif. The *Shoah*, its history and its lessons, are a constant and haunting presence in Jewish existence. If this second interpretation is accurate, then Roth's position is quite similar to Wiesel's: the Holocaust must form the background for any authentically Jewish American novel.

Richard Elman

Richard Elman is a professional writer whose books, essays, novels, and reportage treat a wide variety of themes including American culture, politics, and Jewish existence in modernity. *A Coat for the Tsar* (1959), Elman's first Jewish novel, dealt with the moral dilemma of a pre-Holocaust Russian Jew who was the sole survivor of a pogrom. *Fred & Shirl & The Kids* (1972) is a partly autobiographical sketch of Jewish childhood and early married life in New York. Elman's trilogy about the destruction of a Hungarian Jewish family—*The 28th Day of Elul* (1967), *Lilo's Diary* (1968), and *The Reckoning* (1969), analyzed in this chapter—is a sustained treatment of the Holocaust. Elman has written that he would not know how to write about a (nonfictional) subject unless he was "deeply moved"—"through rage, or compassion, or, perhaps amazement and a sense of wonder." His literary and personal interest in the *Shoah* and in Judaism seems, however, to be a thing of the past. For example, he told a 1980 interviewer that:

> I didn't want to write about Jews anymore. I had written about them. A man is more than what he was when he grew up. He becomes what his experience has been. I wanted to write about my experiences and also about my fantasies. And I try not to repeat myself.[8]

Elman's literary exploration of the Holocaust provides a clear example of the pitfalls awaiting those who lack a knowledge of either Judaism or the *Shoah*. His Holocaust trilogy masquerades as documentary literature, but as Sidra Ezrahi astutely notes, this is merely a "pretext" to claim authority and authenticity.[9] Focusing on the lives of the Yagodah family, Elman writes about the increasingly desperate situation of Hungarian Jewry. The family's lust, anger, betrayal, and mistreatment of each other is meant to stand for the imminent disaster awaiting the Jews. His Jews are caricatures; self-absorbed, morally dubious individuals indifferent to the vicissitudes of history and the demands of covenant, caring instead only about private gain. In this regard, Jewish Hungary serves Elman much as Jewish America functions in Roth's early stories. Indeed, there are similarities between Hungary then and postwar America; factionalism in the Jewish community, an alarming rate of assimilation, and a high degree of intermarriage. Unlike Roth, however, Elman does not posit a normative Judaism or a symbolic Jew—the hasid—as moral examples. Instead, his Jews are self-hating and the Holocaust's universal message, if it has one, is that the Jews are as terrible as any other group and that holocausts occur everywhere.

The 28th Day of Elul portrays the Jewish dilemma of Alex Yagodah, a survivor living in Israel, who stands to inherit a good deal of money from his uncle's estate providing that he can prove he is a practicing Jew. *Lilo's Diary* purports to be the journal of Alex's cousin and fiancée, a ward of the Yagodahs. It relates her feeling of impending disaster which was shared by the entire family. The journal, and Lilo, were left behind when the Yagodahs fled. *The Reckoning* is subtitled "The Daily Ledgers of Newman Yagodah (Alex's Father) Advokat and Factor." It describes the immoral life led by the head of the Yagodah household. All of the characters in these novels are Jewishly ignorant. Elman, despite his penchant for universalizing messages, does not share Bernard Malamud's tendency to endow characters with the possibility of moral growth through suffering. Only Lilo appears to embrace a qualified form of Judaism as a result of her tribulations.

Elman's definition of a Jew is, as one would expect, the most negative of all the writers considered in *Crisis and Covenant*. "I am a Jew," muses Alex Yagodah. "What else should I call myself save *victim*?"[10] The Holocaust has eliminated all bona fide Jews. Yagodah, mentally composing a response to his late Uncle's attorney, twice claims that "there are simply no more Jews anywhere." Rubenstein's radical death of God position is radicalized further by Elman who contends that authentic Jews—a phrase which is never defined but which is authorally intended to refer to those existing in biblical times— no longer exist. Elman has in fact created a psychological first; an Israeli suffering from Jewish self-hate. Yagodah offers the following meditation: "*It may simply be a legal fiction if we are still willing to pretend that the word JEW means what it always meant* (p. 206).

Alex's spiritual discomfort has apparently been triggered, not by the Holocaust, but by Israel's need to function as a modern state in order to survive. Incredibly comparing Israel and Israelis to the government of Nazi Germany and Nazis, a favorite ploy of the Soviets and their Arab and third-world clients, Elman has Yagodah observe:

> I am forced to believe that it was such events [of the Holocaust] which conditioned all of Israel to the murder of innocent fellahin, the slaughter at Port Said of Egyptian families, the continual border sniping, yes, and the growing militarism, racism, and chauvinism of this place. Events here. Events in Asia. Murders everywhere. But since we were the first great modern multitude of Victims of the State, is it surprising that we should have created a modern state of our own in which victimizing others became a way of life? (pp. 161–62).

Yagodah is factually incorrect. To begin with, the Armenians, and not the Jews, were the "first great modern multitude of Victims of the State." But Elman makes no distinction between Jews, whose very birth was a death sentence, and innocent victims of modern warfare. Nor has he any regard for the moral use of power, a lesson drawn from the Holocaust experience by Fackenheim, Greenberg, Rubenstein, and others who argue that it is immoral ever again to have such a radical imbalance of power between victimizer and victim as existed during the time of the *Shoah*. Rubenstein takes this argument the furthest in contending that secular power and not theological election needs to be at the heart of post-Holocaust Judaism.[11] But the issue is not whether or not power should exist. It does. What Elman misses is the significant question of how power can be morally employed.

Elman's lack of attention to Holocaust specificity permits him to make false comparisons which, at times, border on the obscene. Alex Yagodah opines, for example, that:

> each of us . . . glancing up from our own cramped little lives to speculate about the death of six million (or any other crime of that magnitude) may recognize and abhor the injury, but we are likely to perceive an entirely different set of circumstances or be baffled by such an exotic variety of evidence (p. 206).

Here Elman reveals that he has not perceived the unique status of the Holocaust. Is there, for example, "any other crime of that magnitude?" While scholars have variously interpreted the many contributing factors which led to the extermination of European Jewry, their methods have proceeded not out of bafflement, but from certain assumptions about history, psychology, and religion. Moreover, if one is not to trouble about the "death of six million" because of potential bafflement, then the event diminishes and we no longer are obliged to learn its lessons. This is a far cry from Fackenheim's "Commanding Voice" of Auschwitz. But Elman proceeds to speak for the dead.

> Wouldn't those six million martyrs be equally bewildered if they were to rise from their charnal heaps and view the crimes we are committing daily? They would probably say, "It is just as we had thought. No different. Just as we remember. It is the way we were until our murderers came among us" (pp. 206–7).

The cycle is now complete, living, but especially dead, Jews are brought as witnesses against the Jewish state. This massive failure to come to grips with Holocaust specificity is, I believe, unequalled in American Jewish fiction.

Elman's literary strategy is to reduce historical events to the level of biography, and then to allow individual behavior to overshadow the magnitude of history. This has resulted in an ersatz universalism which makes metaphors of both Judaism and the Holocaust. Elman blames the *Judenräte* for cooperating with the Nazis (as if there were a choice); equates African slavery with Jewish fate in the Holocaust; compares America's bombing of Dresden to Nazi Germany, where Jews "were treated like niggers"; and finds German bureaucrats of murder in Israel "with patches over their eyes."

The afterword to *Lilo's Diary* provides a further example of this process. "The precious stuff of a life begins to reveal itself in the sullen face of a black orphan; or, even the lies of the middle-class careerist."[12] This is certainly true, but irrelevant in the context of the life of a Hungarian Jewess who, on the eve of the Holocaust, has just been sold as a sexual slave to a Christian family. "Men are often haunted by spirits about whom they must invent memories. My contemporaries are the dead children of Europe past and Asia present" (p. 155). Again, Elman has uttered a truism which tells us nothing about the genuine lessons of the *Shoah*. He is unable to specify Jewish children or to distinguish between the reasons for their deaths and other tragic deaths of children. While it makes no difference to the unfortunate victims, more than language is involved in distinguishing between Holocaust, genocides, and mass murders. Cynthia Ozick has captured the essence of the problem of metaphorizing the Holocaust. Specifically criticizing the conceptual weakness of *Sophie's Choice*, Ozick's observation applies with equal force to Elman's method. She writes:

> And though it may be metaphorically true that "humanity" was threatened and "life" itself denied, it was Jews who did most of that vast dying, it was the historic life of the Jewish people in Europe which was brought to an end.[13]

Elman's trilogy fails at precisely the point that it wishes to succeed; universalizing the Holocaust's lessons. In order to do this it is first necessary to acknowledge its Jewish dimension, and then to draw the appropriate lessons and distinctions, such as the immorality of isolating any social group and the danger of withdrawing from the political process, as so many ordinary people did during the Holocaust. Elman's Jews are, moreover, not only divorced from their tradition, but their behavior is more reprehensible than the worst traits of non-Jews. If he wanted to portray Jews in their diversity, should he not have made them recognizable participants in at least their own history? By reducing Jews to stereotypes and the Holocaust to another example of "man's inhumanity to man" (that banal phrase), Elman is trivializing the catastrophe and his characters abandon their search for meaning. Alex Yagodah, for example, shares Herman Broder's assumption that Jewish history has ended thereby foreclosing the Jewish future.

Edward Lewis Wallant

Edward Lewis Wallant's *The Pawnbroker* is one of the earliest works of Jewish American fiction to bring the Holocaust into an American focus.[14] In so doing, however, Wallant achieves mixed results. Ostensibly treating the Jewish catastrophe, *The Pawnbroker* portrays, and subtly suggests, an equation between various types of suffering: physical, psychic, spiritual, Jewish, black, and Puerto Rican. The novel also treats race relations and the Jewish-Christian encounter. In this, Wallant, like Elman, has simultaneously trivialized and wrongly universalized the Holocaust, while paying scarce attention to historical detail. *The Pawnbroker* is, in fact, more representative of a literature of misery than a literature of atrocity. But this is to jump ahead of our analysis. Wallant, who died at the age of thirty-six, wrote four novels, all of which deal with the theme of suffering and redemption. The author himself observes that his novels are character studies which illuminate a person's interior life. Wallant wished his fiction to prompt people to "all look at each other in wonder and pity for what each of us goes through in the most apparently simple life."[15] *The Pawnbroker* thus views the Holocaust not as an epoch-making event but as an instance, albeit extreme, of human cruelty whose effects can be overcome through healing contact with other caring humans.

Sol Nazerman is a death camp survivor whose family perished in the Holocaust. Each year, during August (*Tisha b'Av*), he reacts to the *yahrzeit* (anniversary) of their death, which is on the twenty-eighth day of the month, not by any traditional *halakic* means but rather by experiences of intense psychic distress accompanied by dreams and flashbacks which omit no details. Wallant is chronologically if not historically accurate; the flashbacks begin with a transport to the camps. Nazerman's son David drowns in a pool of feces, which covers the floor of the cattle car. Wedged tightly by the wall of humanity surrounding him, Sol helplessly listens to David's death agony and to his wife Ruth's frantic pleas that he do something. Other Holocaust scenes depict Ruth's pain when she observes Nazerman who is forced to watch her commit fellatio in a Nazi brothel, and his daughter Naomi pierced on a monstrous hook. He recalls his own operation, performed for the amusement of S.S. doctors, and remembers stacking bodies for the crematoria, hoping not to encounter corpses of family and friends, yet replacing his own lost spectacles so that he might at least honor the dead by looking at their faces. Sol is also plagued by memories of a death camp selection, and the electrocution of a fellow prisoner.

Sol's post-Holocaust existence is devoid of all human emotion; he is described with death images, "burial," "graveyard," "something exhumed." Like Wiesel's survivor in *The Accident*, Sol's hopes had been amputated, although he feels no sense of witness for the dead.

A university professor prior to the conflagration, Sol undergoes several status reversals, each of which separates him from his former illusions about the civilizing role of culture and the nobility of ideas. Sol's slide down the slippery moral slope ends in his furtive partnership with Murillio, an Italian Mafia figure for whom the business is a front to launder illicitly obtained money. The pawnshop, itself a symbol of failed dreams, is located in East Harlem, a place of great human oppression. The business affords Sol privacy, his one passion. At work he is remote, staring "sightlessly through the office glass like some exhibited creature from another clime" (p. 19).

In terms of plot, the novel focuses on Sol's relationship with his assistant, a Puerto Rican youth named Jesus Ortiz. There exists a quasi master-disciple relationship between Sol and Jesus, and in this respect—as well as several others—the novel bears considerable resemblance to Bernard Malamud's *The Assistant*. Both novels depict, for example, a robbery in which the assistant is involved, assumption of the other's identity, a description of the workplace as a tomb (Anya Savikin also refers to her feeling that the antique shop is like a tomb), and a symbolic interpretation of Judaism. Ortiz conspires to rob the pawnshop, although insisting that there be no violence. At the last minute, however, one of the robbers fires his pistol. Jesus steps in front of Sol taking the fatal shot in his master's stead. Jesus literally dies for Sol who, overcome by this act of self-sacrifice, begins weeping and feels a long dormant but nameless emotion which he guesses is love.

> All his anesthetic numbness left him. He became terrified of the touch of air on the raw wounds. What was this great, agonizing sensitivity and what was it for? Good God, what was all this? *Love*? Could this be *love*? He began to laugh hysterically, and the voices in the store stopped (p. 200).

Wallant's taut prose cannot disguise the superficiality of his christologized Judaism. This scene suggests one of two readings, neither of which speaks to the centrality of the Holocaust. Jewish suffering in the *Shoah* can only be relieved by mediating the experience through Christian symbolism. Alternatively, Christianity, whose teachings of contempt had sown the bitter seeds of hatred which ripened into the Holocaust, is now (in the person of Jesus) made to undergo a rite of expiation.

The American-born Wallant misreads and domesticates the Holocaust. He suggests that the Harlem ghetto, suburban New York, and the death camps are all points on the continuum of human misery. Overcoming this misery may be accomplished only through community with those people—Jews, Christians, blacks, whites—who care about others. Nazerman, whose name may be read as Nazerene, becomes fully human—in the manner of Malamud's protagonists—only by becoming a kind of Jewish-Christian everyman. Sol's life prior to this redemptive murder was spent in isolation from others. "I am safe," he acknowledges, "within myself." But his illicit money supported two families; his own which consisted of his sister Bertha (who had come to America before the war), her husband Selig, and their children Joan and the despised Morton—like Sol a social outcast. They lived in Westchester where they all, with the exception of Morton (and Sol), aspire to be Americans as opposed to Jews. Bertha is a study in Jewish self-hate; proud that Selig and Joan do not look too Jewish. Sol is also supporting his mistress Tessie Rubin and her ravaged father Mendel, both of whom are survivors. Far removed from American suburban Judaism—both experientially and geographically—the survivors live in a depressing slum area.

Wallant's concern is to elicit the phenomenology of suffering. Cecil Mapp, a black alcoholic, observes of Sol, both at the beginning and at the end of the work, "that man suffer." The time between those observations, however, has witnessed a slow and agonizing spiritual odyssey for the pawnbroker. Sol's stated quest for privacy is challenged by his actions during the two weeks preceding the twenty-eighth of August. For example, he no longer wishes to receive money derived from the whorehouse, since it presumably reminds him of his wife's degradation at the hands of the Nazis. When Sol goes to Murillio to terminate their partnership, an implausible action, the mobster threatens him with death. At another point in the story, he inexplicably goes on a picnic and a Hudson River cruise with Marilyn Birchfield, a Protestant social worker who, like Sol, is lonely and physically unattractive. Later still, Sol uncharacteristically discusses his feelings and problems with Tessie, and he arranges for Mendel's funeral. Wallant employs all of these strategies to indicate that Sol is emerging from his psychic and social isolation. The problem is that the novel overly focuses on sociopsychological explanations of character. Wallant's belief that holocaustal suffering is but one interchangeable component in the vast machinery of human misery reduces the enormity of the event. He has surveyed the forest, but badly missed the trees.

His treatment of the Jewish historical experience is superficial.

Sol, for example, symbolizes the Jewish Holocaust survivor. But the only hint of this identity in the interchanges between himself and Ortiz comes as a result of Jesus's curiosity about the numbers on Sol's arm. Jesus is a rootless youth who has been abandoned by his father and is looking for a history. Curious about Sol's "tatoo," the assistant is rebuffed by Sol's response (p. 19), "It's a secret society I belong to. You could never belong. You have to be able to walk on water" (one of the miracles attributed to Jesus in the synoptic Gospels). While this may be interpreted as Wallant's manner of presenting the indescribable nature of Holocaust experience, it is more probable—given the context of this and his other novels—that Jewish particularity is simply unimportant to the overarching theme of redemption through love. Later in the conversation Sol is asked about Jewish affinity to business and gives a sociohistorical description of the wandering Jew legend, without any mention of covenant vocation. Wallant's most sustained portrait of Sol's connection with Jewish history comes, moreover, in negative images. Sol claims "a sense of kinship, of community with all the centuries of hand-rubbing shylocks" (p. 8). Given the experience of the Holocaust, Wallant's strategy for explaining the Jewish singled-out condition is unthinking and cavalier.

Wallant's portrayal of survivors is—like that of Singer, Bellow, and Elman—an unsentimental one, but he does capture the variety of faith and doubt among the witnesses. Mendel's piety is unshaken, he says blessings before eating and utters the *Sh'ma* prayer on his deathbed. Tessie is a secularist who lights *yahrzeit* candles for her many dead but does not believe in God. Along with Eliezer, Shifra Puach, and Mrs. Saivikin, Tessie contends: "The dead are better off." She wants to scream all day long. Sol rejects both sacred and secular forms of Jewish expression; he trusts neither "God or politics or newspapers or music or art." But, most of all, he does not "trust people and their talk, for they have created hell with that talk, for they have proved they do not deserve to exist for what they are" (p. 87).

Wallant's casting of Sol as a teacher was a wise strategy whose potential the author did not pursue. Sol teaches Jesus technical aspects of the pawnbroking profession and contends that only money is to be trusted.

> Next to the speed of light, which Einstein tells us is the only absolute in the universe, second only to that I would rank money. There, I have taught you the Pawnbroker's Credo, Ortiz (p. 88).

Sol's confession is untrue. He himself objects, as noted, to receiving money from Murillio's brothels. Moreover, it is Sol's insistence on the primacy of money which stimulates Jesus's involvement in the robbery. Sol's intellectualism, unlike Artur Sammler's, is not used to reflect on the meaning of his experience for Jewish existence or for civilization as a whole. His European university career is alluded to by a variety of people who hoped either to make the pawnbroker more socially acceptable, or—in the case of George Smith, a sexual deviate who visited the pawnshop—who were unable to understand that the Holocaust had made a mockery of university teachings about truth, culture, and morality. The knowledge which Sol gained from the Holocaust is far superior to the techniques of pawnbroking, but it is the latter which is emphasized. The idea that survivors are people from whom society can learn about the world and about human behavior is simply not broached by Wallant. The survivor as moral instructor (exemplified by Artur Sammler) is preceded by the concept of survivor as societal embarrassment.[16]

Sol's relationship to Goberman, a fellow survivor, further reveals Wallant's confusion about the Holocaust's uniqueness. Goberman is an unattractive figure (like Elman's Alex Yagodah) who collects money for the Jewish Appeal. He has terrified Tessie with his constant badgering for funds. Sol accuses him of being "an opportunist who can put anything to profit." The pawnbroker recalls that in 1941, in Bergen-Belsen, Goberman was reputed to have betrayed his own family for additional food rations. Goberman nervously denies the charge, but in so doing reveals that it may have been true. Sol calls Goberman "worse than all the Nazis"; he is *dreck* to be washed away and a *Shveinhundt*, one of the names Nazis used for Jews. The readers' final glimpse of Goberman comes as he attempts to steal a Yiddish newspaper while being observed by Sol. While Wallant incorrectly places Bergen-Belsen inmates at the camp in 1941, it wasn't established as a transit center until 1943, the larger issue is his portrayal of Sol's brutal nature and Goberman's camp behavior. Wallant correctly implies that each victim is potentially a victimizer. But his truism has the unfortunate effect of blaming Jews for acting like Nazis, thereby missing the central evil of the Holocaust.

The Pawnbroker was written in the late fifties and reflects societal ignorance concerning the meaning of the survivors' experiences. On the one hand, Wallant seems to be aware of the ineffable difference between the death camps and other types of suffering. Responding to Marilyn Birchfield, who wonders why he is so bitter, Sol puts the matter in proper perspective.

There is a world so different in scale that its emotions bear no resemblance to yours; it has emotions so different in degree that they have become a different *species*. I am not bitter, Miss Birchfield; *I am past that by a million years!* (p. 110).

Wallant's misconception of the role of survivors is, however, seen in his insistence on describing them as physically and psychically deformed. The Nazi medical experiment has left Sol mishapen—"and he wished his ugliness to pierce the smallest of dreams" (p. 34). Sol hates everyone; black, white, yellow "are all equally abominations," and thinks he is "too dirty" for the immaculate Miss Birchfield (field of birch trees). In a telephone conversation, Sol admonishes Marilyn not to become intimate with him because "you would be guilty of necrophilia—it is obscene to love the dead." It is as if being a survivor was something about which one should be ashamed.

The *Pawnbroker* also falsely universalizes the Holocaust. Rightly implicating the role of Christian preachments in the Jewish catastrophe, Wallant attempts a resolution of the intractable dilemma of Jewish-Christian encounter. On the Jewish side, Sol's nightmare vision of Naomi hanging on the hook is altered by the appearance of other faces on the child's body—Morton, George Smith, Jesus Ortiz, Mabel Wheatly (a black prostitute and Jesus's girlfriend), Tessie, Cecil Mapp, other pawnshop customers, and Goberman. Christian complicity in the murder of the Jews is indicated in several ways; the ongoing antisemitism of Jesus Ortiz, Mrs. Ortiz's offense at learning that Jesus was a Jew, and, most importantly, Jesus Ortiz's vision of Sol on the crucifix. Jesus's redemptive death is a literary strategy which attempts to claim that one can say "I am sorry" for the Holocaust, and emphasizes Wallant's historical näiveté. Was the Jewish catastrophe an historical aberration? Did it break the covenant? Or was it the logical outcome of Western civilization? By personalizing a tragedy of such historic proportion, Wallant reduces the event to a series of individual gestures which teach nothing about either the Holocaust or about interfaith coexistence.

Sol's understanding of history and covenant exemplify the problems involved in viewing Judaism symbolically. Nazerman accepts Rubenstein's death of God position; the covenant is a "cruel joke" and Sol's "prayer" to this indifferent deity is to "kill us, but only once, isn't once enough?" (p. 194). But religious language and imagery abound: Sol compares himself to a priest giving his customers "absolution in hard cash," Jesus is described as an acolyte, Sol equates feelings of loss at the time of *Tisha b'Av* with "an old superstition," yiddishisms (for the most part badly mangled) are uttered by Mendel and Sol, there are crucifix scenes, and even one episode where Sol sits in a cafeteria (envying a black man the pleasure of his cigarette) humming a wordless tune or *niggun*—a common hasidic ritual.

Jewish and Christian religious imagery is, however, interchangeable. *The Pawnbroker*, in fact, abolishes formal religion, favoring instead the universal brotherhood of man based not on reason but on compassion. Sol's own metamorphosis is presented by his gradual involvement in the lives of those whom he formerly ignored. His new orientation has, however, nothing to do with covenant or *halaka*. Following Ortiz's creative murder, Sol rejoins the human community in a three stage process characterized by feelings of love and grief, telling Morton that he *needs* him, and being able to mourn. Sol acquires the latter ability when, in a dream, he is transported to a deserted death camp where a black-uniformed officer with empty eye sockets—Murillio—informs him that "your dead are not buried here" (p. 203).

Sol's abandonment of Jewish ritual coincides neither with his training nor his background; his parents had both been observant Jews. But Sol refrains from expressing himself Jewishly. There is, for example, no mention of *kaddish* after Mendel's death. Unlike Sammler, a fellow intellectual who eulogized Elya Gruner in terms of his post-Holocaust covenant commitment, Sol makes no attempt to put Mendel's Holocaust experience into any philosophical, ethical, or moral framework. Sol ends by mourning both his American assistant and his European family. Ironically, there is a prescribed sociology of mourning which would strengthen Wallant's communal emphasis. A minyan, ten men, is required each day for a seven day period at the house of the deceased. At this time, reciting the *kaddish*, affirming belief in God and continuity with tradition, Jews also affirm their kinship bonds. The novel concludes with Sol traveling to Tessie's house to help her mourn. Sol's return to the human community, while specifically involving other Jews—Morton and Tessie—is an affirmation neither of covenant nor of Jewish history, but rather of his own human vulnerability.

The Pawnbroker is an ambitious but flawed Holocaust novel. Hoping to universalize the experience, it ends by ignoring the *Shoah*'s lessons. Wallant authorally admires the black doctor who treated Mendel and those who, like Marilyn Birchfield, attempt, despite their own unhappiness, to help others; although none of the survivors are portrayed as caring people. The difference between the Jewish and the black experience is stated by Ortiz: "Niggers suffer like animals. They ain't caught on. Oh yeah, Jews suffer. But they do it big, they shake up the worl' with their sufferin' " (p. 24). Wallant refrains, however, from exploring the origins of this difference which are rooted in the sinuous and complicated relationship between Judaism and Western culture. Wallant's Jews are indifferent to the covenant—the source of Jewish identity—and therefore cannot be expected to establish a strong Jewish future in America. Wallant, unlike Roth, does not utilize Israel as an emblem of Jewishness. Rightly attacking the bankruptcy of intellectualism (university complicity in the murder process) and culture (Germany was the heart of Western civilization) during the Holocaust, Wallant concludes by substituting an equally elusive and religiously unanchored compassion as antidote for those who live in an Auschwitz universe.

Norma Rosen

Norma Rosen's *Touching Evil* (1969) attempts to portray the Holocaust's effects on non-Jewish Americans. [17] The story concerns two women, Jean Lamb, who had been an undergraduate during the *Shoah*, and her younger friend Hattie, whose awareness of the horror stems from the televised Eichmann trial. Both women watch with ritual intensity the victims' testimony of violence and evil. Unlike Elman and Wallant, however, Rosen neither trivializes nor falsely universalizes the catastrophe. She instead wishes the Jewish experience to be read as a cipher of the human condition; hoping—with Ozick—that those listening at the wide end of the shofar will learn the appropriate lessons. Rosen has written that in *Touching Evil*:

> I was not considering the meaning of the Holocaust for Jewish history. I was considering the meaning to human life and aspiration of the knowledge that human beings—in great numbers—could do what had been done. [18]

Rosen boldly prescribes a normative course for non-Jewish reaction to the Holocaust. Hattie and Jean, for example, are described as having "extracted their private symbols of horror from the welter of horror symbols" (p. 55). For Hattie, pregnant with her first child, expectant women and their infants in the camps, and the figure of the Muslim (*Muselmänner*) are the abiding images. [19] Jean, for her part, was riven by the testimony of a naked blood-covered woman who dug her half-dead way up through the corpses. [20]

The novel's Holocaust reflections are juxtaposed against a background of letters that Jean writes to her absent lover and her encounters with a teenaged Puerto Rican, Jesús, to whom she becomes both mother and lover. Jean's task in the post-Holocaust world is that of reality instructor, teacher of history to those who, like Jesús, may be involved in petty crimes and violence but remain unaware of evil's cosmic dimensions. Shown pictures of the death camps in 1944 by her psychology professor/lover, Jean attests that "a catastrophe has changed the world. The old forms have no more meaning" (p. 74). She vows never to marry or have children. Jean has looked into the abyss of the Holocaust and emerged psychically scarred. She embraces Wiesel's position that one should tremble each time the word Holocaust is pronounced. "In those days," observes Jean, "if someone said 'concentration camp' to me, my body and soul emptied out. I was ready to faint, to fall down" (p. 77). Rosen's post-Holocaust authentic Christian is one who has heard Emil Fackenheim's "Commanding Voice" of Auschwitz. Stanwood, Hattie's brother-in-law, asks about the meaning of all the burning. "Is there," he wonders, "a voice in the fire? Omens in the ashes?" Ezra, Hattie's husband, responds, "Yes, survival" (p. 197). Rosen makes clear that survival has moral implications and thus is much more than what Terrence Des Pres terms Darwinian survival. For Rosen the central question asked by *Touching Evil* is; what kind of daily lives can people live after they have touched an evil so absolute that it overpowers all the old ideas of evil and good?[21]

Hattie's response is twofold; consisting of both a moral and a mystical dimension. She empathizes with her predecessors who gave birth in the camps, and whose infants were bitten by spotted fever lice. Hattie assumes the moral burden of the Holocaust in asserting that "a poison went into the atmosphere. Just as when the atomic bomb explodes. Each generation will be sickened, poisoned with disgust for the human race" (p. 84). After giving birth to her daughter, Hattie shares with Jean her quasi-mystical remedy for the cosmic scourge of the Holocaust. Children are to be constantly reincarnated in a type of endless *gilgul*:

> The children talk about their happiness to be alive at first, and then each tells how he or she died. After each war, each atrocity, each death, the children fly down to their mothers' beds and disappear in them. Then the whole thing is repeated, and the children fly up again. New children . . . new births . . . new times . . . new joys. . . . Centuries and centuries of joyful births and terrible deaths. . . . After a while we begin to see similarities . . . we see the same children over and over . . . those children haven't been lost! (p. 237).

Hattie's newborn is thus understood symbolically as an incarnation of one of the Holocaust's one million five hundred thousand murdered children.[22]

Touching Evil is at its best in arguing an authentic universalism concerning contemporary Holocaust implications. Rosen suggests that the Holocaust will even provide a civilizational icon for our age; "the piled-up stick bodies at the bottom of a lime pit," are "destined to become one of the classic sights of the world like Stonehenge, like the Parthenon in moonlight, like the ruined cities of Angkor Wat, like the Great Pyramid at Giza" (p. 73). Her indictment of the corruption of science is no less accurate; Jean's psychology professor observes that scientists "have replaced the mice in the maze with men." The continuing trauma of the *Shoah* is underscored by Jean who, watching the Eichmann trial, states "I'm up to my ears again in corpses," seeing "those same fleshless bones that fell on me seventeen years ago." Rosen also adopts the Greenberg-Fackenheim position concerning authentic as opposed to inauthentic post-Holocaust existence. There were, for Jean, two kinds of people—"those who knew and those who didn't know. And it had nothing to do with reading newspapers" (p. 77).

Authentically encountering the Holocaust means taking its pain and moral challenge into one's soul and body. This pain includes an indictment of God. Jean asks Jesús how a Catholic would pray for a woman about to give birth, then she composes her own prayer:

> Dear God—God of the medical-experiment cell block . . . God of the common lime-pit grave . . . God of chopped fingers . . . of blinded eyes, God of electrodes attached at one end to a jeep battery and at the other to the genitals of political prisoners, God, most powerful God of all these things (p. 233).

Jesús is bewildered and offended when Jean articulates the connection between God, violence, and history. Rosen knows that any authentic post-Holocaust theology, Jewish or Christian, must account for an implicated deity.

There is, moreover, an indissoluble link between survivors and the ones who, while not there, attempt to grapple with the enormity of the *Shoah*. Jean acknowledges that the central role of post-Holocaust individuals is that of witness. "When I hear my name, 'Miss Lamb,' I feel a tugging of the rope. 'Miss Lamb to the slaughter!' Not as victim, I never thought that, but as witness" (p. 97). Rosen has wisely chosen to stress that responsible Christians are also required to live covenantally in the tension between history and redemption.

The novel is marred, however, in several ways. Rosen's use of Jesús, who disappears and is pursued by Jean, seems a heavy-handed symbol. He is, like Wallant's Jesus, a Puerto Rican tempted by evil friends and morally ambivalent. The novel's depiction of city violence—rapes, demolition of old buildings, displacement of elderly and presumably useless people—cannot possibly compare with the death camps. Yet it is precisely in the juxtaposition that Rosen, like Wallant, runs the greatest risk of being misunderstood. This conceptual confusion increases in the hospital maternity ward where Hattie analogizes her situation to that of mothers forced to deliver in vermin-infested death camps. Hattie compares the apparent indifference of hospital personnel to the attitude of the S.S. Edward Alexander has perceptively criticized this as being "so enveloped in feminist rhetoric that many a reader will forget that their point is to finalize the identification between Hattie and the women whose stories she has heard in the Eichmann trial, not to present women as the oppressed race."[23]

Perhaps the greatest difficulty with *Touching Evil* lies not in the book's literary strategy or its understanding of the Holocaust, but rather in its subject matter. Can the *Shoah* be imagined by those who were not present? Rosen herself has termed such individuals witnesses through the imagination. Specifically, she asks that the burden of knowledge about extraordinary evil be carried by Christians in isolation from contact with any Jews except those testifying at the Eichmann trial. It would have increased the novel's power and realism to have interaction between Jews and Christians in America. It was, after all, the isolation of the two groups from each other which fanned the flames of hatred and ignorance. Since Rosen correctly argues that the Jewish historical experience carries a message for all of humanity, one wonders why Jews are excluded from *Touching Evil*.

Bernard Malamud

Bernard Malamud's *The Fixer* (1966) is the author's metaphoric literary encounter with the Holocaust.[24] Unlike either "The Lady of the Lake" or "The German Refugee," which directly engage the Jewish catastrophe, *The Fixer* focuses on the historically antecedent events associated with the Mendel Beiliss blood libel trial. Yakov Bok (Mendel Beiliss) is wrongly imprisoned and cruelly treated; the relentless perversion of humanitarian, legal, and moral processes all prefigure the *Shoah*. Malamud captures the pervasive societal sickness of antisemitism, merging its two most virulent forms: the premodern religious hatred which centered on the blood libel accusation (Jews ritually employed the blood of Christian children) and the modern secular claim of reactionary governments that there exists an international Jewish conspiracy to take over the world. This latter claim is itself based on *The Protocols of the Elders of Zion*, a forgery composed by the Czar's secret police. Maurice Samuel's *Blood Accusation*, an historical study of the case, appearing in the same year as *The Fixer*, emphasizes that the trial "was a crude preview of the destructive possibilities of the twentieth century."[25]

Yakov Bok, like all of Malamud's Jewish protagonists, is unsophisticated—although not unwise—and Jewishly unobservant. Bok wishes to leave the *shtetl* after being abandoned by Raisl, his faithless and barren wife. He is a simple fixer who can "fix what's broken except in the heart" (p. 7). Shmuel, Bok's hapless but God-fearing father-in-law, is a typical Malamudian *schlemiel* figure; a failure at business who persistently clings to tradition. Disgruntled by the grinding poverty and hopelessness of the *shtetl*—with its *luftmenschen* ("who bothers with leaks in his roof if he's peeking through the cracks to spy on God?" (p. 7)—Yakov confides to Shmuel that he is going to the city because "opportunity here is born dead" (p. 7). Shmuel admonishes his son-in-law that "Kiev is a dangerous city full of churches and anti-Semites."[26] There is no need to leave the Jewish Pale of Settlement, attests Shmuel, "what's in the world is in the shtetl," the human condition. "But here," exclaims the old man, "at least God is with us" (p. 12). Bok is unconvinced and retorts that God is with the Jews only until "the Cossacks come galloping, then he's elsewhere. He's in the outhouse, that's where he is" (p. 12).

Traveling to Kiev, Bok experiences increasing antisemitic hatred. Inadvertently saving the life of a member of the reactionary Black Hundreds, Yakov lies to the man about his Jewish identity hoping thereby to create "opportunities" (not unlike Levin/Freeman in "The Lady of the Lake," although with far graver consequences). Bok is made manager of the antisemite's brickyard, resists the sexual advances of the man's crippled daughter (much in the manner of Joseph and Potiphor's wife, Yakov will later be accused by the daughter of sexual assault), and is subsequently arrested for the ritual murder of a twelve-year-old Christian boy, Zhenia Golov. Imprisoned for over two years, Bok comes to terms with the meaning of history and the responsibility of being a Jew, although in a manner largely divorced from any *halakic* standards.

In terms of structure, *The Fixer* portrays the dialectic between history and covenant as occurring in both a literal as well as a metaphoric prison. Unlike Malamud's earlier Jewish *schlemiel*, Morris Bober, whose grocery store was like a tomb or prison, Yakov Bok is literally imprisoned. This theme is touched on by Wiesel in *The Accident*, where the protagonist is in a body cast for ten weeks. As far as literary strategy is concerned, Malamud like Cohen, Singer, Schaeffer, and Wallant, utilizes the dream as a means of indicating the main character's most vivid encounters. In Bok's case these meetings are with Czar Nicholas II and with a host of dead prisoners who formerly inhabited the fixer's cell. In prison he has a surrealistic vision in which the bloodied head of his dead horse accuses him of forgetting his identity.

Malamud's figures wage a twofold struggle; for his *shtetl* Jews the issue is, as for Ozick, a choice between covenant history and pagan nature. Shmuel, at great personal risk and with the expenditure of his last rubles, visits his imprisoned son-in-law. It is, to begin with, no small irony that after a year's absence and all that has befallen Yakov, the two engage in a theological discussion. But the heart of the matter is Shmuel's belief.

> We're not Jews for nothing. Without God we can't live. Without the covenant we would have disappeared out of history. Let that be a lesson to you. He's all we have but who wants more? (p. 256).

In face of Yakov's theological skepticism, Shmuel offers his own version of Greenberg's man in search of God position. Addressing his son-in-law, the old man admonishes, "if you don't hear His voice so let Him hear yours." Echoing the kabbalistic view of divine-human interdependence, Shmuel contends, " 'When prayers go up blessings descend' " (p. 257). *Shtetl* Jews, however, are not Malamud's focal point.

The Fixer's ultimate objective is to achieve a universal moral community. But the Jewish religion is not a decisive force in determining Malamud's characters' moral strength. Ben Siegel has noted that, "for Malamud, religion's function is to convey the essentials of the 'good heart'; he has little sympathy either for the ghetto-minded Jew or the parochial Christian."[27] Like Nissenson, Malamud's Yakov Bok has made a covenant, not with God, but with himself. Bok also shares with Nissenson's Jake Brody a sense of moral responsibility. Unlike Brody, however, this obligation does not stem from a familiarity with the tradition or its classical sources. Bok's moral growth arises instead from his various prison experiences which have revealed self-sacrificing Christians, *viz.*, Bibikov the Russian prosecutor who quite improbably promises to help Yakov and is therefore himself imprisoned, and subsequently commits suicide, and Kogin, one of the fixer's guards who is killed defending Bok. The fixer is, on the other hand, betrayed by Garfein, his fellow Jewish prisoner. Moreover Raisl—who visits Bok in prison—has had an illegitimate child and is being harassed by the Jewish community in a manner not dissimilar to Yakov's ordeal, although not as physically threatening. Malamud stresses that the ability to grow morally as a result of suffering makes one a symbolic Jew, no matter what one's formal religion or, in Bok's case, lack thereof.

Yakov Bok is a reluctant auditor in the school of history. He learns the lesson which the Nazis taught so brutally, being a Jew was a crime. Yakov muses that:

> There was no "reason," there was only their plot against a Jew, any Jew; he was the accidental choice for sacrifice. Being born a Jew meant being vulnerable to history, including its worst errors (p. 155).

Yakov's encounters with Russian antisemitism contain many Holocaust portents. The boatman who ferries him across the Dneiper provides a good example. A rabid Jew hater, the man is reminiscent of Nissenson's peasant in *My Own Ground*. The boatman repeats all the old lies about Jewish perfidy, Jews as the Devil, and Jews as unassimilable others. The crowning accusation is Jews as deiciders. There is one remedy for the "Jewish Problem" and it consists of several steps: kill all the Jews, pile up their corpses, douse them with benzine and incinerate them—the flames will be such that "people will enjoy all over the world," the ashes must then be hosed away, Jewish possessions are to be divided—having all been stolen in the first place. This is a capsule summary of the Nazi plan. After the speech, while the boatman crosses himself, Yakov's bag of ritual prayer objects, given him by Shmuel, sinks into the river (pp. 27–28).

The Fixer portrays the vicissitudes of Jewish existence in pre-Holocaust Europe by contrasting societal treatment of Jews and Christians. Bok is in prison on a patently false charge which even the government knew was ludicrous. On the other hand, Kogin's son was arrested for the senseless murder of an old man. The son had a trial, was found guilty, and sentenced to twenty years in Siberia. Malamud is also interested in revealing the murderous discrepancy between theological preachments, and actions in the world. For example, Bok wished to ask Lebedev, the antisemite whose life he had saved, how he could cry for a dog and yet want to kill humans who happen to be Jews. This query finds contemporary resonance in the bizarre but common assertion made by defenders of Nazis and by unthinking people that a particular Nazi, although having murdered many Jews, nonetheless loved animals, as if this was a mitigating circumstance.

The Fixer underscores Christianity's moral bankruptcy. A priest entreats Yakov to convert because "there is none so dear in the eyes of God as a Jew who admits he is in error and comes willingly to the true faith" (p. 236). If Yakov agrees, the priest will instruct him in the Orthodox dogma. As a Jew, Bok was guilty. As a convert he would be saved. The moral failure of Christianity—especially Eastern European Christianity—during the *Shoah* is a theme which reverberated throughout Nazi Europe. Archbishop Kametko's 1942 response to an appeal for intervention against the deportation of Slovakian Jews consisted of telling the Nietra Rebbe that extermination is the punishment Jews deserve for the death of Jesus Christ. The Archbishop promised to help only if the Jews converted en masse to Catholicism.[28] Lebedev and the priest contrast starkly with Rutkauskus, the righteous Gentile portrayed in *Anya*.

Bok's covenant understanding places great responsibility on man. God is blamed for historical disasters, but, even more, Yakov blames him "for not existing." Shmuel attempts to counter Yakov's doubt citing Job's stance "Though he slay me, yet will I trust in him." But Yakov is angry not only with God who, to "win a lousy bet with the devil" kills off Job's innocent children and servants. He hates the biblical God for his impotence during the subsequent course of Jewish history. Yakov's image of God is, however, ambivalent. The fixer speculates that perhaps God "would like to be human; it's possible, nobody knows." The intermingling of divine and human is Malamud's way of elevating the role of man in the world. Josephine Knopp argues that Yakov's use of the lower case pronoun to refer to God, indicates either a sign of defiance and disrespect or a means of denoting man's moral equality with God.[29] Knopp's argument is intelligent, but not, I think, decisive. More likely is the explanation that the freethinker Bok is "fatigued by history" and represents the condition of Jews in modernity. Earlier Bok was described as a devotee of Spinoza, who thought that "if there was a God, after reading Spinoza he had closed up his shop and become an idea" (p. 60). Reading the blood-stained pages of a Hebrew Bible, Bok was gripped by the narrative of the ancient Hebrews. Whatever they were doing, the Hebrews always dialogued with the "huffing-puffing God who tried to sound, maybe out of envy, like a human being." Bok embodies the third of Greenberg's three theological models—the person who is angry and contends with God. Unlike Wiesel, however, on whose writings Greenberg bases this model, it is far from certain that Bok's anger allows him to remain within the dialectical framework of covenant and history.

The Fixer details the growth of Yakov Bok's moral responsibility in a manner which decreases the role of traditional Judaism. Leaving the *shtetl*, Yakov and Shmuel encounter a beggar who asks for money. The penniless Shmuel tries to borrow a small amount from Yakov who refuses. The beggar calls Yakov a goy. But in Kiev the Yiddish speaking Bok inexplicably rescues an old hasidic man from attack by Russian youths. In his apartment Yakov offers the hasid bread which he refuses because it is Passover, instead he eats matzah from his sack. Yakov is stunned by the reminder of the liberation from bondage; "moved by a strong emotion" the fixer "had to turn away till it had gone." Malamud employed the Passover symbolism in *The Assistant* with equal effect. There, Frank Alpine, Bober's Christian assistant, had himself circumcised one day in April (the same month in which Bok aids the old hasid). After Passover, Alpine "became a Jew." Yakov's full assumption of moral duty comes with his refusal to commit suicide while awaiting trial. Had he done so, his persecutors would have claimed he was guilty. At this point, Malamud suggests a parallel with the biblical story of Jacob and the angel. In a dream, Yakov wrestles with Czar Nicholas: "They wrestled, beard to beard, in the dark until Nicholas proclaimed himself an angel of God and ascended into the sky" (p. 227). The biblical account, as we recall, has Jacob (Yakov) wrestle with an angel all night. As a result of this combat, Jacob's name becomes Israel, a patriarch of the nation. Yakov Bok's struggle may be intended symbolically to identify him with *k'lal Yisrael*. If so, the parallel is a nonparallel. Unlike Jacob of antiquity, who reverently assumed his new identity and role, this modern Jacob rails against his fate.

> From birth a black horse had followed him, a Jewish nightmare. What was being a Jew but an everlasting curse? He was sick of their history, destiny, blood guilt (p. 227).

The Fixer's disturbing message concerning the Jewish condition in modernity can be summarized in one sentence. Jews are unsafe anywhere. Recalling that his own parents had never left the *shtetl*, Bok remembers that "the historical evil had galloped in to murder them there" (p. 315). For the fixer, Jewishness means servitude, diminished opportunity, and vulnerability (p. 315). The fixer's negative assessment of the tradition is reinforced by Malamud's novelistic transformation of Jewish ritual objects. A prayer shawl becomes important to the imprisoned Bok, not for prayer but for warmth. This stands in marked contrast to Ozick's literary transformation of a shawl into a tallit. The Christian scripture is read alongside the Hebrew Bible. Reading Jesus's Sermon on the Mount, Bok interprets it Jewishly and thinks that because he is innocent, true Christians must release him from prison. Bok's meditation on the God of Israel is twofold; God covenants, therefore he is and, in a linguistic play on the words of the Tetragrammaton (God's answer to Moses's query about the divine identity), "I am who I am," Yakov muses "what he is is what he is: God." Informed of Shmuel's death, Bok weeps, but refrains even from the secular eulogy which Artur Sammler had recited for Elya Gruner.

The novel portrays Jewry in transition. Piety is giving way to politics. The tradition is no longer compelling or even formative for modern Jews. Maurice Samuel notes that a striking feature of the Beiliss case is that "none of the Jews accused, directly or indirectly of complicity in a crime of religious fanaticism was particularly religious or particularly versed in the tradition."[30] Barriers between Jews and Christians were also beginning to erode. The historic Mendel Beiliss, for example, had good relations with his neighbors including Christians and the parish priest. On the other hand, none of these mitigating circumstances was enough to prevent Beiliss' ordeal.[31]

While moral responsibility is possible and even necessary in modernity, belief in God as the ground of moral behavior is diminished. Cautioned by Shmuel not to forget God in Kiev, Yakov angrily replies:

> Who forgets who? What do I get from him but a bang on the head and a stream of piss in my face. So what's there to be worshipful about? (p. 17).

Shmuel mistakenly assumes that his son-in-law is a *meshummed*, an apostate, and warns the fixer to stay a Jew. Yakov is, however, no *meshummed*; he believes in no God. On one level *The Fixer* attempts to answer the question which Jews of modernity have asked with increasing frequency; How is it possible to be a Jew without God? Malamud's literary response does not offer even the comfort of Richard Rubenstein's godless but ritual and communal Judaism. On the contrary, Malamud, in a manner reminiscent of Wallant, posits the notion of a Jewish-Christian everyman whose spiritual quest is ritually as well as theologically unanchored. The author's flirtation, and it seems no more than that, with Jewish specificity comes in the form of Bok's cogent observation that "no Jew was innocent in a corrupt state, the most visible sign of its corruption its fear and hatred of those it persecuted" (p. 315). Malamud's universal moralism quickly asserts itself, however, when in a dream the dead Bibikov reminds Bok that, should he ever be released from prison, "the purpose of freedom is to create it for others" (p. 318).

Malamud's novel foretells a bleak Jewish future in Europe. Bok, chained to the wall like an animal, deprived of the most elemental human dignity muses:

> Overnight a madman is born who thinks Jewish blood is water. Overnight life becomes worthless. The innocent are born without innocence. The human body is worth less than its substance. A person is shit (p. 274).

Essentially, Malamud outlines two historical paths open to Jews. One is the way of escape. His Jewish attorney tells Yakov:

> Rich or poor, those of our bretheren who can run out of here are running. Some who can't are already mourning. They sniff at the air and it stinks of pogrom (p. 305).

The second option is, uncharacteristically for Malamud, revolt. In yet another dream encounter with the Czar, Yakov accuses the autocrat of lacking *rachmones* (compassion). Loading a pistol, the fixer aims it at Nicholas exclaiming that his is an act of revenge for living in a country which the Czar has turned into a valley of bones; for pogroms, for the prison, for the poison, for the body searches, for Bibikov and Kogin, and for a lot more. Awaking from his trance, Yakov thinks there are ways to reverse history. The Czar deserves a bullet in the gut. "Better him than us." Bok's experience has taught him that "there's no such thing as an unpolitical man, especially a Jew." This lesson has practical implications. "You can't sit still," Bok realizes, "and see yourself destroyed." He ends by advocating revolution; "Where there's no fight for it there's no freedom" (p. 335).

The Fixer's image of Jewishness is based on a restrictive notion of moral responsibility. The prison, for example, graphically illustrates Malamud's notion of covenantal restraint. Robert Alter persuasively argues that "Imprisonment . . . (is) a general image for the moral life with all its imponderable obstacles to spontaneous self-fulfillment: it is living in concern for the state of one's soul."[32] Bok shares Artur Sammler's perception of Judaism as a set of thou shalt nots. Moreover, Ostrovsky—his attorney—places the fixer's situation in historical perspective by reminding Bok of Dreyfus's sufferings. Dreyfus had gone through the same thing "with the script in French." We are persecuted notes Ostrovsky, "in the most civilized languages."

Malamud's portrayal of Judaism is severely skewed. What emerges is a tradition unable to cope with the vicissitudes of modernity, and whose grounds for hope or succor can only appeal to *shtetl* Jews who know no better. But Malamud has written a novel which passionately wallows in history. Seeing Holocaust portents in retrospect may seem unimpressive, but it is better than not seeing them. Bok is, for example, singled out as a Jew even in prison, segregated from the other inmates he cannot eat with them and is the object of their enmity. One here is reminded of Benjamin Ferencz's observation. Part of the United States Army unit which liberated the Mauthausen satellite camp of Ebensee, he saw prisoners grouped according to nationality marching in joy, one group, more emaciated than the rest, stood aside. Ferencz asked one of the prisoners about this singled out group and was told, "Oh, they can't march with us. They're Jews."[33] Testimony given by corrupt physicians swearing to the ritual nature of the wounds on the dead child's body, was prominent in the case against Bok. The significant role played by doctors—chief among them Joseph Mengele—in the Holocaust is thus shown to have a precedent in earlier forms of governmental sponsored corruption and violence. The Jew is also portrayed as history's moral touchstone, however unwittingly. *The Fixer*, despite its attachment to history, is strangely mute concerning the role of the contemporary Jewish community which formed a Jewish committee of notables in Kiev to assist the Beillis family. The novel ends with Bok about to stand trial. Mendel Beillis left Russia in 1914 going first to Palestine before emigrating to America where he died in 1934.

Malamud's pre-Holocaust novel should be read as an evocation of the central fact of Jewish modernism; the disruption of the covenant-history dialectic. Yakov Bok refuses his Jewish religious and ritual inheritance. As the covenant recedes in importance or becomes translated into solely anthropocentric terms, history assumes a crucial role in determining Jewish identity. Bok rejects the *shtetl* piety of his father-in-law thereby renouncing, like Nissenson's Jake Brody, both covenant and redemption. For Bok, history confers identity as ineluctably as had covenant for the Israelites. While there is no God to covenant with, there is individual responsibility which transcends the differences between Jews and Christians. Here Bok differs from Brody who intentionally sought solace from his turbulent environment only among other Jews. Malamud distances the *Shoah* chronologically. *The Fixer* is the only one of our novels set entirely in a European context,[34] while at the same time inviting the reader to draw analogies between Russian and Nazi reactionaries. His portrayal of the overpowering nature of history is somewhat tempered by the notion of Jew as potential revolutionary, acting at decisive moments to defend freedom. Malamud has replaced the covenantal deity as guarantor of meaning with the concept of the transreligious man who, growing from his suffering, serves as moral exemplar.

Conclusion

Novelists who view Judaism symbolically avoid easy collective characterization in their literary treatment of the Holocaust. All have acknowledged the difficulty of dealing with the topic by refraining from directly portraying Jewish existence under the Nazis. This hesitation has led them, with the exception of Rosen, to adopt an historically unanchored view of both the Holocaust and Judaism. Consequently, the Holocaust fiction of Roth, Wallant, and Elman bears unwitting witness to the danger, articulated in Neusner's position, of making the Holocaust one's only access to Judaism. By emphasizing solitary quests for meaning, these novelists, again excluding Rosen, have made of community—the central mode of understanding Judaism—a vague, indifferent, or nonexistent feature in their writing. Israel does not play a role either, except for the extreme negativity of Elman's Alex Yagodah and Roth's emblematic use of the country in "Eli, the Fanatic." It is no surprise, therefore, that the Jewish characters in novels of symbolic Judaism appear confused about, uncommitted, indifferent, or hostile to the tradition. Only two of the novelists advocate orienting by the *Shoah*, Rosen quite clearly in *Touching Evil*, and Roth—more equivocally—in *The Ghost Writer*. The others, Wallant, Elman, and the early Roth portray a sense of loss, but in a manner that is a far cry from Hersh Rasseyner's appeal (noted in chapter 2) and which reflects a simplistic view of the problem of evil and suffering.

In contradistinction to the novelists discussed in chapters 3 and 4, survivors portrayed by the symbolic novelists are noticeably unreflective concerning the implications of their Holocaust experience. Cynical and bitter, Sol Nazerman hates the world, but is mute concerning his relationship to Judaism. Alex Yagodah directs his hostility inward, to Jews. The universalizing impulse of Elman, Wallant, and Rosen runs the gamut from *Jüdische selbsthass* (universalizing the guilt of the victimizers such that it accrues to the victims), to redemptive murder as a cure for the sickness that characterizes Jewish-Christian relations, to the more reflective universalizing of Rosen, which assumes that all peoples of good will have been touched by holocaustal evil. Malamud's pre-Holocaust work offers a distinctively modern view of the Jew as archetype; an individual Jew whether atheist, believer, agnostic, or freethinker, stands as representative of the Jewish Nation. Unlike Kotlowitz or Nissenson, however, Malamud refrains from criticizing the loss of a Jewish covenantal center of gravity in the modern world. Instead, he celebrates the emergence of the suprareligious man; a figure who appears to be post-Enlightenment, or at least post-traditional, and who views religion as anachronistic. Men achieve their highest calling when, breaking the restrictive bonds of tradition, and ennobled by their struggles, they attain the moral life.

Collectively speaking, novels which are symbolically Jewish seem unable to confront the singular nature of the Jewish tragedy. The Holocaust as an orienting event has eluded the grasp of Elman, Roth, and Wallant, and ends being diffused by Malamud and Rosen. Four of the novels in this chapter reveal the pitfalls involved when the *Shoah* is trivialized and removed from its historical context. The novelists of symbolic Judaism refrain from presenting a coherent view of covenant or of a covenant deity.

Chapter 6

Holocaust And Covenant

The Central Question for Contemporary Judaism

*C**risis and Covenant* has explored the impact of the Holocaust on covenantal Judaism by investigating literary responses to the extermination of European Jewry. Heschel's direct and poignant query—shall we renew the covenant?—animated each of the literary analyses. Discriminating types of Jewish response—religious, secular, and symbolic—enabled us to see how each of these expressions attempts to cope with the Holocaust and its radical assault on the mystery of Jewish survival. What emerges from this study is a portrait of contemporary Judaism in search of itself. The relationship of the Holocaust to the covenant is central for contemporary Judaism. But the *Shoah* has acted on the tradition in a manner which overturns, weakens, or seriously calls into question the Jewish understanding of covenant, of God, and of man. Reacting to the crisis, covenant-revisionists—both theologians and novelists—have attempted to outline ways in which *homo Judaicus* can persist. Theologically, this has involved an extreme questioning of all the old assumptions. Arthur Cohen speaks for the revisionists' position in asserting:

> We have been forced by the Holocaust—once again—as the first people of the human race to rethink all our premises as once we thought out and affirmed them in the beginning. The flood then, fire and gas in our time: we begin again.[1]

In the literary sphere, those writing about the Holocaust's impact are working at the intersection of theology and literature. They question the meaning of chosenness, acknowledge the continuing trauma of the catastrophe, attribute unquestioned Jewish authenticity to survivors, and offer various speculations concerning the future of covenant Judaism. Paradoxically, varying portraits of the diminishment of covenant religion are coupled with the recognition of covenant as the Judaic norm. The interface between theology and literature has permitted an illumination of Jewish fiction in the light of Jewish theological categories thereby enabling us to achieve a perspective which accounts for the relationship between the *Shoah*, Judaism, modernity, and the covenant.

The investigation here has shown that after forty years the Holocaust continues to resist interpretive certitude, while at the same time increasing numbers of thinkers and writers are grappling with the Event. In a similar manner, the covenant itself has become a source of widely differing speculation. Four of the central characters in the novels analyzed have explicitly abandoned the covenant, but arrived at vastly different conclusions concerning the quality of Jewish continuity. Covenant abandonment means, for Singer's Herman Broder and Elman's Alex Yagodah, the termination of Jewish history. Covenant irrelevance is also asserted in the pre-Holocaust novels of Hugh Nissenson and Bernard Malamud. Nissenson's Jake Brody retains, however, a decidedly prophetic orientation concerning human obligation and the role of compassion. Malamud's Yakov Bok accepts a radically anthropomorphized covenant. Bok is convinced that normative Judaism will be replaced by the religion of universal moral concern whose practitioners will be (in the manner of Isaiah) moral exemplars for all people. The *Shoah* is very far from being assimilated either by American Jewish novelists, or by those who comprise their reading audience. Not surprisingly, confusion about the lessons of the Holocaust, for both Jewish and human history, mounts as one moves from the works of novelists who treat the tradition as a religious and a secular value system to those who view Judaism in symbolic terms. In other words, proceeding from "Judaism as a Religious Value System," to "Judaism as a Secular Value System," and "Symbolic Judaism," there is increasing uncertainty about the catastrophe and about Judaism. Stated formulaically, the further removed a novelist is from accepting the normative dialectic between covenantal promise and historic denial, the more likely is the story to trivialize and/or wrongly universalize the catastrophe. The novels of Elman and Wallant's, *The Pawnbroker*, leap to mind as illustrative of this phenomenon.

Literary and theological bafflement about the Holocaust reflects in part the crumbling of religious certitude in modernity. The sacred canopy under which religious man once lived, and which provided coherent and compelling reasons for the meaning of life and death, has been blown away by the winds of history and undermined by the lure of technology. The former has resulted in a diminution of the image of deity, the latter has given impetus to an inflated view of man. Technological accomplishments have, in fact, resulted in a profound shift in self-understanding. The world of antiquity assigned man the role of self-responsibility; modernity has advanced the notion of self-sufficiency. In greater measure, however, the category-shattering nature of the Holocaust itself has meant that all of the old religious and moral assumptions have been radically put into jeopardy. In Irving Greenberg's cogent phrase; "It is not so critical what position one takes after the Holocaust, as long as one is ashamed of it."[2]

Broadly speaking, the reactions of American Jewish novelists to the Holocaust may be seen as corresponding to three classical models, although with significant differences. Those who treat Judaism as a religious value system appear to take their cue from the psalmist who, facing the temptation of a materially superior culture, reacting to the disaster of exile, beset by fear of divine abandonment, and confronting a radical assault on Jewish covenantal thinking, asked (on behalf of the exilic community): "How shall we sing the Lord's song in a foreign land?" (Psalm 137:4). Novelists who view the tradition as a secular value system seem to share certain characteristics with the biblical Joseph. Like their ancient counterpart, these novelists live in two cultures. Joseph becomes Egyptianized, marries an Egyptian woman, has children, and plays an important role in Egyptian life. He also, on the other hand, retains his Hebrew identity. Israel is finally saved through the disasters that befall Joseph, and the story assumes throughout that a hidden or concealed God works through the ironic web of events, historic and communal, and through familial rivalry. Writers who understand the tradition in symbolic terms reflect assumptions found in the wisdom tradition, especially *Koheleth*, and in the apocryphal *Wisdom of Solomon*. Strongly influenced by Hellenistic culture, these expressions tend toward a universalizing of the human condition. The despair of *Koheleth* is, for example, based on his view that there are continual rounds or patterns that repeat themselves and from which humans do not learn.

Contemporary novelists differ from their predecessors in antiquity concerning both the nature of the external threat to Judaism and the internal theological maturity of the community. The Holocaust intended the end of Jewish continuity, not even a prophetic remnant was to be spared. Jewish-American novelists also seem less interested in singing the Lord's song than in conceptualizing man's role in an indifferent universe. The temptations of the surrounding culture have, moreover, increased as immersion in traditional sources has decreased. One is reminded of Saul Bellow's remark that when he was growing up he had a choice between a yeshiva and a pool hall, and the pool hall won. Nevertheless, most of the novelists in our study have made a significant distinction between American and Jewish culture, or in the case of *The Fixer*, between a universalized Judaism and Russian culture, in their attempts to confront the meaning of Jewish survival.

Holocaust Fiction *Lato Sensu*

Common literary strategies exist among the works of American Jewish novelists who deal with the *Shoah*. With the exception of Ozick's "The Shawl" and Nissenson's "The Law," events of extermination are treated indirectly, and distanced both historically and geographically by their European and Israeli settings, or by their pre- or post-Holocaust American context. Dreams and flashbacks substitute for direct first-hand knowledge of the evil. Traditional figures, both biblical (Job) and rabbinic (the *lamed-vov zaddik*), are employed but also transformed in order to seek guidance in the post-Holocaust world. A partial listing of *lamed-vov zaddikim* includes figures of such diverse religious knowledge and behavioral activity as Simon Stern, Elya Gruner, Erdman, Hester Lilt, and Gus Levy. No matter their diversity, each one of them functions as a link in the chain of Jewish continuity. Their role is to exemplify the possibility of living a Jewish existence in a hostile or indifferent environment. Curiously, however, it is neither Jobian rebellion nor Joseph's stealth which most closely identifies contemporary Jewish-American fiction. One is struck, rather, by the imagery of Jacob's struggle which cuts across the lines demarcating religious, secular, and symbolic Judaism. Novelists in all three categories (Nissenson, Bellow, and Malamud) utilize Jacob's travail as a metaphor for post-Holocaust Jewish expression. Similarly, the mystery of Jewish continuity is addressed across the spectrum of novelistic response. Characters return from the dead—Singer's Tamara, Bellow's Sammler, and Roth's Anne Frank/Amy Bellette—thereby symbolizing the eternality of Israel.

Holocaust responses in the works we have studied share certain other elements as well. The past is, for example, far more determinative for survivors than any activity in the present. Memories of death and murder are constant elements in survivors' consciousness. This is the case for Eliezer and for Herman Broder, but no less so for Artur Sammler and for Anya Savikin. Secular or acculturated survivors not only entered Jewish history with the advent of the Holocaust, but they steadfastly remain Jews, albeit in a highly eccentric manner. For the most part, authentic responses to the Holocaust are authorally permitted only to a community of actual survivors (Schaeffer, Singer, Wiesel). Only Cohen and Ozick have spoken about a communal response which is to incorporate the broader notion of *k'lal Yisrael*. Wiesel's *The Fifth Son* establishes theological guidelines for nonwitnesses who wish to respond. A struggle for the soul of both pre- and post-Holocaust Jewry is portrayed in the novels of religious, secular, and symbolic Judaism. Nissenson's *My Own Ground* and Kotlowitz's *The Boardwalk* give eloquent expression to this struggle. Descriptions of what Terrence Des Pres terms "excremental asssault" also cut across the boundaries of the literature, and appear in *Enemies, Mr. Sammler's Planet,* and *The Pawnbroker*.

Jewish-Christian relations and the State of Israel occupy a good deal of attention in contemporary responses to the Holocaust. Jewish continuity, for both religious and secular Judaism, means strictures against adopting Christian norms. Arthur Cohen's post-Holocaust Jews are, for example, to be as their ancestors, "islands in a Gentile sea." This position is less clear in the case of Sammler, who is attracted by culture more than by religion. On the other hand, Anya becomes physically ill when her daughter begins dating a Christian. Novelists of symbolic Judaism have, for their part, made interaction with Christianity a normative component of Jewish existence, although for Roth, in "Eli the Fanatic," this norm has devastating consequences. Norma Rosen has implicitly staked the Jewish future to Christian realization of what the Holocaust entails theologically, morally, and ethically for Christianity. Attitudes toward Israel vary. The centrality of the Jewish State is asserted by Ozick—in her essays—and implied by Singer. It is crucial for Schaeffer in determining Jewish continuity, but merely emblematic for Roth. Bellow is ambivalent about Israel, while Cohen and Elman offer negative assessments of the Third Jewish Commonwealth. Nissenson creatively utilizes Israel and the messianic assumptions it engenders as he portrays a Judaism searching for redemptive covenant identity. Israel appears irrelevant for the remainder of the novelists we have studied.

In negative terms, all the novelists reject institutional Judaism, expressing varying degrees of disappointment with its rabbinic custodians, and eschew ritualism. They recognize that the European *kehillah* structure has not been duplicated in American Judaism. In fact, the move from communal elegies (*selihot* and *kinot*), to a smaller community of survivors, is diminished even further in the works of Elman, Roth, and Wallant. These novelists respond to the disaster either by privatizing it, or by utilizing highly selective notions of communal terms. Consequently, their novels symbolize the loss not only of the destroyed European Jewish community, but the subsequent failure of American Judaism to find either a comparable or even an adequate replacement. Survivors portrayed in the works of religious and secular Judaism are physically and psychically scarred by their experiences, but have learned ineluctable truths about covenant Judaism; it endures and it makes claims which are irresistible. Sammler is one-eyed, Nathan of Gaza is blind, and Ozick's rebbe is without fingers, but all have acquired deepened insights concerning the Jewish and human condition.[3] Schaeffer's *Anya* takes this message one step further in portraying what may be termed a positive legacy of the Holocaust, *viz.*, Anya Savikin's survival skills include an overwhelming desire to live and a marshalling of coping resources which help her survive. These skills also are employed in America to rescue her daughter from marrying outside the faith. Survivors in the novels of symbolic Judaism, on the other hand, frequently deteriorate into stereotypes who either have learned nothing or who have learned the wrong lessons about Jewish particularity.

Problems and Possibilities

Crisis and Covenant has argued that Holocaust centrality is a touchstone of authentic Jewish writing. Realizing that holocaustal pain is one's own alters an individual's perception of the world and personalizes his/her orientation to the tradition. Novelists whose centrally Jewish characters have absorbed this pain manage, in spite of the experience, to live with the contraries involved in covenant and history. Transmitting the post-Holocaust dialectic these novelists simultaneously modify its contours. Those who are unable to remain within the midrashic framework, on the other hand, abandon the dialectic. There is, for example, a marked decrease in the sophistication of the treatment of evil and the reality of suffering as one moves from Holocaust novels which view Judaism as a religious value system through those which view it as a system of secular values, to fictional accounts of symbolic Judaism. Antisemitism, which is a real and fatal presence in the novels analyzed in "Judaism as a religious value system" and "Judaism as a secular value system," deteriorates into stereotype in the novels of Elman. Writers who treat Judaism symbolically have a naïve understanding of Jewish theology and of the *Shoah*. Against Greenberg's wise observation that after the Holocaust one should refrain from final solutions of any type, these novelists tend to emphasize answers as over and against questions; Wallant's compassionate community, Elman's Jewish self-hate, and Roth's self-centeredness are posited as definitive responses to the post-Holocaust Jewish condition.

The relationship of the present to the past is of the utmost importance in Judaism. *Halaka*, for example, means a normative assumption that there exists a continuum of events and responses which cumulatively encompass Jewish history, Jewish identity, and Jewish destiny. This normative mode presumes a tension between covenant and history. Translating this concern to literature, two types of Jewish future emerge in the post-Holocaust fiction we have analyzed. While deviating somewhat from *halakic* standards, the works of Cohen, Ozick, the early Nissenson, Wiesel, and Singer reflect what Ruth Wisse terms the "midrashic mode"[4]; one which is sensitive to the dialectical relationship between divine promise and historical occurrence, while attributing great responsibility to the human covenantal partner. This fiction remains open to covenantal possibility. A second type of Jewish future is portrayed by those novelists who assume that, post-Holocaust, the dialectic has become a choice between covenant and history. Consequently, Judaism is portrayed as now living only in history for Elman, Wallant, and Malamud's *The Fixer*. Jews are symbolically removed from the possibility of obtaining either spiritual succor or moral sustenance from the Jewish tradition.

It is important to distinguish literary strategies from Holocaust lessons. One issue involves aesthetics, the second concerns survival and theology. Questioning whether a story *works* in the artistic sense should not be confused with questioning the status of the covenant. It is precisely at the juncture of literature and theology that one runs the great risk of misunderstanding both disciplines. The stories we have scrutinized reflect the ongoing search for Jewish identity and vocation in the face of the *Ḥurban* of the Jewish people. One needs, however, to beware of neither placing too great a burden nor too much of an expectation on literature. Elie Wiesel sounds a warning which at first appears paradoxical. He writes:

> as far as I am concerned, there is no such thing as Holocaust literature—there cannot be. Auschwitz negates all literature as it negates all theories and doctrines; to lock it into a philosophy means to restrict it. To substitute words, any words, for it is to distort it. A Holocaust literature? The very term is a contradiction.[5]

The danger of which Wiesel speaks lies in thinking that one can learn everything about the Holocaust by reading fiction, especially that work which was written by those who were not enmeshed in the concentrationary universe. There is, on the one hand, a need to translate the disaster and its continuing impact into literature so that people can ponder the meaning of existence on an Auschwitz planet. But if disaster is literature only, it then risks being relegated to the realm of the imagination; that area where humans have neither total control nor distinct responsibility. Cynthia Ozick warns that the Holocaust is already dangerously literary and legendary. She reminds both writer and reader of a central concept in Holocaust study.

> The task . . . is to retrieve the Holocaust freight car by freight car, town by town, road by road, document by document. *The task is to save it from becoming literature.*[6]

This appeal strikes with great force for those, both novelists and readers, who are witnesses through the imagination. It would be a mistake of the greatest magnitude to assume that one could confront holocaustal horrors without historical knowledge. To do so is not only to ignore the Holocaust's dimensions but to miss its message, desensitizing contemporaries to warning signs in their own culture.

It is appropriate to end our study where it began, by asking about the relationship between the Holocaust, contemporary Jewish-American writers, and American Judaism. Disruption of the covenant-history dialectic is the central fact of Jewish modernity. Until the extermination of European Jewry this fact was perhaps less crucial than it has become in the aftermath of the Holocaust. Wiesel has frequently observed that the Holocaust teaches nothing. It is, I think, more accurate to state that one has much to learn from the disaster and that Wiesel himself offers what is perhaps the most significant lesson: after the Holocaust there are no answers, only questions. Authentic post-Holocaust responses are, therefore, fragmentary rather than comprehensive in nature. The theologians and novelists examined in this study each offers a position or perspective from which to scrutinize, if not to comprehend, the Holocaust. Collectively, their works testify that the struggle for Jewish meaning continues and has intensified in ways that resist being restricted to conceptual categorization.

It is apparent that an increasing number of novels, novellas, and short stories are being written about the implications of the *Shoah* for contemporary Judaism. What American Jewish novelists write and say and think about the Holocaust will, therefore, have a greater impact on American Judaism than that of any other group of American Jews in determining Jewish attitudes not only toward the catastrophe but toward the Jewish past as well as toward its future. American Jewry had, in the past, a vast reservoir from which it could draw important sustenance and revitalization. German Jews of the nineteenth, and Eastern European Jews of the early twentieth century brought to America a dazzling array of ethnic and religious Jewish expression. Today there is no more reservoir. Creative Jewish meaning is therefore going to have to be fostered from within the American Jewish community at precisely the time when that community, while continuing to think of itself in religious terms, is increasingly populated by *maskilim* (those indifferent to covenant Judaism). Knowledge of the tradition is woeful, and study of the Talmud has been superseded by the reading of novels. It is perhaps for this reason that novelists as different in orientation as Wiesel and Malamud both invest the writer with the task of saving civilization.

Responses to the Holocaust in American Jewish fiction have pointed to the all-encompassing nature of the disaster. During the time of destruction, Jews are depicted in the great variety of their extreme situations; the chosen people were in both death camps and slave labor camps, in hiding, and even some fighting as partisans in the forests. The majority of novelists we have studied, however, focus their attention on Judaism's post-Holocaust trauma; depicting the physical, emotional, and theological wounds which have seared the people of Israel. Writing about this endless torment, Wiesel notes that for survivors, the Holocaust continued after the Holocaust. American Jewish novelists are, for their part, nonwitnesses. Their responses to the catastrophe vary according to their degree and intensity of Jewish historical and theological sophistication. Contemporary literary response to the covenant-history dialectic has utilized a variety of covenantal transformations, although the tension between covenant and history was not always perceived as creative or even as being present.

Greenberg's "Voluntary," and Wiesel's "Additional" covenants were seen as offering a measure of post-Holocaust Jewish affirmation to Jews who orient their lives by the Holocaust, even though they be secularists. The role of the Holocaust novelist was revealed as coming under increasing scrutiny. Far from being literature only, Holocaust fiction has itself received special designations which consciously set it apart from other literary efforts. Ozick has spoken of "liturgical" and "redemptive" literature; Fackenheim employs the concept of "mad midrash"; while Wiesel calls for the writing of a new Talmud to distinguish serious fictional encounters with the *Shoah*. *Crisis and Covenant* has shown that at least certain American Jewish novelists have a developed covenantal tone of voice in responding to the crisis of Holocaust. It is not altogether clear, however, if this covenantal tone is a mark of the past or a sign of the future.

Notes

Chapter 1. Introduction: Jewish Existence

1. Buber's comment was made in a 1948 Jerusalem talk honoring his Christian socialist friend Leonhard Ragaz. See Maurice S. Friedman, *Martin Buber: The Life of Dialogue* (Chicago: The University of Chicago Press, 1955), 279.

2. The word Holocaust was first used by Elie Wiesel and began appearing in scholarly publications of the *Yad Vashem* Remembrance Authority in the mid–1950s to describe the extermination of the Jews. Prior to that time, either the Hebrew *Shoah* or the Yiddish *Ḥurban* were employed to convey the sense of cosmic desolation which more accurately portrays the dimensions of what occurred between 1939 and 1945. Throughout this book a variety of terms are used to denote the Nazi murder of six million Jews: catastrophe, cataclysm, Final Solution, destruction, *Shoah*, *Ḥurban*, Auschwitz, *Endlösung*, and Tremendum. The term Holocaust has unfortunate sacrificial connotations and has become domesticated as well. It is used here because it has entered the public domain.

3. Elie Wiesel, "Jewish Values in the Post-Holocaust Future: A Symposium," *Judaism* 16:3 (Summer 1967), 281. Wiesel's views on the post-Holocaust status of the covenant are discussed further in chapter 2.

4. The idea of covenant transformation has been powerfully argued in post-Holocaust Jewish theology. It is, of course, a constant theme of Judaism but one which takes on increased importance in our age. The bibliography here is enormous. Irving Greenberg's work on the dialectical relationship between redemption and history has been influential in my own thinking. The following works of Greenberg—whose own approach is presented in

greater detail in chapter 2—pursue the covenant-history dialectic: "Judaism and Christianity After the Holocaust," *Journal of Ecumenical Studies* 12; 4 (Fall 1975); "Judaism and History: Historical Events and Religious Change," *Shefa* 2; 1 (1979); "New Revelations and New Patterns in the Relationship of Judaism and Christianity," *Journal of Ecumenical Studies* 16: 3 (Spring 1979); "The Third Great Cycle in Jewish History" (New York: National Jewish Resource Center, 1981); "Religious Values After the Holocaust: A Jewish View," in *Jews and Christians After the Holocaust*, edited by Abraham J. Peck (Philadelphia: Fortress Press, 1982); and "The Voluntary Covenant" (New York: National Jewish Resource Center, 1982). Greenberg's viewpoint is richly suggestive in emphasizing a mode of post-*Shoah* theological reconstruction which acknowledges evil while holding open the possibility of redemption.

5. Mircea Eliade, *The Myth of the Eternal Return or, Cosmos and History*, translated by Willard R. Trask (Princeton: Princeton University Press, Bollingen Series XLVI, 1971), 108.

6. Emil Fackenheim, *God's Presence in History* (New York: New York University Press, 1970), 21–25. Fackenheim's entire post-Holocaust theological reconstructive effort depends heavily on the logic of midrashic stubbornness. Fackenheim's analysis of the midrashic framework is discussed at length in chapter 2.

7. Harry James Cargas (ed.), *Harry James Cargas in Conversation with Elie Wiesel* (New York: Paulist Press, 1976), 85.

8. Cited by Eugene B. Borowitz in his *The Mask Jews Wear: The Self-Deceptions of American Jewry* (New York: Simon and Schuster, 1973), 30.

9. Raphael Patai, "Enlightenment: Triumph and Tragedy," in *The Jewish Mind* (New York: Charles Scribner's Sons, 1977), chapter 9 and pp. 461, 462.

10. Jacob Katz, *Out of the Ghetto: The Social Background of Jewish Emancipation, 1770–1870* (New York: Schocken Books, 1978), 191.

11. Ibid., 205–10.

12. Wiesel, "Jewish Values," 285.

13. Ibid.

14. I am indebted to Sidra Ezrahi's discussion of the Lamentation tradition. Many of my remarks on this topic are informed by her careful analysis. See Sidra Ezrahi, "The Holocaust Writer and the Lamentation Tradition: Responses to Catastrophe in Jewish Literature," in *Confronting the Holocaust: The Impact of Elie Wiesel*, edited by Alvin Rosenfeld and Irving Greenberg (Bloomington: Indiana University Press, 1978), and her own book *By Words Alone: The Holocaust in Literature* (Chicago: University of Chicago Press, 1980), especially chapters 5 and 6.

15. Ezrahi, "The Holocaust Writer," 136.

16. There were, however, defiant *kinot* as well. Ezrahi notes the twelfth-century *kinah* of Menahem ben Jacob who wrote, "Who is like unto thee among the speechless, O God/who can be compared with thee in thy silence?" (Ezrahi, "The Holocaust Writer," 231). Contending with God while remaining firmly rooted in the tradition is a feature of Judaism which traces its origin to biblical religion (for example, Abraham, Moses, and Job). The best-known modern expression of this protest from within is the hasidic tale and the remonstrations of Levi Yitzhack of Berditchev. In the post-Holocaust world the writings of Elie Wiesel most profoundly voice this type of protest.

17. Israel Efros (ed.), *Selected Poems of Hayyim Nahman Bialik* (New York: Bloch Publishing Co., 1965).

18. Sidra Ezrahi, *By Words Alone: The Holocaust in Literature* (Chicago: University of Chicago Press, 1980), 101.

19. Ezrahi, "The Holocaust Writer," 138.

20. Arthur A. Cohen, *The Tremendum: A Theological Interpretation of the Holocaust (New York: The Crossroad Publishing Company, 1981), 2.*

21. Jacob Neusner, *"The Implications of the Holocaust," The Journal of Religion* 53: 3 (July 1973); *Stranger at Home: The Holocaust, Zionism and American Judaism* (Chicago: University of Chicago Press, 1981), 1–2, 61–91; and *The Jewish War Against the Jews: Reflections on Golah, Shoah, and Torah* (New York: KTAV Publishing House, Inc., 1984), 7 and Chapters 6–8.

22. Greenberg terms critics who claim too much attention is paid to the *Shoah*, "pre-mature Messianists," who thought that the Holocaust's lessons were already learned. The best evidence that the Holocaust has not been overstressed, writes Greenberg, is the world-wide surge in anti-Jewishness. Irving Greenberg, "Are We Focusing On The Holocaust Too Much?" (New York: National Jewish Resource Center, 1983), 2.

23. Chaim Grade, *My War with Hersh Rasseyner*, translated by Milton Himmelfarb, *Commentary* 16:5 (November 1953), 437.

24. Irving Greenberg, "Judaism and Christianity After the Holocaust," *Journal of Ecumenical Studies* 12: 4 (Fall 1975), 521–23.

25. Eichmann's comments are reported by Rudolf Hoess in his auto-biography *Commandant of Auschwitz*, translated by C. FitzGibbon (Cleveland: World Publishing Company, 1960), 242.

26. Lily Edelman, "A Conversation with Elie Wiesel," in *Responses to Elie Wiesel*, edited by H. J. Cargas. (New York: Persea Books, 1978), 11.

27. Daniel J. Elazar, *Community and Polity: The Organizational Dynamics of American Jewry* (Philadelphia: Jewish Publication Society of America, 1976), 71.

28. Edelman, 12. Wiesel is quite critical of the American Jewish community, both for what he perceives as its lack of sufficient response during the Holocaust and for its current spiritual deficiency. Concerning the former, Wiesel has written:

> Never before have so many Jews been abandoned by so many Jews. . . . The massacre in Europe had almost no bearing on American Jewish life. The annihilation of thousands of Eastern European communities was almost not at all reflected in what was going on in the thousands of American Jewish communities. Tea parties, card games, musical soirees continued to take place. Of course, money was raised, but entertainment was not omitted from the Program (Wiesel, "Jewish Values," 282).

Wiesel is no less pessimistic regarding contemporary Jewish expression in America. He writes:

> Man can understand only through words. Jews have never believed in statues, we have never believed in buildings. Judaism is words. If the American Jewish community is experiencing so many difficulties and so many defeats, especially with our young, it is perhaps because there are too many buildings. Judaism is not buildings. Jewish building is in words. (Edelman, 21)

29. Alvin H. Rosenfeld, *A Double Dying: Reflections on Holocaust Literature* (Bloomington: Indiana University Press, 1980), 19.

30. Robert Alter, *After the Tradition: Essays on Modern Jewish Writing* (New York: E. P. Dutton and Company, 1969), 18.

31. Norma Rosen, "The Holocaust and the American-Jewish Novelist," *Midstream* XX: 8 (October 1974), 58. See also Edward Alexander's essay "The Holocaust in Jewish American Fiction: A Slow Awakening," in his *The Resonance of Dust* (Columbus: Ohio State University Press, 1980). Alexander sees the absence of satire in the writings of the new left in Jewish American fiction as a serious defect.

32. Edelman, 11.

33. Elie Wiesel, *A Jew Today*, translated by Marion Wiesel (New York: Random House, 1978), 163.

Chapter 2. Holocaust As Watershed

1. Abraham J. Heschel, *Man's Quest for God* (New York: Charles Scribner's Sons, 1954), 151.

2. Elie Wiesel, *Legends of Our Time*, translated by Steven Donadio (New York: Holt, Rinehart and Winston, 1968), 183.

3. Arthur A. Cohen, "The American Imagination After the War: Notes on the Novel, Jews, and Hope," B. G. Rudolph Lecture, Syracuse University, March 1981, p. 8.

4. Wiesel, *Legends of Our Time*, 190.

5. Richard Rubenstein, *The Cunning of History* (New York: Harper and Row, 1978), 91.

6. Alvin H. Rosenfeld, *A Double Dying: Reflections on Holocaust Literature* (Bloomington: Indiana University Press, 1980), 13.

7. Alice L. Eckardt and A. Roy Eckardt, "The Holocaust and the Enigma of Uniqueness: A Philosophical Effort at Practical Clarification," *The Annals of the American Academy of Political and Social Science* 450 (July 1980), 165–78.

8. Lucy S. Dawidowicz, *The War Against the Jews 1933–1945* (New York: Bantam Books, 1976), 463 and XXIII.

9. Steven T. Katz, "The 'Unique' Intentionality of the Holocaust," *Modern Judaism* 1: 2 (1981), 161–83.

10. Yehuda Bauer, *A History of the Holocaust* (New York: Franklin Watts, 1982), 332.

11. Arthur A. Cohen, *In the Days of Simon Stern* (New York: Dell Publishing Co., 1974), 457–58.

12. Raul Hilberg, *The Destruction of the European Jews* (Chicago: Quadrangle Books, 1967), 1–4.

13. Elie Wiesel, *A Jew Today*, translated by Marion Wiesel (New York: Vintage Books, 1979), 182.

14. Arthur A. Cohen, *The Tremendum: A Theological Interpretation of the Holocaust* (New York: The Crossroad Publishing Co., 1981), 53.

15. Irving Greenberg, *Voluntary Covenant* (New York: National Jewish Resource Center, 1984), 15, 33.

16. Cohen, *Tremendum*, 10, 11.

17. Ibid., 21.

18. Ibid., 22.

19. Arthur A. Cohen, "The American Imagination," 34.

20. Emil L. Fackenheim, *God's Presence in History: Jewish Affirmations and Philosophical Reflections* (New York: New York University Press, 1970), 70.

21. Fackenheim, *God's Presence in History*, 84.

22. Ibid., 24.

23. Emil Fackenheim, "The Holocaust and the State of Israel: Their Relation," in *Auschwitz: Beginning of a New Era?* edited by E. Fleischner (New York: KTAV, 1977), 211.

24. Emil Fackenheim, *The Jewish Return Into History* (New York: Schocken Books, 1978), 269.

25. Irving Greenberg, "Judaism and Christianity After the Holocaust," *Journal of Ecumenical Studies* 12: 4 (Fall 1975), 529.

26. Ibid., 533.

27. See chapter 1, note 16.

28. Greenberg, *Voluntary Covenant*, 21.

29. Ibid.

30. Richard L. Rubenstein, *After Auschwitz: Radical Theology and Contemporary Judaism* (Indianapolis: The Bobbs-Merrill Company, 1966), 223.

31. Ibid., 46.

32. Richard L. Rubenstein, "Homeland and Holocaust," in *The Religious Situation: 1968*, edited by D. R. Cutler (Boston: Beacon Press, 1968), 41.

33. Rubenstein, *After Auschwitz*, 68.

34. Elie Wiesel, *Legends of Our Time*, 8.

35. Elie Wiesel, "Jewish Values in the Post-Holocaust Future: A Symposium," *Judaism* 16:3 (Summer 1967), 285.

36. Michael Berenbaum, "The Additional Covenant," in *Confronting the Holocaust: The Impact of Elie Wiesel*, edited by A. Rosenfeld and I. Greenberg (Bloomington: Indiana University Press, 1978), 168–85.

37. Ibid., 171.

38. Michael Wyschogrod, "Some Theological Reflections on the Holocaust," in *Response* 25 (Spring 1975), 68.

39. T. W. Adorno, "Engagement," in *Noten zur Literatur* 111 (Frankfort am Main: Suhrkamp Verlag, 1965), 109–35.

40. Primo Levi, *Survival in Auschwitz*, translated by S. Woolf (New York: Collier Books, 1961), 113.

41. Fackenheim, *God's Presence in History*, 72.

42. George Steiner, *Language and Silence* (New York: Atheneum, 1967).

43. George Steiner, *The Death of Tragedy* (New York: Alfred A. Knopf, 1961).

44. George Steiner, *The Portage to San Cristobal of A. H.* (New York: Simon and Schuster, 1981).

45. Hannah Arendt, *The Origins of Totalitarianism*, new edition (New York: Harcourt Brace and World, 1966), 437.

46. This is a problem with political as well as theological reverberations. The recent Hitler revival, fascination with violence, and books denying or falsifying the Holocaust are worrisome signs. Yehuda Bauer deals with one aspect of the situation, exposing "neo-Nazi gutter history" in his *The Holocaust in Historical Perspective* (Seattle: University of Washington Press, 1978), chap. 2. Lucy S. Dawidowicz, "Lies About the Holocaust," *Commentary* 70:6 (1980), explores the political and moral implications of the so-called revisionists' position.

47. *Musselmen* or *muselmänner* were camp slang terms for prisoners who had lost all will and desire to live.

48. Irving Greenberg, "Judaism and Christianity After the Holocaust," 550. It is curious that Rubenstein—given the emphasis which he places on the importance of ritual for the community—chooses to ignore the Holocaust ritually, while retaining the bar mitzvah and other rites.

49. *New York Times* interview with Michiko Kakutani 7 April 1981.

50. Nessa Rapoport, *Preparing for Sabbath* (New York: William Morrow and Co., 1981). I am grateful to Professor Thomas Friedmann for discussions on this point.

51. An important exception to this observation is Stefan Kanfer's *The Eighth Sin* (New York: Random House, 1978), a novel dealing with the Post-Holocaust life of a gypsy survivor and his search for revenge against a gypsy collaborator. The novel acknowledges the Holocaust's shattering impact on Western culture, and takes, with utmost seriousness, the issues of evil, divine abandonment, and human indifference.

52. Cynthia Ozick, "A Liberal's Auschwitz," in *The Pushcart Prize: Best of the Small Presses*, ed. Bill Henderson (Yonkers: Pushcart Book Press, 1976), 153. This piece should be read together with Alvin H. Rosenfeld's powerful critique "The Holocaust According to William Styron," *Midstream* XXV: 10 (December 1979), 43–49.

53. Yehuda Bauer, *The Holocaust in Historical Perspective*, 49.

54. Joseph Blau, *Modern Varieties of Judaism* (New York: Columbia University Press, 1966), 27.

55. I utilize the spellings antisemitism and antisemitic, as opposed to

the more common forms anti-Semitism and anti-Semitic, throughout *Crisis and Covenant*. James Parkes, pioneer scholar of Jewish-Christian relations, described the spelling "anti-Semitism" as "pseudo-scientific mumbo jumbo." There is, noted Parkes, no entity called "Semitism" against which "anti-Semitism" is directed. Parkes concludes his remarks by stating that " 'anti-semitism' is entitled to neither a hyphen nor a capital." See A. Roy Eckardt's "The Nemesis of Christian Antisemitism" in *Jewish-Christian Relations in Today's World*, edited by James E. Wood, Jr. (Waco, Tx.: Baylor University Press, 1971), 45. The Nazis themselves knew full well that antisemitism referred only to Jews. Yehuda Bauer observes that there was active cooperation between Hitler and Hajj Amin el-Husseini, Mufti of Jerusalem and leader of Palestine's Arabs. Nazis, writes Bauer, made Arabs "honorary Aryans." Bauer rightly terms antisemitism "a semantic cover" for Jew-hatred. (Bauer, *A History of the Holocaust*, 44).

56. Norma Rosen, "The Holocaust and the American-Jewish Novelist," in *Midstream* XX: 8 (October 1974), 57.

57. Irving Greenberg, "Polarity and Perfection," in *Face to Face* 6 (New York: Anti-Defamation League, 1979), 12.

58. Helen Fein, *Accounting for Genocide* (New York: The Free Press, 1979), XVII.

59. Lucy Dawidowicz, "Toward a History of the Holocaust," *Commentary* 47; 4 (April 1969), 56.

60. "Jewish Values in the Post-Holocaust Future," A Symposium, *Judaism* 16:3 (Summer 1967), 286.

61. Edward Alexander, *The Resonance of Dust* (Columbus: Ohio State University Press, 1979), 146.

62. Harry James Cargas (ed.), *Harry James Cargas in Conversation with Elie Wiesel* (New York: Paulist Press, 1976), 87.

63. Yosef Hayim Yerushalmi observes that despite the unprecedented historical research generated by the Holocaust, the castastrophe's image is "being shaped, not at the historian's anvil, but in the novelist's crucible." Yerushalmi, *Zakhor: Jewish History and Jewish Memory* (Seattle: University of Washington Press, 1982), 98.

64. Jacob Katz, *Tradition and Crisis* (New York: Schocken, 1971), 3.

Chapter 3. Holocaust Responses I

1. Ruth R. Wisse, "American Jewish Writing Act II," *Commentary* (June 1976).

2. Cynthia Ozick, "America: Toward Yavneh," in *Judaism* 19: 3, 276. Ozick's oft-quoted statement overlooks developments in American culture which go a long way toward situating the Jewish-American novelists' Jewish self-awareness. A perceptive and revealing analysis of this issue is found in the remarks of Professor Thomas Friedmann. He argues that the younger generation of American Jewish writers—including Ozick and Cohen—focus on "Jewish Jews" owing largely to the liberating influence of the growing ethnocentrism of the decade." Specifically concerning Ozick's shofar imagery, Friedmann writes:

> There are beauty and artistic merit in Ozick's argument for the narrow focus, but the more significant reason why more Jewish writers will follow "the lesson of the shofar" is the psychological necessity for doing so. As all other ethnic groups in America have done, Jews, too, are finally accepting the argument of self-preservation. "If I am not for myself, who is?" And Jewish writers in America have begun to act according to the instinct of self-preservation too. This is why they are turning, and must continue to turn, inward. Into community, into history, into racial spirit. Having grown up independent of the chains of all mankind, they are free to bind themselves within the boundaries of their kind.

Thomas Friedmann, "Back to the Edges, the Center Will Not Hold: One Reason for the Emergence of a New Consciousness in American Jewish Literature," *American Jewish Archives* XXX (November 1978), 129.

3. Cynthia Ozick, "America Toward Yavneh," *Judaism* 19:3 (Summer 1970), 279. Ozick has subsequently tempered her initial prediction, writing in *Art & Ardor* (New York: Alfred A. Knopf, 1983) that she is "no longer greatly attracted" to the essay's conclusions (p. 152). She later distinguished the historical from the personal, and ascribed the article's conclusions as belonging to the former. (Letter to the editor of *Commentary* 77: 5 [May 1984], 8).

4. Ozick, "America Toward Yavneh," p. 278.

5. Arthur Kurzweil, "An Atheist and His Demonic God: An Interview with Hugh Nissenson," *Response* (Winter 1978–79), 16.

6. Emil Fackenheim, *God's Presence in History: Jewish Affirmations and Philosophical Reflections* (New York: New York University Press, 1970), 95.

7. Emil Fackenheim, "The Human Condition After Auschwitz: A Jewish Testimony a Generation Later," B. G. Rudolph Lecture, Syracuse University, April 1971, p. 13.

8. "The Shawl," in *The New Yorker* (May 26, 1980), 33–34.

9. "The Law," in *A Pile of Stones* (New York: Charles Scribners Sons, 1965).

10. Eliach's book is flawed, however, in giving accounts only of those who were saved from the Nazis. There is no theological reflection concerning the countless numbers of pious Jews whose lives were exterminated.

11. *In the Days of Simon Stern* (New York: Dell Publishing Co., 1973), 193. All references are from the Dell edition and appear in the text.

12. *Teshuvah* (turning) is the Hebrew word for repentance. In Ozick's "Bloodshed," the rebbe advocates "turnings" for the truly penitent (see this chapter, p. 50).

13. Cohen utilizes the dream as a vehicle for presenting Simon's most complex and elaborate encounters. In addition to Elijah, Simon meets and discourses with President Roosevelt in this manner. Elie Wiesel and Isaac Bashevis Singer also employ the dream in similar fashion (see this chapter, pp. 76-77, 86) as do Susan Schaeffer, Hugh Nissenson, and Cynthia Ozick (see Chapter 4), Edward Lewis Wallant and Bernard Malamud (see chapter 5). The sociologist Peter Berger notes that dreams exemplify "marginal situations," a "standing, or stepping, *outside* reality as commonly defined." Frequently the realities represented in marginal situations are invested with higher cognitive status. Dreams, for example, can be related to daily existence as warnings, prophecies, decisive encounters with the sacred, and as having specific consequences for everyday conduct in society. Peter L. Berger, *The Sacred Canopy* (Garden City, N.Y.: Doubleday and Company, 1967), 43.

14. Alvin H. Rosenfeld, *A Double Dying: Reflections on Holocaust Literature* (Bloomington: Indiana University Press, 1980), 32.

15. Wiesel's Simha-the-Dark commits a similar offense (see this chapter, p. 71, 76) as do Ozick's Joseph Brill and Nissenson's Reb Isaacs (see chapter 4).

16. The Jewish notion of *lamed-vov zaddikim* appears first in the Babylonian Talmud (Sanhedrin 97b and Sukkot 45b). This figure is frequently employed in Holocaust fiction. Ernie Levy is a highly stylized *lamed-vov zaddik* in Andre Schwarz-Bart's *The Last of the Just*, translated by Stephen Becker (New York: Atheneum, 1960). Secular writers have also been attracted by this concept. For example, Saul Bellow, Robert Kotlowitz, Cynthia Ozick, and Susan Schaeffer all utilize this figure. (their relevant works are discussed in chapter 4).

17. See the *Taku* references throughout the Talmud. *Taku*, an acrostic, refers to Elijah the Tishbite who will solve all problems which currently appear unresolvable.

18. Edward Alexander's claim that Cohen's work is most appealing in its call for a collective response to the Holocaust is somewhat inaccurate. The community to which Cohen refers is not a geographic or even an historical one. Alexander's otherwise perceptive analysis is found in his essay "The Holocaust in Jewish American Fiction: A Slow Awakening," in *The Resonance*

of Dust, edited by Edward Alexander (Columbus: Ohio State University Press, 1980), 121–46, see esp. 142–45.

19. Ozick, *Art & Ardor*, 248.

20. Although many scholars have commented on the structural similarity between "Bloodshed" and Philip Roth's "Eli the Fanatic," Ozick's tale significantly differs from Roth's in its focus on a Jewish mystical theology rather than as a sociological critique of American Judaism's covenant abandonment. I discuss Roth's tale in chapter 5.

21. *Azazel* has been variously identified as a dwelling place of satyrs, imps, and Lillith. In the second Temple period *Azazel* was identified with the fallen angels. A useful summary of the interpretation and theories regarding the scapegoat is found in Hayyim Schauss's *The Jewish Festivals, History and Observance*, translated by Samuel Jaffe (New York: Schocken, 1973), 300–301.

22. *Bloodshed and Three Novellas* (New York: Alfred A. Knopf, 1976), 66. All text references are from this edition.

23. Theron Raines is the critic. He is cited on p. 7 in the Preface to *Bloodshed and Three Novellas*.

24. Cynthia Ozick, "The Shawl," *The New Yorker*, May 26, 1980, pp. 33–34.

25. "Levitation" was originally published in *Partisan Review* 46:3, 1979 and is reprinted in *Levitation: Five Fictions* (New York: Alfred A. Knopf, 1982). All references are from this edition. One measure of the importance with which Ozick views her Holocaust tales can be seen in the fact that both "Bloodshed" and "Levitation" title their respective collections.

26. Elie Wiesel, "Talking and Writing and Keeping Silent," in *The German Church Struggle and the Holocaust*, edited by Franklin H. Littell and Hubert G. Locke (Detroit: Wayne State University Press, 1974), 273.

27. "The Pagan Rabbi" was originally published in *The Hudson Review* (Autumn 1966) and is reprinted in *The Pagan Rabbi and Other Stories* (New York: Schocken Books, 1976). The citation is from this edition, 3.

28. Robert Alter, "Sentimentalizing the Jews," *Commentary* 40: 3 (September 1965), 75.

29. Hugh Nissenson, *A Pile of Stones* (New York: Charles Scribner's Sons, 1965). All text references are from this edition. The present analysis of Nissenson is an expanded and extensively revised form of certain ideas which appeared in my earlier essay, "Covenant and History: The Holocaust in the Fiction of Hugh Nissenson," *Journal of Reform Judaism* XXXI: 3 (Summer 1984), 47–65.

30. The dialectical nature of God's relationship to Jacob/Israel is lucidly

analyzed by James G. Williams, "Israel as a Way of Being in the World," chapter 5 in Williams' book *Women Recounted: Narrative Thinking and the God of Israel* (Sheffield, Eng.: Almond Press, 1982).

31. Many high-ranking Nazis, Himmler, Hoess, and others, came from religious families and some had contemplated clerical careers. See Raul Hilberg, *The Destruction of European Jewry* (Chicago: Quadrangle Press, 1967). This is one reason Fackenheim and Greenberg contend that the Holocaust has shattered traditional religious and secular distinctions.

32. *The Accident*, translated by A. Brochardt (New York: Hill and Wang, 1962). Text references are from this edition.

33. R. J. Z. Werblowsky, "Judaism, or the Religion of Israel," in *The Concise Encyclopedia of Living Faiths*, edited by R. C. Zachner (New York: Hawthorn Books, 1959), 44.

34. Seminar at Syracuse University, Spring 1982.

35. Harry James Cargas, "What is a Jew?" Interview of Elie Wiesel in *Responses to Elie Wiesel*, edited by H. J. Cargas (New York: Persea Books, 1978), 151.

36. Byron L. Sherwin, "Elie Wiesel and Jewish Theology," *Judaism* (vol. 18:1 (Winter, 1969), 40.

37. *The Fifth Son*, translated by Marion Wiesel (New York: Summit Books, 1985). Text references are from this edition.

38. See the following works; Robert Greenfield's *Temple* (New York: Summit Books, 1982) and Thomas Friedmann's *Damaged Goods* (New York: The Permanent Press, 1984). It is interesting to note that these novels also are set in late 1960's America. Greenfield's work concerns the grandson of a survivor but distances survivors from Americans. Friedmann's autobiographic novel displays an insider's eye for the ritual of Orthodox life in America. He skillfully relates the complexities involved in survivor parent-child relationships.

39. Harry James Cargas (ed.), *Harry James Cargas in Conversatioon with Elie Wiesel* (New York: Paulist Press, 1976), 48.

40 Elie Wiesel, *One Generation After*, translated by Lily Edelman and Elie Wiesel (New York: Random House, 1970), 198.

41. Elie Wiesel, *A Jew Today*, translated by Marion Wiesel (New York: Vintage Books, 1979), 16.

42. Gershom G. Scholem, *Major Trends in Jewish Mysticism* (New York: Schocken Books, 1965), 275.

43. Irving Greenberg, "Are we Focusing On The Holocaust Too Much?" (New York: National Jewish Resource Center, 1983), 2.

44. Cynthia Ozick's Hester Lilt, a secularist, also utilizes Rabbi Akiba as a model, but for post-Holocaust American Judaism (see chapter 4).

45. Wiesel, *A Jew Today*, 16.

46. For a detailed discussion of the angel and its relationship to Lurianic Kabbalah see Gershom G. Scholem, *On Jews And Judaism In Crisis* (New York: Schocken Books, 1976), 232–34. Schoelm notes, however, that for Luria, the awaking of the dead and the joining together and restoring of what has been smashed and broken is the task not of an angel but of the Messiah" (pp. 233–34). The angel, unlike Wiesel's messanic hope, is ultimately defeated by history.

47. Wiesel, "Talking and Writing and Keeping Silent", *The German Church Struggle and the Holocaust*, 277.

48. Elie Wiesel, *The Gates of the Forest*, translated by Frances Frenaye (New York: Schocken Books, 1982), 225.

49. Isaac Bashevis Singer, *Enemies, A Love Story* (New York: Fawcett Crest Books, 1972). Text references are from this edition.

50. According to traditional sources, souls of the righteous travel to the Holy Land no matter where they are buried. This practice, sometimes called in Hebrew *gilgul mehilot* (rolling in tunnels) is a tenet of faith among the pious. A good summary of sources concerning this phenomenon is found in Zev Vilnay's *Legends of Jerusalem The Sacred Land* (Philadelphia: The Jewish Publication Society of America, 1977), 1: 337.

51. William James, *The Varieties of Religious Experience* (New York: The New-American Library, 1958), 326.

52. Isaac Bashevis Singer and Ira Moskowitz (illustrations), *A Little Boy in Search of God: Mysticism in a Personal Light* (New York: Doubleday and Co., 1976), 25 and 27.

53. Singer refers to the rite of *kapporot* which involved transferring one's sins to a rooster or hen which is then swung around the petitioner's head. On the magical-mystical efficacy of this rite see Hayyim Schauss, *The Jewish Festivals, History and Observance*, translated by Samuel Jaffe (New York: Schocken Books, 1973), 164–67, 206–7).

54. Alfred Kazin, *Bright Book of Life* (Boston: Little, Brown and Company, 1973), 159.

Chapter 4. Holocaust Responses II

1. Jacob Katz, *Tradition and Crisis* (New York: Schocken Books, 1971), 215.

2. Arthur Hertzberg, *The French Enlightenment and the Jews* (New York: Columbia University Press, 1968), 5.

3. Nathan Glazer, *American Judaism*, 2nd ed., rev. (Chicago: University of Chicago Press, 1972), 142.

4. Niger's remarks are cited by Eliezer Whartman, "Jewish Secularism in America—at the End of the Road?" *In the Dispersion* 7 (1967), 98.

5. Mordecai Kaplan, *Judaism as a Civilization* (New York: Macmillan Co., 1934).

6. Emil Fackenheim, *God's Presence in History* (New York: New York University Press, 1970), especially the discussion on pp. 45–47.

7. Mark Helprin's short story "Tamar" also exemplifies this genre while shifting the scene to 1939 London. Helprin's anonymous narrator, a Palestinian Jew, comes to the British capital on a mission of assistance for European Jews. Despite their learning and culture, Jewish peers and the Jewish upper class in Britain were extremely vulnerable and unable to see the Jewish situation as clearly as the young Palestinian Jew. Mark Helprin, *Ellis Island and Other Stories* (New York: Delacorte Press, 1981).

8. "The Lady of the Lake" was originally published in *The Magic Barrel* (New York: Farrar, Straus, 1958). All text references are from the 1972 Pocket Books edition.

9. "The German Refugee" was originally published in the *Saturday Evening Post* 236:38–9, 1963. Text reference is from the story as it was reprinted in *Idiots First* (New York: Delta, 1965).

10. Saul Bellow, *Mr. Sammler's Planet* (Harmondsworth, Eng.: Penguin Books, Ltd., 1978). Text references are from this edition. The book was originally published in 1970 by Viking Press.

11. Irving Greenberg, "Judaism and Christianity After the Holocaust," *Journal of Ecumenical Studies* 12: 4 (Fall 1975), 535.

12. Sidra Ezrahi, *By Words Alone* (Chicago: University of Chicago Press, 1980), 74ff.

13. Richard Rubenstein argues this position with unfailing rigor. He asserts it on religio-theological grounds in *The Cunning of History* (New York: Harper & Row, 1978), and more recently on an economic-political basis in

The Age of Triage (Boston: Beacon Press, 1983). Rubenstein's view is that genocide is a necessary result of modernity's production of surplus people.

14. Hannah Arendt's remarks are contained in her book *Eichmann in Jerusalem: A Report on the Banality of Evil* (New York: Viking Press, 1963).

Jacob Robinson critiques Arendt's banality thesis, observing:

Whether or not Miss Arendt's theory has merit as a generalization, it clearly is neither substantiated by, nor relevant to, Adolf Eichmann's "unprecedented" case. For he was no average man and possessed no ordinary criminal skills, nor did he ever show in his actions a repugnance for what he was doing. It is hardly legitimate for a historian to generalize from a single, uncommon case.

Jacob Robinson, *And the Crooked Shall be Made Straight; The Eichmann Trial, The Jewish Catastrophe, and Hannah Arendt's Narrative* (New York: The Macmillan Co., 1965), 58. A different type of literary reaction to the Eichmann trial is given in Norma Rosen's novel *Touching Evil* (New York: Harcourt Brace and World, 1969), (see this volume, ch. 5).

15. Bellow's choice of this particular passage is a curious one. Erubin 13b is one of only a small group of statements which support a negative evaluation of existence. This text goes against normative Judaic affirmations of life. See C. G. Montefiore and H. Loewe (eds.), *A Rabbinic Anthology* (Cleveland: World Publishing Company; Philadelphia: The Jewish Publication Society, 1963), 538–39.

16. Edward Alexander, "Saul Bellow: A Jewish Farewell to the Enlightenment," in Alexander's *The Resonance of Dust* (Columbus: Ohio State University Press, 1980), 171–93.

17. Saul Bellow, *To Jerusalem and Back* (New York: Viking Press, 1976), 58.

18. In a typically perceptive remark the historian Lucy Dawidowicz notes that the ability to face the idea and reality of death, coupled with a wholesome sense of Jewish identity, permits Israeli Jews to confront the historical data of the Holocaust in a manner unavailable to native American Jews. "Toward a History of the Holocaust", *Commentary* 47:4 (April 1969), 56. Dawidowicz's observation, correct though it may be, does not account for the fact that Israeli novelists have, thus far, been no more successful than their American counterparts in treating the Holocaust novelistically.

19. Although the bibliography here is extensive the following works are useful in approaching the complexity of the issue: Solomon F. Bloom, "Dictator of the Lodz Ghetto," *Commentary* 7 (1949); Michael Checinski, "How Rumkowski Died," *Commentary* 67 (1979); *Helen Fein, Accounting for Genocide* (New York: The Free Press, 1979); Lucy Dawidowicz, *The War Against the Jews*

(New York: Holt, Rinehart and Winston, 1975). Leslie Epstein has written a novel loosely based on Rumkowski, *King of the Jews: A Novel of the Holocaust* (New York: Coward, McCann & Geoghegan, 1979).

20. Bellow, *To Jerusalem and Back*, 26.

21. Susan F. Schaeffer's letter to Dorothy Seidman Bilik, cited in the latter's *Immigrant-Survivors: Post-Holocaust Consciousness in Recent Jewish American Fiction* (Middletown: Wesleyan University Press, 1981), 100, 196. Schaeffer has not pursued the Holocaust beyond *Anya*.

22. Susan F. Schaeffer, *Anya* (New York: Avon Books, 1974). Text references are from this edition.

23. Alexander, "The Holocaust in American Jewish Fiction: A Slow Awakening," in *The Resonance of Dust*, 134.

24. Primo Levi, *Survival in Auschwitz*, translated by S. Woolf (New York: Collier Books, 1961), 36.

25. Hermann Goering, Reichsmarshall of the Luftwaffe, provides a case in point. Impressed by the administrative and technical skills of Erhard Milch, who was born of a Jewish mother, Goering wished to appoint Milch to his staff. Goering had the woman sign an affidavit attesting that Erhard Milch was the illegitimate son of his father and not an offspring of her marriage. Thus Aryanized, Milch became a trusted confidant of the Third Reich hierarchy, rising to the rank of General Field Marshall of the Luftwaffe.

Erhard Milch's Nuremberg testimony concerning his Aryanization appears in volume 9 of *The International Military Tribunal*, Proceedings 8 March 1946–23 March 1946 (Nuremberg: The International Military Tribunal, 1947), 93f. A useful summary of Milch's career is found in Louis L. Snyder's *Encyclopedia of the Third Reich* (New York: McGraw-Hill, 1976), 229–30.

I am grateful to Professor Robert W. Ross who first brought Milch's case to my attention.

26. Thomas Keneally's *Schindler's List* (New York: Simon and Schuster, 1982) portrays the real life career of Oskar Schindler who saved many Jewish lives during the *Shoah*. Undistinguished both before and after the war, Oskar Schindler's extraordinary wartime behavior reveals that one can never know who the hidden righteous man will be during the time of testing. The actions of people like Oskar Schindler give credence to those who contend that the religious-secular dichotomy is meaningless in light of the ovens of Auschwitz.

27. Cynthia Ozick, "Rosa," *The New Yorker*, March 21, 1983, 38–71.

28. Primo Levi, *Survival in Auschwitz*, 82.

29. Cynthia Ozick, *The Cannibal Galaxy* (New York: Alfred A. Knopf, 1983). Text references are from this edition.

30. Ozick addresses her concern about the role of women in Judaism in a variety of places. For good summary statements see *Lilith* 6 (1979), "The Jewish Half-Genius," *Jerusalem Post*, international edition, August 8, 1978, 10, 11, and certain of the essays in *Art and Ardor* (New York: Alfred A. Knopf, 1983). For an analysis of Ozick's evolving feminist concerns see Louis Harap's "The Religious Art of Cynthia Ozick" *Judaism* 33: 3 (Summer 1984), esp. 359–61.

31. *The New Yorker*, Nov. 10, 1980. I am grateful to Professor Sarah Blacher Cohen for calling my attention to this short story.

32. For analyses of Holocaust pedagogy in the university context, see Alan L. Berger "Academia and the Holocaust," *Judaism* 31: 122 (Spring 1982), "Reflections on Teaching the Holocaust: The American Setting," *Shofar* 2;2 (Winter 1984), and "Holocaust: The Pedagogy of Paradox," ch. 23 in *Towards Understanding and Prevention of Genocide*, edited by Israel Charny (Denver: Westview Press, 1984).

33. At the International Conference on the Holocaust and Genocide held in Tel Aviv in 1982 those assembled at one workshop were told that the principal of a religious school in a large eastern city did not permit his teacher to attend an in-service training session on methods of teaching about the *Shoah* because the "Holocaust made God look bad."

34. Emil Fackenheim, *The Jewish Return Into History* (New York: Schocken Books, 1978), 10.

35. Emil Fackenheim, *To Mend the World* (New York: Schocken Books, 1982), 17.

36. Hugh Nissenson utilizes an orphan to symbolize the Jewish condition of modernity in America. See analysis of *My Own Ground* on pp. 137–144.

37. Edmond Fleg, *Why I Am a Jew*, translated by Louise W. Wise (New York: Arno Press, 1975).

38. André Neher, *The Exile of the Word*, translated by David Maisel (Philadelphia: Jewish Publication Society, 1981), 144.

39. *My Own Ground* (New York: Farrar, Straus and Giroux, 1976). Text references are from this edition. See footnote 29 in chapter 3.

40. Hugh Nissenson, *In the Reign of Peace* (New York: Farrar, Straus and Giroux, 1972). This, his second collection of short stories, pursues the theme in an Israeli context.

41. Schlifka's understanding of the concept of soul root rests on a distorted interpretation of this mystical notion whose origins lay in the Lurianic kabbalah. Gershom Scholem writes that the kabbalistic version had cosmic significance:

each individual is enjoined to raise the holy sparks which belong specifically to his spiritual root in the great soul of Adam, the common soul of all mankind.

Gershom G. Sholem, *The Messianic Idea in Judaism* (New York: Shocken Books, 1971), 246.

42. Edward Alexander perceptively comments on the persistence of the "universalist-humanist delusion" among American Jews. Correctly tracing its origins to the Enlightenment and the French Revolution, Alexander notes that the Jews of Europe were convinced that they must abandon their Jewish identity in order to assimilate with "humanity." "No conviction," writes Alexander, "has ever been more resistant to negative evidence than the belief of the Jewish Leftist in the promises held out to him by declarations of human rights." Edward Alexander, *The Resonance of Dust*, 124.

43. Ruth R. Wisse, "American Jewish Writing, Act II," *Commentary* 61 (June 1976).

44. Alvin H. Rosenfeld, "Israel and the Idea of Redemption in the Fiction of Hugh Nissenson," *Midstream* XXVI (April 1980), 56.

45. There is a subgenre of Holocaust literature whose authors, while consciously refraining from direct portrayal of the catastrophe, nonetheless intend their works to be read as Holocaust fiction. Examples of this subgenre include Mark Helprin's "Tamar," Robert Kotlowitz's *Someplace Else*, Jay Neugeboren's *The Stolen Jew*, and *An Orphan's Tale*, and Isaac Bashevis Singer's *Shosha*.

46. Portraying the death of Jewish children in pre-Holocaust Europe is a theme in Isaac Bashevis Singer's work as well and emphasizes the gravity of the threat to Jewish continuity.

47. Arthur Kurzweil, "An Atheist and His Demonic God: An Interview with Hugh Nissenson," *Response* 36 (Winter, 1978–79), 20.

48. Commenting on the kabbalistic ideology, Scholem writes that Rachel is "exiled from God and lamenting," while Leah is in a "perpetually repeated reunion with her Lord." Consequently, only the *tikkun* Rachel was a true rite of lamentation, one which acknowledges the exile of the *Shekhinah*. The rite for Leah emphasized not exile but the redemptive promise. Some kabbalists, notes Scholem, added a third part to the ritual, a *tikkun ha-nefesh* or rite for the soul. The mystic's goal in this rite was to unite God and the *Shekhinah* by intense concentration "with every single organ of [the kabbalist's] body." Gershom G. Scholem, *On the Kabbalah and its Symbolism*, translated by R. Mannheim (New York: Schocken Books, 1965), 149 and 150.

49. This theme is a constant one in Nissenson's fiction. "The Crazy Old Man," reports an incident in which Kolya, a Russian blacksmith, had raped

and murdered a Jewish woman he had known for forty years. The old man, a hasidic Jew, observes that "violence made all the difference between us, the goyim and the Jews" (p. 39). This tale is not without problems however: the old man's view of the Holocaust is that God relented and saved a remnant because they did not fight back. The story's denouement comes when the old man shoots an Arab soldier being interrogated by two Israeli-born officers in order to spare them the deed. He had done so because, in the words of one of the officers, "I had been born in the country into which his God had returned the Jews to give them their last chance" (p. 47). In this case, the old man makes the same error committed by Rabbi Isaacs, he thinks that redemption requires "forcing the end of history." "The Crazy Old Man," *In the Reign of Peace*.

50. Robert Kotlowitz, "Baltimore Boy," in *Growing Up Jewish*, edited by Jay David. (New York: Pocket Books, 1970), 239. Text references are from this edition.

51. *The Boardwalk* (New York: Alfred A. Knopf, 1977). Text references are from this edition.

52. Scholem, *On the Kabbalah and Its Symbolism*. 105.

53. Emil Fackenheim, *God's Presence in History* (New York: New York University Press, 1970), 81.

Chapter 5. Holocaust Responses III

1. In Search of Kafka and Other Answers," *New York Times Book Review* 15 February 1976, p. 6.

2. "Eli, the Fanatic" was originally published in *Commentary* 27: 3 (1959). Text references are from the version reprinted in *Goodbye Columbus* (Boston: Houghton Mifflin Co., 1959).

3. Interestingly, Roth chose the Yiddish proverb "The heart is half a prophet," as the epigraph for his *Goodbye Columbus* tales.

4. *The Ghost Writer* (New York: Farrar, Straus and Giroux, 1979). Text references are from this edition.

5. Benno Weiser Varon, "The Haunting of Meyer Levin," *Midstream* XXII: 7 (August/September 1976), 19. Varon tellingly notes that Otto Frank, who authorized the sanitized Broadway version of his daughter's diary, was "not a proud Jew" (like Anne), but "a German assimilationist" (p. 20). Otto Frank had brought his daughter a copy of the New Testament as a Chanukah present.

6. Elie Wiesel, *A Jew Today*, translated by Marion Wiesel (New York: Vintage Books, 1979), 220.

7. Irving Greenberg, "Judaism and Christianity After the Holocaust," *Journal of Ecumenical Studies* 12; 4 (Fall 1975), 529.

8. "Richard Elman" entry in *American Jewish Biographies* (New York: Lakeville Press Book, 1982), 93. Elman is the rule-proving exception to the assertion that novelists of symbolic Judaism persist in writing about the Jewish tradition.

9. Sidra Ezrahi, *By Words Alone* (Chicago: University of Chicago Press, 1980), 46.

10. *The 28th Day of Elul* (New York: Charles Scribner's Sons, 1967), 276. Text references are from this edition.

11. Richard L. Rubenstein, "Homeland and Holocaust: Issues in the Jewish Religious Situation," in *The Religious Situation: 1968*, edited by D. R. Cutler (Boston: Beacon Press, 1968), 103.

12. *Lilo's Diary* (New York: Charles Scribner's Sons, 1968), 155. Text references are from this edition.

13. Cynthia Ozick, "A Liberal's Auschwitz," *The Pushcart Prize: Best of the Small Presses* (Yonkers, N.Y.: Pushcart Book Press, 1976), 153.

14. *The Pawnbroker* (New York: Macfadden Books, 1965). Text references are from this edition.

15. Wallant letter quoted by Theodore Solotaroff in *Book Week* (5 April 1964), 5.

16. Ozick's Rosa Lublin symbolizes yet another negative societal attitude, depersonalizing survivors by treating them merely as objects of study.

17. *Touching Evil* (New York: Harcourt, Brace & World, 1969). Text references are from this edition.

18. Norma Rosen, "The Holocaust and the American-Jewish Novelist," *Midstream* XX: 8 (October 1974), 58.

19. The only other literary reference to the *Muselmänner* among the novelists in this study is found in Ozick's "Rosa" (see chapter 4, p. 123).

20. Bellow employs a variant of this account but has a man, Sammler, rather than a female escape from the pit. This true tale was told at the Eichmann trial by Rivka Yoselewska. Gideon Hausner, *Justice in Jerusalem* (New York: Schocken Books, 1968), 73–74.

21. Rosen, "The Holocaust and the American-Jewish Novelist," 60.

22. Rosen's usage of the *gilgul* concept in a Christian setting is interesting

to note. Isaac Bashevis Singer is the only other novelist in our study who speaks of *gilgul*, and he does so out of his familiarity with Jewish mystical sources (see chapter 3, p. 83).

23. Edward Alexander, "The Holocaust in American Jewish Fiction: A Slow Awakening," in *The Resonance of Dust*, edited by Edward Alexander (Columbus: Ohio State University Press, 1979), 132.

24. *The Fixer* (New York: Farrar, Straus & Giroux, 1966). Text references are from this edition.

25. Maurice Samuel, *Blood Accusation* (New York: Alfred A. Knopf, 1966), 268.

26. The Nazis were familiar with Kiev's history of reactionary Jew-hatred. Surely it is no accident that the murderers chose Babi Yar, a ravine on the city's outskirts, as the site of their mass slaughter of Kiev's Jews.

27. Ben Siegel, "Victims in Motion: Bernard Malamud's Sad and Bitter Clowns," *Northwest Review*, V (Spring 1962), reprinted in *Recent American Fiction: Some Critical Reviews*, ed. Joseph J. Waldmeir (Boston: Houghton Mifflin Company, 1963), 206.

28. Reported by Michael Dov Weissmandl in Greenberg, "Judaism and Christianity," 525.

29. Josephine Knopp, *The Trial of Judaism in Contemporary Jewish Writing* (Urbana: University of Illinois Press, 1975), 116.

30. Samuel, *Blood Accusation*, 58.

31. Samuel underscores the irony that the day of Beiliss's arrest coincided with *Tisha b'Av* (p. 62). Nazis took pleasure in initiating special *aktions* against the Jews on Jewish holidays.

32. Robert Alter, *After the Tradition. Essays on Modern Jewish Writing* (New York: E. P. Dutton & Co., 1969), 122.

33. Benjamin Ferencz, *Less Than Slaves* (Cambridge, Ma.: Harvard University Press, 1979), 88.

34. Leslie Epstein's *King of the Jews: A Novel of the Holocaust* (New York: Coward, McCann & Geoghegan, 1979) is the only other Holocaust novel written by an American whose frame of reference is entirely European (see chapter 4, note 19).

Chapter 6. Holocaust and Covenant

1. Arthur A. Cohen, "Our Narrative Condition," *Present Tense* VII:4 (Summer 1980), 59.

2. Irving Greenberg, "Lessons to be Learned from the Holocaust." Unpublished manuscript read at the International Scholar's Conference on the Holocaust. Hamburg, Germany, 1978, 3.

3. Ozick's Joseph Brill does not fully conform to this generalization.

4. "American Jewish Writing, Act 11," *Commentary* 61: 6 (June 1976), 43.

5. Elie Wiesel, *A Jew Today*, translated by Marion Wiesel (New York: Random House, 1978), 197.

6. Cynthia Ozick, "The Uses of Legend: Elie Wiesel as Tsaddik," *Congress Bi-Weekly*, June 9, 1969, 19.

Index